Place in Research

Bridging environmental and Indigenous studies and drawing on critical geography, spatial theory, new materialist theory, and decolonizing theory, this dynamic volume examines the sometimes overlooked significance of place in social science research. There are often important divergences and even competing logics at work in these areas of research, some which may indeed be incommensurable. This volume explores how researchers around the globe are coming to terms—both theoretically and practically—with place in the context of settler colonialism, globalization, and environmental degradation. McKenzie and Tuck outline a trajectory of *critical place inquiry* that not only furthers empirical knowledge, but ethically imagines new possibilities for collaboration and action.

Critical place inquiry can involve a range of research methodologies; this volume argues that what matters is how the chosen methodology engages conceptually with place in order to mobilize methods that enable data collection and analyses that address place explicitly and politically. Unlike other approaches that attempt to superficially tag on Indigenous concerns, decolonizing conceptualizations of land and place and Indigenous methods are central, not peripheral, to practices of critical place inquiry.

Eve Tuck is Associate Professor of Educational Foundations and Coordinator of Native American Studies at the State University of New York at New Paltz.

Marcia McKenzie is an Associate Professor in the Department of Educational Foundations and Director of the Sustainability Education Research Institute at the University of Saskatchewan.

Routledge Advances in Research Methods

Place in Research
Theory, Methodology, and Methods

Eve Tuck and Marcia McKenzie

Routledge
Taylor & Francis Group

LONDON AND NEW YORK

First published 2015
by Routledge
711 Third Avenue, New York, NY 10017

and by Routledge
2 Park Square, Milton Park, Abingdon, Oxfordshire OX14 4RN

*Routledge is an imprint of the Taylor and Francis Group,
an informa business*

First issued in paperback 2015

Library of Congress Cataloging-in-Publication Data
Tuck, Eve.
   Place in research : theory, methodology, and methods / by Eve
Tuck and Marcia McKenzie.
      pages cm. — (Routledge advances in research methods ; 9)
   Includes bibliographical references and index.
   1. Space—Social aspects—Research.   2. Social sciences—Research.
I. McKenzie, Marcia.   II. Title.
   HM654.T83 2015
   114—dc23
   2014012806

ISBN 978-0-415-62672-9 (hbk)
ISBN 978-1-138-63968-3 (pbk)
ISBN 978-1-315-76484-9 (ebk)

Typeset in Sabon
by Apex CoVantage, LLC

For our Elders, the Land, and our Children

Contents

Figures

Tables

Preface

In *Wisdom Sits in Places* (1996), ethnographer Keith Basso tells the story of visiting a particular place with two Apache men, hosts and informants on a cultural geography research project in which participants helped to collectively map Apache place-names near Cibecue. They were visiting a circular swale, "ringed by willows and filled with luxuriant grass," located near a creek that flowed toward Cibecue (p. 8). It was Basso's second day of the study, and his second day of travel through Apache land with Charles Henry, who was serving as Basso's escort, showing him places, telling him their proper Apache names, and sharing some about their significance, and cultural and historical meanings. They were accompanied by Morley Cromwell, Henry's cousin, who translated between Apache and English.

Henry and Cromwell shared with Basso that the place is called *Water Lies With Mud In An Open Container*, telling him the name in Apache. Basso tried to repeat the name, in Apache, but fobbed it, apologizing. This had become a running theme, even so early in their time together; Henry would tell him the place-name, and Basso, with some embarrassment, would try to repeat it, but he was defeated again and again. "I'm sorry, Charles," Basso said at the edge of the swale, "I can't get it. I'll work on it later, it's in the machine [referring to the voice recorder he was carrying]. It doesn't matter" (p. 10).

To this, Henry responded with frustration—because it did indeed matter—with Cromwell quickly translating:

> What he's doing isn't right. It's not good. He seems to be in a hurry. Why is he in a hurry? It's disrespectful. Our ancestors made this name. They made it just as it is. They made it for a reason. They spoke it first, a long time ago! He's repeating speech of our ancestors. He doesn't know that. Tell him he is repeating the speech of our ancestors. (p. 10)

Basso, taken aback and unsettled by the admonition, paused to allow the full effect of the words to reach him.

But, before Basso could respond, Henry supposed aloud in a self-deprecating gesture that the missed communications might have been his fault (joking about his own missing teeth). With this generous act, Basso was invited to try again to form the name in his mouth again, this time with a sense of the seriousness that the words of ancestors require.

Basso continues to tell this story, and many other stories of his work with Apache men and women to map the words of their ancestors for the places they inhabit throughout the rest of the book. Explaining the need for such a project, Basso contends that ethnographers, "much like everyone else, take sense of place for granted, and ethnographic studies exploring their cultural and social dimensions are in notably short supply" (1996, p. xiv). Calling the project an ethnography of place-making, Basso uses the story of his own learning about places' names as the speech of ancestors to draw attention to the multidimensional significance of place(s), as "durable symbols of distant events and as indispensable aids for remembering and imagining them" (p. 7).

As we describe in Chapter 1, the book before you also seeks to draw attention to the multidimensional significance of place(s) in social science research, not just as "durable symbols or the distant past" (Basso, 1996, p. 7), but as sites of presence, futurity, imagination, power, and knowing. This is an important time to write about place, not just because social science, in general practice, doesn't give place its due, but because we write from and into the overlapping contexts of globalization and neoliberalism, settler colonialism, and environmental degradation. We do not see the practices of social science and these overlapping contexts as disconnected. Rather, to use Kim Tallbear's (2013) term, they are *coproduced*, meaning science and society are actively entangled with each other. They are mutually constitutive in that "one loops back in to reinforce, shape, or disrupt the actions of the other, although it should be understood that because power is held unevenly, such multidirectional influences do not happen evenly" (p. 11).

As Angayuqaq Oscar Kawagley observed,

> Throughout the world many people are beginning to recognize significant changes that are underway, be it with weather and climate shifts, ecological contamination and disruptions, depletion of natural resources, societal inequities with the rich getting richer and the impoverished growing in large numbers, population expansion among the poor growing exponentially, and violence on the increase. The negative effects of these changes are exacerbated by the hyper-consumerism of Western society, which has perpetuated the impoverishment of many Third World countries through exploitation of low production and manufacturings costs. Recognition of these transformational factors in many societies has contributed to people demanding changes in the way we live and in our use of nature. (Kawagley, 2006, p. 123)

Coproduction of practices of social science, globalization and neoliberalism, settler colonialism, and environmental degradation comprises both the barrier and the possibility to making the changes needed for the sustainability of (human) life on the planet. As we suggest in Chapter 3, decolonization may be something the land does on its own behalf, even if humans are too deluded or delayed to make their own needed changes.

Our work together on critical place inquiry builds on our separate trajectories and identities as an Unangan scholar (Eve Tuck) and as an environmental scholar from Canada (Marcia McKenzie). Both of us work primarily in education, as it intersects with Indigenous studies (Eve) and environmental studies (Marcia). Though education is the field in which we most often do research and writing, we look to, read in, and think through work happening in other social science fields in order to inform our work. While we may think of education as an intellectual home base, this book is designed to draw upon (and speak to) a variety of social science fields.

Working in our respective intersections, we met at a conference planning meeting in Chicago in 2009. The theme of the conference we were helping to plan included the language of "complex ecologies" to refer to the conditions and systems of educational research and practice. We were mutually concerned about the organization's apparent imperviousness to environmental and social issues suggested in the irony of using the language of ecology without any mention of actual ecosystems. In our view, "complex ecologies" was being employed as a metaphor, emptied of its connections to place, land, and environment. Given the mounting pressures of climate change, oil spills, and other environmental issues that are affecting the land and lives of Indigenous and non-Indigenous people around the globe, we saw a need to draw attention to this problematic lack of attention at a conference supposedly concerned with children, youth, and education.

In response to this concern, together with another colleague, Jillian Ford, we designed a highlighted session on "demetaphorizing complex ecologies," featuring a mix of environmental and Indigenous scholars and practitioners, some working locally and others based elsewhere. Our hope was that the panel would be an opportunity to establish mutual concerns, but also would identify gaps and challenges between these two fields. What initially seemed a small but promising act of transdisciplinary collaboration and intervention into institutional norms, however, became more complicated as speakers from the distinct trajectories of environmental and Indigenous scholarship mobilized contradictory language and understandings in their panel presentations. The worldviews, epistemologies, and lexicons mobilized by environmental scholars and Indigenous scholars were not only contradictory, but perhaps even incommensurable.

For example, in a paper by Angayuqaq Oscar Kawagley (read by his close friend and colleague, Ray Barnhardt), Kawagley observed, "We know that Mother Nature has a culture, and it is a Native culture" (see also Kawagley, 2010, p. xiii). Environmental education scholars on the panel used the forum to consider how humans might establish deeper relationships with nature. Two powerful perspectives emerged from the discussion, and both seemed to grapple with the same notion of the inseparability of humans with nature. The first, expressed by Kawagley and other Indigenous scholars on the panel, insisted that Indigenous peoples have always had relationships to land that are distinct and sovereign from relationships imposed by settlers. This perspective emphasized a recognition of the inseparability of humans and nature as concomitant with Indigenous cosmologies and epistemologies. The other perspective, expressed by environmental scholars, was that further environmental degradation could only be prevented through more ethical and respectful relationships of humans to place. This perspective was notably silent on the claims of Indigenous peoples to have prior, intact relationships to their land, but instead seemed to desire to form new relationships to the very same territory, without recognition of those prior claims. Audience members came away from the panel energized by the very apparent disconnections, silences, and obvious contradictions, but still others were offended, seeing some assertions made by both sides as exclusive and even disrespectful.

A few years later, at the same conference, we organized another session that brought Indigenous and settler scholars together to discuss the differences between settler colonial relations to place and Indigenous relations to land. Here, too, some of the incommensurabilities between environmental studies literatures and Indigenous studies literatures emerged. This time, the incommensurabilities were not embodied by the panelists, as in the prior panel, but instead were observed in the papers by panelists Megan Bang, Troy Richardson, K. Wayne Yang, Dolores Calderon, and Kate McCoy. Together, their papers pointed to the ways in which social sciences, when not cognizant of settler colonial structures, can replicate some of the epistemic violences of settler colonialism and exhibit some of the tendencies of that structure to accumulate at all costs (see also Tuck & Guishard, 2013).

Several years and several collaborations later, we have had more opportunities to become aware of the ways in which environmental research in education, as in most other fields across the social sciences, continues to be mired in assumptions and practices that perpetuate forms of colonialism and racism, despite well-meaning intentions to the contrary. A recently co-authored introduction to a special issue on "Land education: Indigenous, postcolonial, and decolonizing perspectives on place and environmental education research" discusses this further in relation to the field of (environmental) education (Tuck, McKenzie, & McCoy, 2014).

Environmental and Indigenous concerns are not mutually exclusive domains: on the contrary, they are necessarily entwined. This reality has entered popular discourse and is strengthening social movements resisting extractive and polluting industries; fighting for public access to clean water; and responding to climate change, climate justice, and other social and environmental issues affecting communities around the globe. However, with the typical siloing of scholarly fields, to date there has been little discussion across these domains in academia. As we have suggested, where there are attempts, situated within historical blank spots and systemic oppression, those working in these areas do not always effectively hear one another. Steeped in challenges and more to be done, we are hopeful that the discussions of this book will help contribute to broader engagement of the possibilities for contingent collaborations and valuable incommensurabilities (Tuck & Yang, 2012) across these domains and their importance for considering place in social science research. As part of that, we also hope to contribute to understandings that social science research that better addresses place is one part of what is needed to redress the consequences of colonialism and enable the sustainability of (human) life on the planet.

Acknowledgments

Together we acknowledge St. Paul Island, Alaska; Cornwall and Hershey, Pennsylvania; Brooklyn, New York; Cortlandt Manor, New York; Shabomeka Lake, Ontario; and Saskatoon, Saskatchewan.

We acknowledge those who labored alongside us to make this book possible: Jean Kayira, Jeff Baker, Sofia Saiyed, Valerie Zink, Ranjan Datta, and Mark Brigland-Pritchard. Thank you also to Nicola Chopin, Philip Vaughter, Ranjan Datta, Jen McRuer, Kathleen Aikens, Heather Lake, Jeh Custerra, and Kristin Hargis for the support and time needed to complete this project.

We acknowledge Max Novick, our expert editor at Routledge.

We acknowledge our collaborators, those who do this work with us, who think with us on the walking, and who have helped inform our thinking towards this book: K. Wayne Yang, Monique Guishard, Kate McCoy, Brian K. Jones, Kondwani Jackson, Mistinguette Smith and the Black/Land Project, Joe Henderson, Alex Wilson, Jonas Greve Lysgaard, Karen McIver, Hamish Ross, Alan Reid, and Randy Haluza-DeLay.

We acknowledge our colleagues and friends who encouraged us along the way, including Sarah Buhler, Lise Kossick Kouri, Ellen Quigley, Danny Beveridge, Janet McVittie, Dianne Miller, Bob Regnier, Leigh Patel, Kathleen Nolan, Julie Gorlewski, Kate McCoy, Stephanie Waterman, Cindy Cruz, Ro Millham, Jessica Bissett Perea, Kiersten Greene, Jen Jack Gieseking, Jenn Milam, Beth Blue Swadener, JoAnn Schmier, Karanja Keita Carroll, and Michael D. Smith.

Our families have our deepest recognition: Kevin, Kieran, Beverly, Melody, John, Justin, Sarah, Beverly, Ted, Masura, Lenore, Eugene, John, Kae, Dale, Jean, John, Nancy, Gregory, and Helena.

1 Introduction to Place in Research

"What do people make of places? The question is as old as people and places themselves, as old as human attachments to portions of the earth."

Keith Basso, *Wisdom Sits in Places*, 1996, p. xiii

Social science research is always situated physically, in some instances in particular locations, in others, across borders. Social science research is always undertaken by researchers and participants embedded in *places*, places that are both local and global, shaped by and constitutive of culture and identity. Thus, research in the social sciences is always concerned with epistemologies, questions, and methods that impact place and land, and the human and natural communities that inhabit them. These realities of research have been largely overlooked in many fields: as we detail in this book, place is significant in research.

Our articulation of the practices and trajectories of place in research is situated on the cusp of a renewed interested in "place" in the social sciences, evident both in the increased attention to decolonizing research and Indigenous methodologies, as well as in relation to "spatial" and "material" turns in the social sciences more broadly. Although there is a renewed interest in place, this does not always mean that place is engaged meaningfully. Throughout this book, we aim to deepen readers' considerations of place to grapple not only the physical and spatial aspects of place in relation to the social, but also more deeply with how places and our orientations to them are informed by, and determinants of, history, empire, and culture. As David Harvey (1989) has observed, "How we represent space and time in theory matters, because it affects how we and others interpret and then act with respect to the world" (p. 205). This book seeks to develop complex and historicized orientations to place in research through providing social science researchers with rationales, discourses, examples, and methods of critical place inquiry, or in other words, research that more fully considers the implications and significance of place in lived lives. Beyond the furthering of social science empirical knowledge, we advocate for theoretically and ethically responsive research in the context of the globalization of the planet, its populations, and places. The chapters that follow will help readers understand and make decisions about conducting research that critically engages places and people's relationships with them.

Thus, in this introduction and in the chapters that follow, we elaborate theorizations and practices of *critical place inquiry* in the social sciences. By this we mean research that takes up critical questions and develops corresponding methodological approaches that are informed by the embeddedness of social life in and with places, and that seeks to be a form of action in responding to critical place issues such as those of globalization and neoliberalism, settler colonialism, and environmental degradation. In what follows, we examine ways in which place is being deployed conceptually and empirically in social science research, methodologies and methods through which meaningful engagement of place can be undertaken, and the ethical and political implications and possibilities of critical place inquiries as public scholarship.

WHY IS THIS IMPORTANT NOW? INDIGENOUS AND ENVIRONMENTAL COLLABORATIONS

An increased focus on place in critical research matters because it enables greater attention to the ways in which land and environmental issues intersect with social issues and social life. Just some examples of these intersections include the following:

- Issues of borders, displacement, and (re)place-making for diasporic and refugee populations
- War and militarism in relation to territorial identification or expansion
- The role of spatial and place-based practices in colonialism and settler colonialism, from practices of property ownership to those of the environmental poisoning of fish and wildlife on Indigenous traditional territories
- Access to healthy food, equitable education, or the uneven geographic distribution of other social services within urban environments based on racialization, gender, or economic disparities
- Municipal and regional inequities in the distribution of environmental harms, such as the location of industrial or nuclear waste storage
- Global North-South inequities in which those regions and populations hardest hit are those least responsible for climate change
- Human-caused harm and extinction of other forms of life
- Intergenerational injustices entailed in loss of places and species, and the increasing possibility of human extinction due to climate change

The conditions for these and other interwoven social and environmental forms of injustice have been created by long histories of hierarchical divisions among peoples, to other species, to the land. Legacies and ongoing practices of Empire and globalization, racialization and privilege, and destructive land management practices, exacerbated by industrialization, capitalism, and increasing global mobility, have created circumstances in which inequalities on almost all scales are increasing (e.g., inequalities in financial wealth within most countries, global economic inequalities between countries, interspecies injustice, intergenerational injustice) (IPCC, 2013).

Neoliberalism, as a term used to describe currently dominant global and globalizing governance systems, promotes "free-market" conditions that prioritize corporations and economic growth over considerations of social equity or environmental protection. As Peck (2013) suggests, neoliberalization processes should be viewed as operating alongside other dominant trajectories, such as those of globalization, as well as taking hybrid forms in relation to more localized histories and priorities. While variegated across nations and social contexts, various formations of neoliberalism can be understood to share an emphasis on privatization, public-sector austerity, tax cuts, and regulatory restraint. For our discussions here, we particularly want to point out a less articulated characteristic of neoliberalism as a current formation of capitalism and Empire, which is the reliance on territory and the natural environment to fuel unsustainable and colonialist economies.

One component of this largely absent analysis of political systems in relation to land is the relationship between capitalism and the biophysical. This comprises a focus in Neil Smith's (2008) book *Uneven Development: Nature, Capital and the Production of Space*, which Noel Castree (2007) summarizes as follows:

> Smith argues that the biophysical world is both a condition of, and propellant to, capital's uneven development in space and time. This is true not only in the case of nature-dependent industries and areas (think of agricultural, forestry and mining districts, or fisheries communities). It is more generally true for capital writ-large, since ultimately all aspects of capitalist society are nature-dependent in some way, shape or form: the making, moving, selling, servicing, consuming and disposal of any and all commodities necessarily requires raw materials, energy sources, physical spaces and waste disposal opportunities. It follows, for Smith, that uneven development is simultaneously a political economic and biophysical process. Capital's restless search for new investment opportunities and new markets routinely entails: (i) the abandonment of no longer productive zones (where the conditions of production may be deteriorating and too costly or risky to fix); (ii) biophysical changes in 'virgin' territories because new energy- and raw-material intensive infrastructures may emerge combined with new productive activities that may themselves make large biophysical demands; and (iii) the use of these territories as absorption zones for surplus capital from growth

regions, including myriad resource-commodities like trees, foodstuffs and minerals in search of market opportunities. At moments of crisis—economic, political and reproductive—environmental problems in one area can become the impetus for new rounds of biophysical transformation elsewhere as capital switches (often speculatively) into new growth areas. But even in non-crisis conditions, Smith argues, the compulsion to work existing biophysical assets harder and seek-out new ones is part-and-parcel of capitalism's normal functioning. (pp. 32–33)

However, despite (neoliberal) capitalism's reliance on the biophysical, Castree (2007) suggests that most recent assessments of neoliberalism, such as David Harvey's (2005) *A Brief History of Neoliberalism*, or Andrew Glyn's (2006) *Capitalism Unleashed*, pay little attention to associated considerations of climate change, water resource management, biodiversity loss, or other biophysical issues, focusing instead on topics such as employment, trade, and welfare provision. Going beyond these macro-analyses to consider more specialized books, journals, and working papers, Castree found that the majority of the critical literature on neoliberalism was disproportionately focused on issues other than environmental ones:

> For instance, a search of the ISI Web of Knowledge at the time of writing reveals over 500 peer review publications containing the world 'neoliberalism' as a title or keyword. However, a search using additional terms such as agriculture, farming, fisheries, forestry, water resources, mining and so on reveals that only about one fifth of these writings focus on the relationship to the non-human world in some way, shape or form. (p. 9)

Our more recent searches for this book indicate a maintained relative lack of focus on the relationships between neoliberalism or capitalism and land or environment, particularly in meta-analytic discussions.

A second aspect of problematic relationships between dominant political systems and the land are the historical and ongoing land-based practices of colonialism and, in particular, settler colonialism. As will be described at length in Chapter 3, the legacies of the spatial practices of European colonization over the past 500 years in many parts of the globe continue to be supported by governments, but also social practices more generally, which establish and reify hierarchies of settler over Indigenous. Seeking to uncover the traces and effects of (settler) colonialism, scholarship in settler colonialism is quickly growing in scope and impact, and we draw on it extensively in this volume to problematize settler relations to land as they affect Indigenous peoples, land, and other life forms, including as linked to current environmental devastation and curtailed possibilities for future generations. Settler and colonial futurities based on expansionist, capitalist, and racist assumptions necessitate practices of decolonization in order to re-prioritize Indigenous and land-based futurities (Tuck & Yang, 2012).

Based in these intersecting absences in much social science research, this book highlights research that does elaborate and address the embeddedness of social life, including economic policy, with land and environment. This includes work on global mobilities and post-carbon social theory (Elliot & Urry, 2010), power geometries and politics of place (Katz, 2004; Massey, 2005), the land-based mechanisms of settler colonialism (Byrd, 2011; Wolfe, 1999), and the political contexts of environmental injustice (Walker, 2012). We draw on these and other examples of research theorizing place, as well as those discussing implications for methodologies and methods of critical research, in order to advocate for greater consideration of place in social science research, particularly at this critical juncture of human and planetary history.

Thus, this book seeks to convince readers to take place more seriously in social science inquiry in order to further research and associated action on human and land-based injustice, to current and future generations. The entire volume is dedicated to providing rationales, exemplars, and looks to the future for making place (more) significant in social science inquiry. We highlight examples from across social science research that take up place not only as the topic of the research in many cases, but as central to the process of making research-based knowledge and action. Throughout the volume we attend to theories and conceptualizations of place, methodologies of place, and methods of place. Our hope is that in these pages, readers will find inspiration and guidance in designing social science research that engages place meaningfully.

The approach of this book is uncommon because it seeks to bring decolonizing Indigenous studies, environmental scholarship, and related critical areas concerned with place into conversation with one another. These comprise areas of study that address many similar topics, but that remain quite distinct in epistemology, discourse, and practice. There are often important divergences and even competing logics at work in these areas of research, some that may indeed be incommensurable. The book brings these areas into conversation, without papering over the differences, but also without maintaining false dichotomies. Instead, as collaborating authors located in environmental and Indigenous studies, we bridge these and related domains to examine place in social science research, and in doing so, define and contribute to the emerging area of critical place inquiry.

This book seeks to offer cross-disciplinary insight into how researchers around the globe are theoretically and empirically engaging, or re-engaging, place in social science research. The book maps the emergence of what we call critical place inquiry; marks the historical, economic, colonial, and ecological conditions that necessitate such inquiry; offers new directions for methodologies and methods of place inquiry; and highlights research efforts around the world that inform how one can understand and inhabit place through research. In so doing, the book examines and provides insight into the *why, what, and how* of developing critical place research in the social sciences.

UNDERSTANDING PLACE

Although it may at first seem self-evident, place is a complex concept, and most often is defined in relation to space. Agnew (2011) suggests that space, "is regarded largely as a dimension within which matter is located or a grid within which substantive items are contained" (p. 317). Karen Barad (2007) observes,

> The view of space as container or context for matter in motion— spatial coordinates mapped via projections along axes that set up a metric for tracking the locations of the inhabitants of the container, and time divided into evenly spaced increments marking a progression of events—pervades much of Western epistemology. (p. 223)

The Western philosophical tradition of the term *space*, as it is used now, arose in the seventeenth century, emerging from Newtonian and Leibnizian conceptualizations. In the Newtonian conceptualization, space is itself an independent entity, no matter what or if it is occupied by objects or events (Agnew, 2011, p. 318). In this view, space is concrete, and indeed it is this concreteness that makes it real. In contrast, in the Leibnizian conceptualization, space is relational and dependent, holding no powers itself. In this view, space is active, yet "entirely parasitic on the relations between objects and events occupying places" (Agnew, 2011, p. 319).

Donna Haraway's (1997) critique of models of spatialization updates the Leibnizian construction:

> Spatialization as a never-ending, power-laced process engaged by a motley array of beings can be fetishized as a series of maps whose grids nontropically located naturally bounded bodies (land, people, resources—and genes) inside "absolute" dimensions such as space and time. The maps are fetishes in so far as they enable a specific kind of mistake that turns process into nontropic, real, literal things inside containers. (p. 136)

The description of spatialization offered by Haraway is an extension of the Leibnizian construction of space because it does not characterize space as static or concrete or absolute, but instead as dynamic, interactive, indeed, as a process. Haraway's updating of the Leibnizian construction depicts it as power-laced rather than as having no powers of its own; this rejoinder allows for analyses of how power and place are coproduced. Haraway's and others' extensions of Leibnizian constructions of space have inspired much of contemporary spatial theory, especially theories that expound upon relational and shifting aspects of space.

"Place," although used in multiple ways in the English language (as rank, as temporality, as position), is perhaps most importantly used to convey geographic meaning (Agnew, 2011, p. 318). In many Western definitions of place(s), the focus is on its/their specificity—either by singular spatial metric (latitude-longitude, elevation), or the non-exchangeability of one place with another (Farinelli, 2000). Agnew (2011) explains that after many years of regard and dis-regard as a static concept, place underwent a significant revival in the field of geography in the 1970s and 1980s (p. 320). In part, this was a response to positivism, and was made possible by the insight that "the term place carries with it not only the meaning of spatial location but also those of social position and moral order" (Agnew, 2011, p. 322; see also Tuan, 1974; Barad, 2007). Michael Curry (1998) express the insights of this revival as follows:

> The relationship between an object and where it belongs is not simply fortuitous, or a matter of causal forces, but it is rather intrinsic or internal, a matter of what that thing actually is. When things are not where they belong, they cannot truly be themselves. (p. 48)

Thus, the revival of conceptualizations of place that occurred in the 1970s and 1980s was concerned with the mediating role of place in social relations and in meaning-making (Massey, 1984). This revival has had many ripple effects in the field of geography, but Agnew laments that this "socially and morally inflected sense of place" has not been substantively engaged in fields beyond geography (2011, p. 322).

Although there has been this intensified interest in the physical locations of social life and research, at the same time, theorizations of identity and globalization have led to critiques of terminology and theorizations of place in social research (e.g., Massey, 1994; Rose, 1993). Considering the ways in which factors such as gender, racialization, nationality, or access to financial or technological resources affects people's access to, mobility across, and experiences of place, some scholars have suggested that the defining of places is problematic. Or in other words, "the terminology of 'place' is seen by some as ignoring process, power relations, and remaining too bounded" (Anderson & Harrison, 2010, p. 9). In addition, Agnew (2011) argues that other social sciences still adopt the view of the nation-state, not the community or place, as the main geographic unit of account or concern. He contends that social sciences problematically rely on evolutionary or linear understandings of human history, in which community-place has been superseded by notions of nation-space, putting false weight in narratives of (civilized) society and modernity.

As a final point on Agnew's (2011) work on space and place, he observes that current notions of the world as increasingly "flat" or "placeless" (e.g., Friedman, 2005) are ignorant of deeper meanings of *both* space *and* place. In views of the world as flat—primarily yielded through commentaries on globalization—new technologies, the internet, cellular phones, seem to make place(s) obsolete (Agnew, 2011, p. 317). Globalization, as represented by big-box chain stores that dot the landscape of otherwise very different places, makes it seem that place matters far less than it used to matter. Indeed, writing about place in the social sciences may seem almost quaint, or even passé (Casey, 2009). Talking about the impacts of these circumstances on the field of anthropology, Coleman and Collins (2006) write about the "simultaneous prominence and disappearance of place in contemporary ethnography," explaining the following:

> In a curious sense places have disappeared—or at the least the boundaries around them have become deeply problematized as connections between culture and territory, identity and fixed community, are challenged. It may be a sign of the times that a recent textbook on "key concepts" in social and cultural anthropology by Rapport and Overing (2000) lacks an entry on the concept of place, but does have one on *non*-places. (see Augé, 1995, p. 2)

Thus, theorists and researchers attendant to issues of space and place must work against the seemingly common-sense conclusions of popular analyses of globalization, which, not operating from a complex conceptualization of space and place, attempt to foretell the end of place. As Edward S. Casey insists,

> We do not live in space. Instead, *we live in places*. So it behooves us to understand what such place-bound and place-specific living consists in. However lost we may become by gliding rapidly between places, however oblivious to place we may be in our thought and theory, and however much we may prefer to think of what happens in a place rather than of the place itself, we are tied to place undetachably and without reprieve. (Casey, 2009, p. xiii, italics original)

Beyond the under-theorizing of place, it is typical for place to be superficially addressed in social science inquiry. Many social science professional mores require researchers to clearly define *what* was learned and *how* it was learned. *When* is important too, especially in fields in which the most cutting-edge and recent research is given favor, and others in which longitudinal studies are valued. *Where*, however, is not always given much attention, beyond a few notes at the outset of a dissertation or publication, and then usually only by place name. Basso (1996) writes,

> Places, to be sure, are frequently mentioned in anthropological texts ("The people of X . . . ," "The hamlet of Y . . ." "The market-place at Z . . ."), but largely in passing, typically early on, and chiefly as a means of locating the texts themselves, grounding them, as it were, in settings around the world. And with that task accomplished the texts move ahead, with scarcely a backward glance, to take up other matters.

Practicing ethnographers, much like everyone else, take sense of place for granted, and ethnographic studies exploring their cultural and social dimensions are in notably short supply. Human attachments to places, as various and diverse as the places to which they attach, remain, in their way, an enigma. (p. xiv)

Thus, in much social science research, place is just the surface upon which life happens (and from which data are collected) (Massey, 1994). If mentioned at all, it is usually as the backdrop of the inquiry, described briefly beneath headings like "the research site," or "the research context." Consider the number of studies that use designations such as "urban," "rural," "Southern," or "small," to describe where the work has taken place. Such terms are used frequently, but rarely are further examined through the research.

Thus we suggest that discussions of place are located on the periphery in most social science inquiry, not as core components of the analysis or in the selection and development of a research methodology and methods of data collection and analysis. If place is mentioned at all, it is typically inserted at the outset in discussion of the research site, rather than engaged as part of the analysis or considered in terms of the specifics of research methodology or methods. Although much work has been done to bring concepts of place and space forth from their earlier seventeenth-century conceptualizations, it is those conceptualizations and not their revivals that are still employed most commonly in social science research (Agnew, 2011). This has implications for the richness of theories of space and place engaged in social science research, but also for how the relationships between space and place are usually understood.

RECENT TURNS IN SOCIAL SCIENCE RESEARCH

Although Agnew (2003, 2011) worries over the minimal engagement of disciplines outside of geography in issues of space and place, there have been important "turns" in social sciences that somewhat unsettle his assessment. Here, and returned to throughout this volume, we discuss the increasing influence of Indigenous and decolonizing perspectives, the spatial turn, and the new materialist or ontological turn.

Indigenous and Decolonizing Perspectives and Methodologies

In recent decades, perspectives of Indigenous scholars have found their way to greater numbers of readers, achieving more and more influence. This trend is evident in the wide circulation and use of books like Linda Tuhiwai Smith's *Decolonizing Methodologies* (1999/2012); Denzin, Lincoln, and

L. T. Smith's *Handbook on Critical and Indigenous Methodologies* (2008); and the creation of numerous professional associations, graduate programs, and academic journals on Indigenous studies around the globe in the past 15 years.

Shawn Wilson (2008) emphasizes the ways in which Indigenous methodologies are typified by a kind of internal consistency, meaning Indigenous cosmologies, cosmogonies, worldviews, and ethical beliefs are evident in every aspect in Indigenous inquiry. In Indigenous approaches, it is the people who decide what should be studied, and researchers are held accountable not only to developing useful knowledge, but also to adhering to cultural expectations and to fostering ethical relationships along the way. In part, this is because of the long history that Indigenous peoples have had with unethical researchers, but also the unethical ways that Indigenous materials, samples, stories, and intellectual property have been improperly handled and dispersed in academe (see also L. T. Smith, 1999/2012; Tuck & Guishard, 2013).

Although many historians and other observers have characterized Indigenous intellectual traditions as almost exclusively oral traditions, recent works (Brooks, 2008; Erdrich, 2003) have tried to dislodge that narrative, insisting instead that there have always been intimate, synthesizing relationships between oral and written and image-based meaning-making (called knowledge production, in the academy). Indeed as Erdrich (2003) has noted, the words for *book* and *rock painting* are almost the same in Ojibwe language, and as Brooks (2008) has noted, the words for *draw, write,* and *map* have the same root in Abenaki language; through tracing the roots of the words in Abenaki, Brooks is able to conclude that *the book and the map are the same thing* (2008, p. xx–xxii).

Looking to Indigenous languages helps to demonstrate the differences between understandings of space and place (and time) that exist between Western/colonial frameworks and Indigenous knowledge systems. Linda Tuhiwai Smith (1999/2012) observes that,

> The Maori word for time or space is the same. Other indigenous languages have no related word for either space or time, having instead a series of very precise terms for parts of these ideas, or for relationships between the idea and something else in the environment. (p. 52)

In contrast to the diversity of understandings of space, place, and time in Indigenous knowledge systems, Smith depicts Western philosophies of space as being divorced from time. This separation,

> is particularly relevant in relation to colonialism. The establishment of military, missionary or trading stations, the building of roads, ports, and bridges, the clearing and the mining of minerals all involved processes of marking, defining, and controlling space. There is a very

specific spatial vocabulary of colonialism which can be assembled around three concepts: (1) the line, (2) the center, and (3) the outside. The 'line' is important because it was used to map territory, to survey land, to establish boundaries, and to mark the limits of colonial power. The 'center' is important because orientation to the center was an orientation to the system of power. The 'outside is important because it positioned territory and people in an oppositional relation to the colonial center. (p. 55)

Thus, one major outgrowth of the increased attention to Indigenous perspectives and methodologies in academic discourse is the recognition that alternative, long-held, comprehensive and theoretically sophisticated understandings of place exist outside, alongside, against, and within the domain of the Western philosophical tradition. These understandings of place, often framed in terms of *land,* derive from entirely different epistemological and cosmological foundations and, thus, cannot be easily combined or absorbed into Western argumentations. They come from, and go to, a different place.

This is not an assertion that Indigenous conceptualizations of land are pristine, devoid of Western philosophical influence, or even that keeping Indigenous theory pristine from colonial and settler influences is possible or most desirable (Smith, 2012). But the persistence/existence of Indigenous theorizations and methodologies of land serve as rejoinder to Western theorizations of place, to mark how theories of the West have also been shaped by its colonial and settler histories and current pursuits.

As we discuss more fully in Chapters 2 and 3, Indigenous conceptualizations of land are diverse, specific, and particular. They often derive from Indigenous cosmologies, meaning Indigenous conceptualizations of land are abundant with aspects of relationships to and within the universe.

Scott Morgensen (2011) asserts that Indigenous methodologies are tied to a larger project of Indigenous decolonization; they do not merely model Indigenous research, but "denaturalize power within settler societies and ground knowledge production in decolonization" (p. 805). Decolonizing perspectives, informed by Indigenous perspectives, seek to undo the real and symbolic violences of colonialism. Decolonization is determined to thwart colonial apparatuses, recover Indigenous land and life, and shape a new structure and future for all life. Like colonization, which has shared components and instruments across sites but is uniquely implemented in each setting, decolonization requires unique theories and enactments across sites. Thus, decolonization is always historically specific, context specific, and place specific (Fanon, 1961; Tuck & Yang, 2012). As Elizabeth Povinelli (2011) has observed, "potentiality and its perpetual variations never occur in a general way, but in specific arrangement of connecting concepts, materials, and forces that make a common compositional unity" (p. 16). Decolonization is always about land (Tuck & Yang, 2012).

The Spatial Turn

Edward Soja (2010) observes that social scientists have long prioritized historical and sociological perspectives and have overlooked spatial and geographical perspectives. Attention is paid to how processes and personhood develop over time rather than in relation to space. The spatial dimension has been treated as fixed, as having some influence, but quite external from human processes and consciousness (p. 2). Yet, Soja notes that a spatial turn, "an unprecedented diffusion of critical spatial thinking across an unusually broad spectrum of subject areas," is underway.

> Often these applications of a spatial perspective are superficial, involving little more than a few pertinent spatial metaphors such as mapping this or that or using such words as cartography, region, or landscape to appear to be moving with the times. In some fields, however, such as in current debates in urban archaeology and development economics, radically new ideas have been emerging from an understanding of sociospatial causality, the powerful forces that arise from social produced spaces such as urban agglomerations and cohesive regional economies. (Soja, 2010, p. 14)

Soja suggests that the spatial turn is poised to profoundly change all aspects of inquiry, including ontological and epistemological considerations, theory formation, empirical research, and applied knowledge (p. 15). However, it has also met some resistance from scholars who find historical and sociological perspectives to be superior, as well as scholars who seemingly adopt a critical spatial perspective but ultimately lack "the rigor and depth of their own well-developed . . . ways of thinking and writing about space," and tend to "give greater stress to how social processes such as class formation, social stratification, or racist or masculinist practices shape geographies than to how geographies actively affect these social processes and forms" (Soja, 2010, p. 4).

Exciting examples of how the spatial turn has been taken up in other fields include George Lipsitz's (2011) *How Racism Takes Place* in American Studies/Black Studies, and Pauline Lipman's (2011) *The New Political Economy of Urban Education* in Educational Studies. Both engage a political economy approach, but the influence of spatial theorizing makes a dynamic contribution. Lipsitz, informed by geographer Laura Pulido's (2000) work, observes the place-bound nature of white identity in the United States and how "practices that racialize space and spatialize race" shape almost every aspect of urban life (2011, p. 6). Lipman's (2011) work traces how Harvey's (2003) notion of accumulation by dispossession is spatialized through real-estate driven educational reform that closes schools in Black neighborhoods and paves the way for gentrification.

In *For Space*, Doreen Massey insists that how we imagine space has consequences: seeing space as commensurate with voyages and discovery, as something to be traversed, as the same as the land and oceans, as a surface, as given, will have ramifications (2005). In imagining space as a surface upon which human life happens, it becomes possible to view other variations of human life as simply phenomena atop this benign surface; this may not at first appear to be problematic, but it is insofar as phenomena on the surface may be seen to be waiting to be discovered, conquered (p. 4), but also managed, exploited, rescued, pathologized.

One invisibilized trick of globalization, Massey (2005) observes, is that via frames of development, openness, and (soon to be) new markets, it prompts a sleight of hand with regard to space and time, in which geography is turned into history, and space into time (p. 5). Thus, what a contemporary spatial analysis seeks to do, is to "refuse to convene space into time" (p. 5). The abiding question of the turn to spatial analysis is how to think about space more explicitly (p. 7).

There are three propositions that are central to Massey's (2005) argument for space: (1) Space is constituted through interactions; (2) Without space there is no multiplicity, without multiplicity there is no space; and (3) Space is always under construction (p. 9). As a whole, Massey makes some important conceptual moves that help to explain the overarching project of the spatial turn. These conceptual moves include

- Remaking space as multiplicity, as much more than a surface
- Rethinking relationships between space and time
- Articulating the significance of space
- Considering the consequences of lack of depth in theorizing space
- Pushing back against the false inevitability of globalization
- Identifying possibilities for spatial justice (Soja, 2010), particularly through geographies of care (Massey, 2005)

The project of the spatial turn is one that presses against prior ways of taking up social science questions, not because space is less challenging than time, but because space presents us with the

> challenge of our constitutive interrelatedness—and thus our collective implication in the outcomes of the interrelatedness; the radical contemporaneity of an ongoing multiplicity of others, human and nonhuman; and the ongoing and ever-specific project of the practices through which that sociability is to be configured. (Massey, 2005, p. 195)

Still, in our view, there are some descriptions of the spatial turn in which arguments for the primacy of space in social science inquiry offer problematic characterizations of place. For example, in a generally very considered volume titled *Education and the Spatial Turn: Policy and Geography Matters*, editors Gulson and Symes (2007) write the following about the differences between space and place,

Places generally have names; they figure on maps, have boundaries and parameters—there is an element of fixity pertaining to them. Place lends itself to more 'objective,' scientific accounts of space—even though what constitutes a place is itself a construct, subject to myriad judgements as to where its boundaries and populations begin and end. (p. 2)

Gulson and Symes continue, "places do not have practices in quite the same way [that spaces do]. Space in this sense is more of a verb than a noun" (2007, p. 2). These observations come from the introduction to Gulson and Symes's (2007) edited volume. In it, they are introducing readers to the central premise of the book: theories of space and spatiality have much to offer analyses of education, including in terms of policy, social inequality, and cultural practices. Of course, we recognize that, by way of introducing theories of space to readers unfamiliar with the field, Gulson and Symes are working to articulate and differentiate space from place—as authors such as Agnew, 2005; Harvey, 1996; and Massey, 2005, did before them. Our contention is that place is not adequately described in this contrast. Places are not always named, and not always justly named. They do not always appear on maps; they do not have agreed-upon boundaries. They are not fixed. Places are not more readily understood by objective accounts. Finally and most importantly, places have practices. In some definitions, places *are* practices (see Deyhle, 2009).

The New Materialist Turn

The recent new materialist, neo-materialist, or ontological turn has emerged through orientations that object to the hegemony of the linguistic paradigm in poststructuralism, "stressing instead the concrete yet complex materiality of bodies in social relations of power" (Braidotti in Dolphijn & van der Tuin, 2012, p. 21). Building on interdisciplinary scholarship on non-representational theory (e.g., Thrift, 2008), actor network theory (e.g., Latour, 2005; Law, 2004), feminist ontologies (e.g., Haraway, 1985; Grosz, 1994), and other trajectories of critical materialism (e.g., Harvey, 2000; Žižek, 2010), nearly all social science disciplines are now experiencing a renewed interest in "the world," in its physical or material manifestations (Burns & Smith, 2011; Coole & Frost, 2010). Despite the variations across these approaches, particularly in whether they attend to the political or are "critical," most gather place or land into broader categorizations of actors or objects that are viewed as also influencing and influenced by social life (e.g., technology, institutions, animals, other humans). As an aggregate, new materialism is strongly interdisciplinary, with intellectual roots in Continental philosophy and Anglo-American thought (Dolphijn & van der Tuin, 2012, p. 89). One of its major impulses, in no small part due to the influence of feminist philosophy, is to reject dualistic separations of the mind from the body, and of nature from culture (p. 21).

Prominent new materialist theorist Karen Barad (2007), following Ruth Wilson Gilmore's (1999) suggestion to replace a politics of location with a "politics of possibilities," seeks to

> dislocate the container model of space, the spatialization of time, and the reification of matter by reconceptualizing the notions of space, time, and matter using an alternative framework that shakes loose the foundational character of notions such as location and opens up a space of agency in which the dynamic intra-play of indeterminacy and determinacy reconfigures the possibilities and impossibilities of the world's becoming such that indeterminacies, contingencies, and ambiguities coexist with causality. (p. 225)

This serves as a cogent definition of the spatialization project of new materialism. The refusal of space as an "Euclidean grid of identification" (Barad, 2007, p. 240), is a generative move toward a topological analysis and representation of changing dynamics of space, time, and matter.

In their introduction to an edited volume on *New Materialisms* (2010), Diana Coole and Samantha Frost posit that the "massive materiality" of human existence is often taken for granted, perhaps in part because once we begin to think about matter, "we seem to distance ourselves from it, and within that space that opens up, a host of immaterial things seems to emerge: language, consciousness, subjectivity, agency, mind, soul; also imagination, emotions, values, meaning, and so on" (p. 2). New materialism is concerned with how matter comes to matter: "Materiality itself is always already a desiring dynamism, a reiterative reconfiguring, energized and energizing, enlivened and enlivening" (Barad in Dolphijn & van der Tuin, 2012, p. 59).

In response to the focus on subjectivity that has typified much of the social sciences in recent decades, Coole and Frost (2010) call for a reappraisal of material reality, material causality, and the significance of corporeality. They wonder if the recent proliferation of new ways to theorize and research material reality in fields like geography, political science, economics, anthropology, and sociology are evidence of the inadequacies of text-based approaches encumbered within the prior so-called "cultural turn" (pp. 2–3). Indeed, Coole and Frost see the reconfiguring of understandings of matter as a prerequisite "for any plausible account of coexistence and its conditions in the twenty-first century" (p. 2).

Discussing the influence of feminist philosophies on new materialism, Rosi Braidotti (in Dolphijn & van der Tuin, 2012) highlights the centrality of corporeality in this frame: "The body or the embodiment of the subject is to be understood as neither a biological nor a sociological category, but rather as a point of overlap between the physical, the symbolic, and the sociological" (p. 33). The turn to new materialisms coincides with theorems and findings in post-classical physics, which indicate the ways in which matter and its defining are elusive (Coole & Frost, 2010, p. 5). Unanswered and perhaps unanswerable questions that abound in post-classical physics and post-classical natural sciences parallel a reinvigorated discussion of ontology in the social sciences—discussions that pertain to the underlying beliefs about being and existence, about relationships and meaning.

The new materialist turn also reflects the emergence of "pressing and ethical political concerns that accompany the scientific and technological advances predicated on new scientific models of matter and, in particular, living matter" (Coole & Frost, 2010, p. 5). Coole and Frost continue,

> From our understanding of the boundary between life and death and our everyday work practices to the way we feed ourselves and recreate or procreate, we are finding our environment materially and conceptually reconstituted in ways that pose profound and unprecedented normative questions. In addressing them, we unavoidably find ourselves having to think in new ways about the nature of matter and the matter of nature, about the elements of life, the resilience of the planet, and other distinctiveness of the human. (p. 5)

An important characteristic of new materialists that differentiates them from the historical materialists of the nineteenth and twentieth centuries is their emphasis on active processes of materialization, particularly the active role that humans (and human bodies) and non-humans play in materialization, undoing the barriers established through Cartesianism (p. 8). Matter, of which human beings are both part and cogenerate, is agentic, with its own modes of self-transformation, self-organization, and directedness (p. 10).

Finally, theory formation in new materialism is concerned with cartography rather than classification. Classification is avoided because it is "territorial and fully dualistic," whereas cartography allows for the unfolding of cultural theory, nonlinear coding practices, cutting across matter and signification (Dolphijn & van der Tuin, 2012, p. 111). Not primarily interested in representation, signification, and disciplinarity, new materialism is fascinated by affect, force, and movement as it travels in all directions. "New materialism argues that we know nothing of the (social) body until we know what it can do" (p. 113, parenthesis original).

With regard to how the materialist turn approaches theories of space and time, we heed Barad's warnings away from geometrical considerations of place, instead attending to topological questions of boundary, connectivity, interiority, and exteriority (2007, p. 244):

> Analyzing the multidimensional, multiply connected heterogenous geo-political-economic-social-cultural "landscape" on the basis of geometrical considerations will not suffice. Not even if what is meant by geometry is retrofitted for postmodern sensibilities by insisting on the relative and socially constructed nature of presumably geometrical terms (e.g. scale).

Nor is it sufficient to figure responsibility in terms of positionality or other efforts to locate oneself within the relevant social horizon. The inadequacy of geometrical analysis in isolation from topological considerations lies in the very nature of "construction." (2007, p. 245)

We wholly agree that "geometric" understandings of space and place are reductive, and, like Massey's (2005) critique of those who see space as a "surface" upon which human life takes place, we press back against theorizations of space as given, as static, as passive, as backdrop. Yet, Barad dismisses the entirety of discussions of space and place as though all of them adhere to geometrical constructions. We also see that there are very different discussions of place emerging from Indigenous literatures on material land and sovereignty. Thus, we take Barad's critique of geometrical constructions of space seriously, but are not yet willing to cede the notions of place and land for topology.

WHEN TURNS BECOME TRENDS: BARRIERS TO CRITICAL PLACE INQUIRY

The increasing influence of Indigenous and decolonizing scholarship, spatial theories, and new materialism on the theories, methodologies, and methods of social science cannot be disputed. However, although one might suppose that such innovations and recalibrations might prompt a more robust discussion of place in the social sciences, this is not often the case. In many cases, flattened ontological or materialist frameworks de-emphasize the agency of people and politics in attempting to better attend to the interconnected "networks" or "mangles" of practice in researching social life; while the spatial turn has emphasized global flows of people, information, and products, in many instances this has resulted in a turning away from a focus on place in theoretical or empirical study. In contrast, Indigenous intellectual contributions rarely fail to engage in issues of land and place—especially via conceptualizations of tribal identity, sovereignty, and treaty rights—yet when these discussions are taken up by non-Indigenous and settler scholars, the saliency of land/place is frequently left out of the picture.

Thus, it is our view that scholars influenced by these turns often do not go far enough to attend to place. Although there are rich theorizations of place that throb at the center of each of these turns in social science, in their wider adoption and redaction, place gets reduced and reified. There are important exceptions to each of these characterizations, of course, but ironically, works across social science that now are attending to issues of being and existence can rely upon conceptualizations of place that are markedly shallow or emptied. The challenge is to get rich theorizations (and methodologies and methods) of place to travel within and alongside the adoption and adaptation of these turns, and other turns now forming and emerging.

In addition, another barrier to more hearty conceptualizations/articulations of place in social science research was identified more than 20 years ago by Neil Smith and Cindi Katz, who argued against haphazard use of metaphors, specifically spatial metaphors. Writing about the wider adoption of the poststructural turn (via the works of Deleuze and Guattari, for example), Smith and Katz (1993) cautioned social scientists about the metaphors we use, and how those metaphors are translated in our discussions (see also Simonsen, 2004).

> We argue that many current spatial metaphors, such as 'positionality', 'locality', grounding', 'displacement', 'territory', 'nomadism', and so forth require urgent critical scrutiny. The appeal of these spatial metaphors lies precisely in the new meaning they impart, but it is increasingly evident that these metaphors depend overwhelmingly on a very specific and contested conception of space and that they embody often unintended political consequences. (Smith & Katz, 1993, p. 68)

Metaphors, Smith and Katz argue, are never politically neutral nor benign; they are never empty of significance. Use of place- and space-derived metaphors does little to attend more responsibly to issues of place. Instead, metaphorical representations of place invoke place superficially, too easily.

DESCRIBING CRITICAL PLACE INQUIRY

In thinking about critical engagements with place in research, we draw on the developments of postmodern, spatial, new materialist, and other "turns" of the social sciences for their insights on the movement and relationality of place. As is detailed further in Chapters 2 and 3 on conceptualizing and practicing place, we suggest we need to move beyond understandings of place as neutral backdrop, or as a bounded and antiquated concept, or as only physical landscape, to instead theorize and practice place more deeply in social science research. Critical place inquiry can involve and include a range of research methodologies, as we discuss in Chapter 4, from textual analysis to ethnography to Indigenous approaches to mixed and strategic methodologies; what is central is the way the chosen methodology engages conceptually with place in order to mobilize methods that enable data collection and analyses that also engage place explicitly and politically.

Likewise, as we discuss in Chapters 5 and 6, a range of data collection and analyses methods can be used, with promising new directions in the ways in which data from land and other species, as well as emplaced and embodied data from humans, are being collected and considered; as well as mobilized towards more ethical and responsible relations on and with place. Research methodology and methods should be selected in relationship to the specifics of place and research participants and aims. One question that emerges from discussions in Chapters 3 and 6 is the extent to which the aims of decolonizing conceptualizations of land and place and Indigenous methods are central and not peripheral to practices of critical place inquiry.

While critical place inquiry (like all inquiry) is performative, it is also representative; we cannot escape mental processes of thought and language in data collection or analyses. Efforts to get beyond representation are in danger of being solipsistic and apolitical, and seemingly impossible. Instead, as we discuss in Chapter 7, the legitimacy of critical place research can be established by reference to its relational validity, or in other words, its grounding and implications for relations to land, to social context, and to future generations.

Critical place inquiry:

- Understands places as themselves mobile, shifting over time and space and through interactions with flows of people, other species, social practices
- Entails, at a more localized level, understanding places as both influencing social practices as well as being performed and (re)shaped through practices and movements of individuals and collectives.
- Conceptualizes place as interactive and dynamic due to these time-space characteristics
- Recognizes that disparate realities determine not only how place is experienced but also how it is understood and practiced in turn (e.g., in relation to culture, geography, gender, race, sexuality, age, or other identifications and experiences)
- Addresses spatialized and place-based processes of colonization and settler colonization, and works against their further erasure or neutralization through social science research
- Extends beyond considerations of the social to more deeply consider the land itself and its nonhuman inhabitants and characteristics as they determine and manifest place
- Aims to further generative and critical politics of places through such conceptualizations/practices and via a relational ethics of accountability to people and place

In outlining these considerations of critical place inquiry, the goals or aims of the book are as follows:

1) *To render a cross- and transdisciplinary discussion of theory, methodology, and methods of place.* Although it is not the dominant perspective, scholars in particular disciplines have been advocating for increased attention to place for several decades. We have read across disciplinary literatures in order to bring together arguments and justifications for the significance of place in social science inquiry. Thus, a contribution this book makes is to bring together discussions from several disciplines, including environmental scholarship, Indigenous

studies, and geography, to see what is said across these and other domains, what is said with disciplinary specificity, and what may be incommensurable among these approaches.

2) *To offer a discussion of the implications of place theorizing for the more applied activities of determining research methodology and methods.* Much of the existing literature focuses on conceptual articulations of place and space, which leave it to the reader to determine avenues for application in empirical research. This volume provides examples and discussion of theories, methodologies, and methods of critical place inquiry from across disciplines and across places. Although not providing explicit instruction on how to do critical place inquiry (because such a task would always be incomplete and because critical place inquiry is always specific to place), the volume provides readers ample points of inspiration for considering ways to elevate the significance of place in their inquiry projects at multiple dimensions and junctures.

3) *To take seriously the conceptual and empirical contributions of Indigenous epistemologies in critical place inquiry.* In recent years, important moves have been made to critique the gaps between critical approaches and Indigenous approaches to knowing and research (Grande, 2004; L.T. Smith, 1999/2012) and to bridge those gaps, at least by placing Indigenous theories alongside critical theories and methodologies (Denzin, Lincoln, & L.T. Smith, 2008). Yet, much of critical theory remains unresponsive to the critiques raised by Indigenous scholars (see Grande, 2004; Tuck & Fine, 2007; Tuck & Gaztambide-Fernández, 2013, for more discussion on this). This book forwards a framework of critical place inquiry that places Indigenous theories, methodologies, and methods at the center, not on the periphery. It does this not by simply incorporating Indigenous work, as is often done in liberal multicultural discourse; instead, it engages Indigenous work on its own terms, in adherence to its own commitments and conditions. Rather than simply pasting Indigenous work on to an existing framework, this book builds the framework to respond and attend to Indigenous work.

4) *As a point of minor contribution, this book makes an accumulative argument for the saliency of place over space.* The prominence of the philosophical differentiation between space and place arose in the nineteenth century. Space is more preferred right now in social science discourse because, as outlined, typically space is conflated with global, modern, and progressive, whereas place is conflated with local, traditional, and nostalgic. (Agnew, 2011; Jessop, Brenner, & Jones, 2008)

> Place is the setting for social rootedness and landscape continuity. Location/ space represents the transcending of the past by overcoming the rootedness of social relations and landscape in place through mobility and the increased similarity of everyday life from place to place. (Agnew, 2011)

As we make clear throughout this volume, it is the specificity, the rootedness of place, that makes it so important in social science and in human imagination. We urge readers and colleagues to reconsider place and its implications, not because it offers a generalizable theory or universal interpretation, but because generalizability and universality are impossibilities anyway, in no small part because place matters and place is always specific. Finally, as we discuss throughout this volume, the environmental consequences of deluding ourselves into believing that place no longer matters are stark and creeping.

OVERVIEW OF THIS BOOK

The remainder of the book is divided into two major parts: one on conceptualizations of place (Chapters 2 and 3), and one on methodologies and methods of critical place inquiry (Chapters 4, 5, and 6). The closing chapter of the book (Chapter 7) discusses the ethical implications and imperatives of critical place inquiry.

In the first part, Chapter 2 discusses and provides a commentary on some of the theories or conceptualizations of place that are being engaged in critical social science research on "place," broadly understood, including drawing from Indigenous perspectives and the spatial and new materialist turns. Chapter 3 elaborates conceptualizations of place understood as land, drawing on decolonizing Indigenous studies to emphasize the importance of critical place researchers addressing the colonial and settler colonial locations of their research.

The second part of the book discusses the ways in which these conceptualizations of place are being operationalized in the methodologies and methods of critical scholarship on and in place. Chapter 4 discusses a range of possible methodologies of critical place studies, including archival research; narrative research; phenomenology; ethnography; "post," experimental, and strategic approaches; and Indigenous methodologies. In Chapter 5 we then discuss the possibilities of specific methods of data collection and analysis as used across approaches to critical research on place. We highlight several issues that cut across various methods: These include the "where" of the methods, other embodied aspects of data and data collection and analysis processes, and the participatory and performative aspects of methods and what is learned and done through the research process. The chapter also discusses specifics of data collection and analysis methods that are being engaged in critical research in place, including oral, digital, mapping, and textual methods. Chapter 6 zooms in specifically on Indigenous methods of critical place inquiry.

The final chapter of the book, Chapter 7, focuses in on ethical considerations of critical place inquiry, including what the research "does," both through the research process as well as its potential end products. Included in this discussion are considerations of research with the populations that live in relation to place, including considerations of research as relation. We discuss how considerations of theory, methodology, and methods of place in research may enable us to respond more ethically and urgently to the priorities of accountability to land, people across places, and future generations.

Enduring questions of this volume include the following: What might change if place were taken more seriously in social science research? How might we reconceive the expected practices of social science so that, if place is not addressed with depth, the work seems incomplete? What might become possible if Indigenous understandings of place were engaged more fully by social scientists across other fields? And what would it mean to do critical place inquiry that interrogates ongoing structures of settler colonialism and other forms of spatialized oppression? These questions are posed throughout this book, and different possibilities arise in response. What we know, though, is that these questions must be asked in graduate courses, among research collaborations and partnerships, in conference sessions, and all the places in which we learn to do inquiry. There is a crucial disconnect between the looming consequences of ignoring place and the practices of social science that diminish place; a disconnection that has been fostered over generations of settler colonialism and social science research. Place is significant, and our inquiries will become more significant through this recognition.

Part I

2   Conceptualizing Place

Daniel Miller's (2008) *The Comfort of Things* presents thirty portraits of thirty people who all live on the same street in South London. The portraits focus on how the individuals know and express themselves through the material objects that fill their homes. Miller observes that contemporary life is brimming with ever more stuff, shopping, consumption, and possessions. Miller's project is to determine whether all of the stuff of modern life really does mean that we are more materialistic and less connected to other humans, as has been assumed.

Miller proposes that although London is increasingly culturally diverse, much of living takes place behind the closed doors of private homes. The way that he and his colleague Fiona Parrott set about learning more about what happens behind those closed doors was to knock on them and ask their inhabitants, not about their lives or personhood, but about their stuff (2008, p. 1–2). Miller writes in the appendix,

> There is absolutely nothing special about this South London street, where Fiona Parrott and I carried out research for a year and a half. It's a slightly odd task to look for a place which has no particular features and offers you no reason to choose it. But not a hard one. Most streets in London appear from the outside to be pretty ordinary.

Miller goes on to explain the factors of their choice of "Stuart Street": it was convenient for both of them to travel to, it seemed to house people living within a mix of incomes, it showed signs of gentrification, it had diverse sorts of housing, it was somewhat long. While at first "cold" knocking on the doors and asking to interview strangers was difficult, Miller and Parrott soon came to know more and more people on the street so that they "couldn't walk for five minutes without meeting people we knew and stopping for a chat" (p. 299).

> (A)fter seventeen months even the local corner shopkeepers admitted that we seemed to know more people on the street than they did, and we felt we had been able to achieve the kind of relationship which

approximates to the anthropological ideal: an ethnographic study of an area. Yet the street hardly features in this book. Each portrait seems to be a separate encounter with a separate household. This is because, while we may have come to know a great many people that lived on the street, in the main they did not know each other. They just lived by juxtaposition. (Miller, 2008, pp. 299–300)

BEYOND GEOGRAPHY?

We find Miller's method, of studying a single street, to be quite compelling. We can see how this approach might inspire other works of social science, across disciplines. The portraits that emerged from the project do indeed provide insight about how participants expressed themselves through their belongings, but also insights about how things do and do not get in the way of human relationships.

Yet, as we delve more deeply into the discussions of this book, what are we to make of the account that Miller provides of this study? What does it mean to say that this supposedly place-based method revealed little about the street itself?

Putting aside these questions for a moment, it makes sense to point out that much of social science takes place in a place—a neighborhood, a school, a city, a hospital, a village. Yet, those places rarely are heavily featured in the articles, reports, and books that emerge from those studies. One of the driving preoccupations of this book is to wonder why this is the case, but also to consider the ways in which social science has been constructed to ignore place.

To these wonderings, Miller (2008) observes,

> Social science, whether consciously or not, aimed not only to explore but also enact the Durkheimian view of the world. The phrase 'social science' affirms the existence of something called society, which can be the subject of scientific study. Durkheim himself was concerned that, if modern life was lived under the conditions of Nietzsche's death of God, then people needed to keep faith with some alternative transcendent object—ideally, society itself. Otherwise, as is implied by his study of suicide, there was a danger that life itself would seem, and indeed become, pointless. (p. 283)

In its very name, social science is, obviously, focused on the social as the most important frame. Place is but one of many subjects of study that are underserved by the somewhat artificial and arbitrary division between science, social science, and humanities domains. From this, Miller draws some interesting rationales for why "the street" or community (or place) didn't figure more prominently in the findings of this project. We quote him at length because he speaks to an experiential component of globalization that is rarely articulated so fully.

> The street presented in this book does not, however, suggest that concepts such as society or community play much of an immediate role in the lives of people who reside in a modern metropolis such as contemporary London. In a way, the state operates too efficiently. The underlying forces which provide basic education, health services, public order, the media and the condition for the development of an economy can deliver our daily goods without us having to know anything much about how this came to be. . . . We do not seem to require any active allegiance to, or alignment with, some abstract image of society or community, which lies closer to our daily lives . . . On the smaller side-streets, households give at least the impression that people know each other, while on Stuart Street itself this is rare. We need to face up to the degree to which in contemporary London, people do not live their lives in order to accord either with the cosmology of a religion or with the cosmology of a belief in society. For the most part, these are the random juxtapositions of households, as determined by forces such as house prices, transport systems and proximity to work, school, and leisure. The political economy determines these circumstances, but not how people live within them. (p. 284)

Again, Miller's account of the epistemic and experiential side-effects of globalization are provocative. His positing that the "state operates too efficiently" so that building community is no longer thought necessary has its parallels in ways that the significance of place has been characterized in the literature as less important now than in the past due to globalization.

The World Is Flat is the title of a 2005, then 2006, then 2007 runaway international bestseller by Thomas Friedman that promises in the subtitle a brief history of the twenty-first century. In insisting that the world is flat, Friedman references the discourse of discovery of a new world to describe how globalization and technology have reshaped the global labor market. To say that the world is flat is to say that it has none of the prior time and space barriers to labor and commerce of prior generations. Ultimately, the book argues that access to technology is equalizing global commerce and that employees, companies, and nation-states will struggle to remain relevant as the significance of geographical borders diminishes. Friedman goes to Columbus himself to narrate his own realization of this new world order:

> Columbus was happy to make the Indians he met his slaves, a pool of free manual labor. I [Friedman] just wanted to understand why the Indians [in India] I met were taking our work [jobs that used to be in the United States but are now located in India] . . . Columbus reported to his king and queen that the world was round, and he went down in

history as the man who first made this discovery. I returned home and shared my discovery only with my wife, and only in a whisper.

"Honey," I confided, "I think the world is flat.[1]" (Friedman, 2007, p. 5)

Friedman is trying to be cute and clever here. There is no irony at all in Friedman's neocolonial employment of the discovery narrative, or when he proclaims that Bangalore is a suburb of Boston and that Canton, Ohio, may as well be Canton, China. These are but two examples of how a theorist (Miller) and a social commentator (Friedman) have interpreted globalization and its implications for the significance of place.

Yet, as Neil Smith wrote in the first edition of *Uneven Development: Nature, Capital, and the Production of Space* in 1984 (20 years before Friedman's Columbus-like epiphany), globalization has made space and place *more* significant, not less. Globalization has meant deindustrialization and regional destabilization in some parts of the world, and industrialization in other parts of the world. It has meant a new international division of labor, observable at the scale of the globe and the nation-state. It has meant an intensification of nationalism and a new geopolitics of war:

The popular geographical wisdom is that we live in a shrinking world, that cheap and sophisticated transportation systems have diminished the importance of geographical space and geographical differentiation, that traditional regional identities are being evened out—in short, that we are somehow beyond geography. What I argue here is the derivation of the theory of uneven development is that whatever the partial truths conveyed by the popular wisdom, the contrary is true. Geographical space is on the economic and political agenda as never before. (N. Smith, 1984/2008, p. 4)

Smith observes that (Western) theorists have struggled to make more evident the role of space in society, whereas capital seems to have achieved it in practice on a daily basis (p. 7).

No matter how badly Friedman wants to declare it, the world is not flat, perhaps especially within the uneven power topologies of globalization. Miller's (2008) more carefully constructed interpretation that place is somehow now less significant than in prior generations still bears little resemblance to the world that we see, in which place matters more and more. Globalization, specifically its unevenness, makes considerations of place more important, not less (see also Katz, 2004; Casey, 2009). Friedman and Miller, although offering dramatically differently constructed arguments and justifications, represent the range of undertheorizations of place that dominate the popular and scholarly discourses on globalization. Such undertheorizations can have stark consequences with regard to continued forms of colonial violence (e.g., the U.S.'s now frequent use of drone attacks orchestrated by soldiers holding video game controllers from another continent) and environmental violence (e.g., the destruction of earth and water through the extraction of bitumen from tar sands in Canada).

Within the context of Smith's discussions of the geographic imperatives of globalization, the remainder of this chapter examines considerations of reconceptualized and renewed understandings of place, as grounded and relational, and as providing roots for politics that are deeply specific to place and yet connected to other places. These considerations are drawn from new and renewed trajectories of materialist and spatial scholarship; as well as from longer trajectories of decolonizing and Indigenous scholarship and practice. Through this discussion, we trace and elaborate some of the possibilities for theorizing in and through critical place inquiry. Our hope here is not necessarily for a coherent whole—conceptualizations featured in this chapter overlap and juxtapose with each other. Instead, we aim to draw attention to the compelling ways in which geographers and other social scientists are conceptualizing place and space in order to provide inspiration to readers wanting to develop the same in their work.

We also point to the work of Raewyn Connell (2007) who has emphasized the importance of the place-based aspects of theory. Connell suggests how "Northern theory" typically informs social science research, resulting in viewpoints and problems of "metropolitan society, while presenting itself as universal knowledge" (p. vii). "Social thought happens in particular places," and as a result, attention also needs to be drawn to the "periphery-centre" relations embedded in much social science research (p. ix). In elaborating this, Connell discusses "Southern" social theorizing that has developed in four locations where colonial relations have been challenged: postcolonial Africa, modernizing Iran, post–Second World War Latin America, and India post-1970s. While many of the conceptualizations of place that follow in this chapter come from Anglo-American and Continental theories, or, in other words, are of "the metropole," we also explicitly center Indigenous perspectives and scholarship throughout the volume. Connell's point regarding which theories are prioritized in social science, where they originate from, and what legacies are tied to those theories is a crucial one for critical place inquiry. The place-based theory, methodology, and methods of research one mobilizes require ongoing scrutiny for their inherent legacies and effects.

Discussed in this chapter alongside other theories, in the following chapter we focus specifically on elaborating decolonizing conceptualizations of place. In part this is because our volume seeks to interface spatial theories, methodologies, and methods with Indigenous theories, methodologies, and methods. The challenge is to formulate a description of the theoretical foundations of critical place inquiry that are accountable to Indigenous peoples and futurity.

MOBILITY AND PLACE

With new technology and social media connecting people across distances, increased travel and migration, and associated global circulations of everything from entertainment to social and economic policy, it is clear that the world is increasingly globally connected and that this suggests the significance of space and scale. Thus, growing emphasis has been placed across the social sciences on understanding, tracking, critiquing, and otherwise examining the flows of people and information through and across these "scapes" or spheres of social life (Appadurai, 1996). Sub-areas such as mobility studies have focused more broadly on the movements and implications of this global fluidity (e.g., Urry, 2007), whereas other work has attended to the impacts on and associated characteristics of particular locations through, for example, the study of "global cities" (e.g., Sassen, 1991) or of "non-places," such as airports, store chains, or other replicating and anonymous environments (e.g., Augé, 1995).

Still others have focused on historical mobilities and diasporas, which figure metaphorically and literally in the coproduction of identity, time, and place. Katherine McKittrick (2006), in her work to counter-narrate "ungeographic" narrations of Black women's bodies and experiences, writes,

> The ships of transatlantic slavery moving across the middle passage, transporting humans for free labor into "newer worlds" do not only site modern technological progression, which materially moved diasporic subjects through space, that is, on and across the ocean, and on and across landmasses such as Canada, the United States, the Caribbean; these vessels also expose a very meaningful struggle for freedom in place. Technologies of transportation, in this case the ship, while materially and ideologically enclosing black subjects—economic objects inside and often bound to the ship's walls—also contribute to the formation of an oppositional geography; the ship as a location of black subjectivity and human terror, black resistance, and in some cases, black possession. (p. xi)

Attending to instances of "time-space compression," or the relative collapsing of space and time through increased mobility of people and information, has become a compelling trope in framing and understanding social analyses.

"Place," understood as more localized enactments of social and material practice, has in some ways also received more attention as a contrary alternative (Harvey, 1996). Viewed as providing stability and familiarity in the face of globalizing forces, place is made distinct from space (as well as mobility) in popular experience as well as in much scholarly work. Over the past several decades we thus see references to place in contrast and sometimes as remedy to globalizing spatial flows (Cresswell, 2004). However, with such engagements with place sometimes seen as outdated or reactionary in the scholarly literature, there has been relatively little deeper theorizing and discussion of place as others have pointed out previously (e.g., Coleman & Collins, 2006; Nayak, 2003; Casey, 2009).

Of those who have theorized place more deeply, Doreen Massey's work is helpful in her critiques of the oversimplified division of space from place and in considering why and how "place" is an important and useful framing for politics and thus for critical social science research, as will be discussed later in the chapter. Suggesting that her 1991 essay on "a global sense of place" has been taken up as advocating for the concept of place to be abandoned, Massey (2009) clarifies that her position has been different from those who suggest that "everything is now flow." For example, "Hardt and Negri say that you can't have a concept of place that doesn't have boundaries. Therefore it is one of those old, modernist containments that we must abandon, because it divides global humanity, it divides the global multitude . . . I would say . . . there never was place that was a container" (p. 416). Massey instead articulates an orientation to place that acknowledges the connections across local places and their influences on global circulations of knowledge and practice:

> "how can we resolve the binary between place and space?" Well one way is precisely by integrating them relationally. But if you do that then it means you *have* to accept the implication of the local in the construction of the global. The global doesn't just exist 'up there'. It is made in places and there is hardly a place on the planet that in some ways isn't party to that making. (p. 412)

Massey (2005) also suggests the ways in which places are themselves moving and changing over time, whether through connections with other places and the global or through physical processes, from shifting tectonic plates to climate change. Using the example of the 3,000-foot-high rock block of Skiddaw in the Lake District in England, Massey discusses how natural landscapes that we often think of as timeless and fixed have been formed through history as well as geography. The rocks of Skiddaw were originally placed in the sea in the southern hemisphere around 500 million years ago. Over time they have migrated north, changing their form into a "mountain," a relatively recently 10 million years ago. Not at all static over time or space, 'Skiddaw' continues to migrate and change form. Asking where 'here' is if there are no fixed points, Massey (2005) responds that "It won't be the same 'here' when it is no longer now" (p. 139). This is certainly also a poignant realization as we face human-induced climate change and learn of the projected transformations in ecosystems, species, and human patterns and practices in the places we know and perhaps cherish, within the much more rapid timeframe of our own lifetimes.

Such a relational understanding of place to space, and of place to time, suggests the ways in which what we think of as particular 'places' can be understood as articulations of time-space, or of the interweaving of history and geography (Massey, 1994; L.T. Smith, 1999/2012; Byrd, 2011). This is an understanding of place as open, "as a particular constellation within the wider topographies of space, and as in process, an unfinished business" (Massey, 2005, p. 131).

"Mobility" then is integral to place, as flows of people, technology and other human practices, and other species move through places, as well as in how the places themselves, with a long view, can also be understood to be moving. As the next section elaborates, more localized mobilities with specific places are also means through which these places are understood, formed, upheld, and resisted.

PRACTICE AND PLACE

Understanding place as lived space (Soja, 1999), meeting place (Massey, 2005), site of social reproduction (Katz, 2004), or as personality (Deloria & Wildcat, 2001; see also Chapter 3, this volume) suggests the variety of considerations of relationships between place and social practice, across disciplines and epistemological frames. Neil Smith observes of (Western) philosophies, "We are used to conceiving of nature as external to society, pristine and pre-human, or else as a grand universal in which human beings are but small and simple cogs. But here again our concepts have not caught up with reality" (1984/2008, p. 7). In both of these (Western) constructions—nature as outside, or humans as simple cogs—humans do not perceive themselves as part of/as shaped by place, or vice versa, as shaping place through our everyday social practices.[2] In this section, we discuss how our embodied and emplaced practices of movement, and stillness, are among the ways that place shapes us individually and collectively, and in turn, through which we shape and reshape place (see also Cajete, 2000, p. 185, on the human body as a metaphor for landscape).

Tewa scholar Gregory Cajete (1994) writes, "*Mitakuye Oyasin* (we are all related) is a Lakota phrase that . . . reflects the understanding that our lives are truly and profoundly connected to other people and the physical world . . . knowledge gained from first-hand experience in the world is transmitted or explored through ritual, ceremony, art, and appropriate technology" (p. 26). These positings of nature and land as not external, indeed as ultra-connected to human life, emphasize how land with its physical features, climate, other species, and other aspects can act on and in conjunction with social histories and introduced influences to form current human practices of ritual and ceremony; architecture, planning, and design; educational traditions; and leisure pastimes. The specificity of social practice as aligned with the time-space considerations of specific places was well documented through the twentieth century in a range of fields of study (e.g., Cresswell, 2004; Harvey, 2001; Ingold, 2000, 2011; N. Smith, 1984/2008; Wilson, 2008). As we have already noted, while the practices of globalization may have in some ways eroded the place-specific aspects of social practice, increasingly both communities and scholarly research are emphasizing the ways in which identities and social practices remain significantly determined by place-specific considerations (e.g., Katz, 2004; Nayak, 2003; N. Smith, 1984/2008).

Inasmuch as place influences social practice, likewise social practice can be understood to influence place. More obvious instances of this include the ways that environmental, planning, or other social policies or lack thereof, influence the ways that humans shape the places in which they live and work. In Canada, for instance, in 2012 federal omnibus budget bills C-38 and C-45 were passed changing more than 130 federal laws without parliamentary debate or First Nations consultation, causing 99% of Canada's waterways to lose their protection via navigation and environmental assessment standards (e.g., 32,000 protected lakes to just 97, and from 2.25 million protected rivers to just 62) (Land, 2013). These conditions led to the instigation of the initially localized and then global "Idle No More" Indigenous sovereignty and environmental movement, as exemplar of a different genre of social practice that influences decisions and actions on and about land.

In another example, Cindi Katz (2004) has elegantly documented the ways in which "development" practices and policies shape the places and everyday lives of young women as they come of age in a village in central eastern Sudan. Katz's 'countertopography' creates a parallax with Harlem, New York City, to illustrate the simultaneous disruptions of place and everyday life afforded by development practices, or "refusing to let geography hide consequences" (p. 259), but also to push against the abstractions of globalization with a place-based political imagination (p. xiv).

> In focusing on Sudan with the insistent counterpoint of New York, I have tried to make clear that the increasingly globalized expression of capitalist relations of production, the tenor of neoliberal global economic restructuring, and the broad retreats from the social wage that have been associated with them have common local and regional effects, such as deskilling, community destabilization, and a reordered relationship between production and reproduction. (p. 259)

Katz's work goes on to illuminate how our individual and collective daily lives thus influence place through the social practices we maintain, support, resist, and build. This includes our interactions with material aspects of the world such as what we literally mow, plant, dismantle, obstruct, build, walk around, or walk through.

In *The Practice of Everyday Life,* Michel de Certeau (1984) explores the "ways of making" enabled through everyday practices such as walking. While the spatial order is organized into places in which one can move as well as walls or barriers that prevent passage, he suggests it is the walker that actualizes some of these possibilities but also moves around them, inventing other pathways, crossing, drifting, improvising. De Certeau thus explores the ways in which people's everyday practices or "ways of operating" are relationally determined and guided by established rules, and yet what an individual does with these determinations can differ—how through ways of using these "products," one can create another different production. A concrete example of this is provided by research on youth skateboarding practices and how they remake established places in new ways for ends different than those intended or expected (e.g., Anderson, 2010; see also Katz, 2004; Soja, 2010).

In addition to forms of movement as practices that influences place, de Certeau (1984) also discusses the place-making aspects of story, suggesting that stories are a means of enabling solidified or structured places to become habitable ones. Belief is one form of storying that allows a certain play "within a system of defined places" (p. 106). He writes,

> It is through the opportunity they offer to store up rich silences and wordless stories, or rather through their capacity to create cellars and garrets everywhere, that local legends . . . permit exits, ways of going out and coming back in, and thus habitable spaces. . . . One can measure the importance of these signifying practices (to tell oneself legends) as practices that invent spaces. . . . Stories diversify. (pp. 106–107)

Related to this point, Indigenous scholars (Archibald, 2008; Brooks, 2008; Wilson, 2008) and non-Indigenous scholars conducting research with Indigenous communities (Basso, 1996; Dehyle, 2009) have extensively theorized the role of storytelling as a practice of shaping and being shaped by place among Indigenous peoples. Some Indigenous scholars have emphasized the role that cosmology and cosmogony stories have played in Indigenous conceptualizations of collective identity and place (Archibald, 2008; Cajete, 2000; Deloria & Wildcat, 2001), indeed how Indigenous people came to be a place (Tuck & Yang, 2012; See also Basso, 1996).

> After the people had emerged into the fourth world from former worlds of development, stories relate distinctions of tribes or races of human-kind, each of whom is given special instruction and sent to a particular cardinal direction. Almost all emergence myths recount the migration[3] of the people through the landscape with stories where important lessons about relationships, ideals, and moral teachings must be learned. (Cajete, 2000, p. 33)

Stories thus carry out a labor; creating, maintaining, and/or shifting narratives about the places in which we live and how they produce us and us them. As de Certeau (1984) writes, "In a pre-established geography . . . everyday stories tell us what one can do in it and make out of it . . . [The story] opens a legitimate *theater* for practical *actions*. It creates a field that authorizes dangerous and contingent social actions" (pp. 122, 125).

Through better understanding how social practice is shaped by place as well as an influential factor in the making and remaking of place through time and over space, place becomes both less stable as well as potentially more powerful. As Tim Cresswell (2004) writes,

> Place provides a template for practice—an unstable stage for performance. Thinking of place as performed and practiced can help us think

of place in radically open and non-essentialized ways where place is constantly struggled over and reimagined in practical ways. . . . Place in this sense becomes an event rather than a secure ontological thing rooted in notions of the authentic. (p. 39)

Or in the language of Tim Ingold (2008), places do not exist so much as they occur.

As overviewed in Chapter 1, many "new materialist" accounts emphasize the productivity of "matter" (e.g., human and non-human actors, including other species, material objects, technology, etc.) and the events of their interactions. Coole and Frost (2010) write, "Materiality is always something more than 'mere' matter: an excess, force, vitality, relationality, or difference that renders matter active, self-creative, productive, unpredictable" (p. 9). This in other words, is a "materiality that materializes" (Coole & Frost, 2010, p. 9). And while the work of Cresswell, Massey, or other critical geographers is considered by some to be "new materialist," there have been critiques by these and other scholars of approaches that flatten human and non-human relations in more micro-focused analyses that de-emphasize the politics of materiality (Nayak & Jeffrey, 2011). Focusing on embodied performance rather than language-based representation, non-representational theories (NRT) and other "object oriented ontologies" (Burns & Smith, 2011) can be understood as insisting that,

> the root of action is to be conceived less in terms of willpower or cognitive deliberation and more via embodied and environmental affordances, dispositions and habits. This means that humans are envisioned in constant relations of modification and reciprocity with their environs. . . . Arguably, what [distinguishes] such accounts [is] their refusal to search for extrinsic sources of causality or determination, an out-of-field 'power', an efficacy and opportunism (or otherwise) of practices and performances. It is from the active, productive, and continual weaving of the multiplicity of bits and pieces that we emerge. (Anderson & Harrison, 2010, pp. 7–8)

However, we agree with others who have suggested that performances and practices cannot exist outside of "extrinsic sources," such as cultural configurations of power and past colonial histories (Nayak & Jeffrey, 2009). As the next section discusses, experiences of embodiment and emplacement are not universal. We must also consider the role of power in our day-to-day understandings and experiences of materiality and place.

POWER AND PLACE

We have discussed how places are themselves mobile, shifting subtly or significantly over time and space and through interactions with "global flows" of people, other species, and social practices. At a more localized level, places can be understood as both influencing social practices from ceremony to design, as well as being performed and (re)shaped through practices and movements such as walking, protesting, or institutionalization. In this section, we discuss the ways in which power and place are coproduced, indeed are co-constitutive. Spatial organizations give coherence and rationality to maldistributions of power and resources (McKittrick, 2006), geographic processes that result in what David Harvey (2003) has called accumulation by dispossession. Capitalism and the production of capital has perhaps always required the displacement and perpetual landlessness of some for the accumulation of others; Harvey argues that it is not the process of accumulation of dispossession that has changed, but its location (as the "development" of the global south opens new markets) (see also Povinelli, 2011, p. 18).

For these reasons, Linda Tuhiwai Smith (1999/2012) has critiqued colonial naming and mapping practices that have worked simultaneously to dispossess Indigenous peoples of land and establish settler colonial nation-states. L. T. Smith, McKittrick (2006), Brooks (2008) and others have embraced Chandra Mohanty's (2003) notion of *cartographies of struggle* to speak to the importance of attending to the intersecting but never synchronous lines of simultaneous oppressions. More than the duality of mapping,[4] of drawing oppositions with the line, cartography is the art and science of making and remaking maps, of creating and being created by, of recognizing and conceptualizing marginality, sites of struggle, domains, place, and sovereignty (L. T. Smith, 1999/2012). Learning from this critique and from the notion of cartographies of struggle, we resist ontological analyses that, much like earlier phenomenological study, focus at the micro and yet universal level, while ignoring the situated realities of historical and spatial sedimentations of power. Rather we draw on work from feminist studies (Mohanty, 2003; Rose, 1993), Black feminist scholarship (McKittrick, 2006), Indigenous and settler colonial studies (Byrd, 2011; McCoy, Tuck, & McKenzie, 2014), urban studies (Lipsitz, 2011), critical Marxist (Harvey, 2005; Katz, 2004), critical geography (Gilmore, 2006), and other critical scholarship to understand place as experienced differently based on culture, geography, gender, race, sexuality, age, or other identifications and experiences; and to understand how these disparate realities determine not only how place is experienced but also how it is understood and practiced in turn. These place-specific differences do not amount only to "diversity," but rather in many cases exemplify and help establish forms of inequity, colonization, and other forms of oppression (Haluza-Delay, O'Riley, Cole, & Agyeman, 2009; McKittrick, 2006).

Writing alongside Gilmore's important 2002 article, "Fatal couplings of power and difference: Notes on racism and geography," Katherine McKittrick (2006) insists,

> The simultaneous naturalization of bodies and places must be disclosed, and therefore called into question, if we want to think about alternative spatial practices and more humanly workable geographies. Borrowing

from Ruth Wilson Gilmore, I want to suggest that geographies of domination be understood as "the displacement of different," wherein "particular kinds of bodies, one by one, are materially (if not always visibly) configured by racism into a hierarchy of human and inhuman persons that in sum form the category of 'human being'" (Gilmore, 2002, p. 16). Gilmore highlights the ways in which human and spatial differentiations are connected to the process of making place. The displacement of difference does not describe human hierarchies but rather demonstrates the ways in which these hierarchies are critical categories of social and spatial struggle. (p. xv)

McKittrick does not allow for categories of body/identity/place to be regarded as separate. Her work pushes us to see how practices of subjugation, including racism and sexism, are spatial acts and to consider effective ways of mapping them. Indeed, it may only be possible to see how racism and sexism are not bodily or identity based, but are spatial acts (p. xviii) through embodied methods of critical place inquiry (see Chapter 5, this volume). Indeed, McKittrick posits that disclosing how geographies are socially and differentially produced, that is, how subjugation is a spatial act, is "one way to contend with unjust and uneven human/inhuman categorizations is to think about, and perhaps employ, the alternative geographic formulations that subaltern communities advance" (p. xix).

In *How Racism Takes Place*, George Lipsitz (2011) shows that attributing the ongoing material disparities between white people and people of color to race alone can result in interpretations of social data that pathologize people of color as "unfit for freedom" (p. 1). Building upon his prior (Lipsitz, 1998) arguments that focusing *only* on Black disadvantages pulls attention from unearned privileges enjoyed by white people (in health care, criminal justice, banking, and education systems), Lipsitz argues that "largely because of racialized space, whiteness in this society is not so much a color as a condition" (p. 3). Whiteness operates as a spatialized and structured advantage. Lipsitz examines residential and school segregation, spatial isolation from employment, mortgage and insurance redlining, taxation and transportation policies, and the location of environmental amenities and toxic hazards to learn how place and race are coproduced in urban United States (p. 5).

Winona LaDuke's (1999) *All Our Relations* traces the origins and impacts of the "toxic invasion of North America" (p. 2): the dumping of toxic waste, clearcutting, species contamination and extinction, violent resource extraction, nuclear testing, and other industrial encroachments on Indigenous land in now-United States. Mapping and narrating the consequences of polychlorinate biphenyl (PCB) in mothers' milk in Akwesasne Nation, the "development" of the Everglades in Seminole Nation, coal mining on Northern Cheyenne territory, nuclear waste dumping on multiple Indigenous lands and reservations, the correspondence of the slaughter of buffalo and the dispossession of Indigenous land, LaDuke makes evident the entanglements of uneven development and dismantling of Indigenous land and sovereignty. Environmental degradation and its disproportionate effects on Indigenous land and peoples is an extension of the violence and biopolitics of settler colonialism.

The title of this section borrows from the title of a 2001 volume by Vine Deloria, Jr. and Daniel Wildcat, *Power and Place: Indian Education in America*; power in this volume is theorized within an Indigenous metaphysics and practices that "actively acknowledge the power that permeates the many persons of the earth in places recognized as sacred not by human proclamation or declaration, but by experience in those places" (p. 13). Power in this framing cuts another way entirely, toward those who have long-standing relationships with place(s) rather than those who purport to conquer them.

Doreen Massey (1991) coined the term *power geometries* to discuss the inequities associated with "a global sense of place." While global mobility has increased through travel and technology, these factors clearly are not experienced by everyone with the same benefits. While some have the privilege of choosing to travel, others are not able to due to financial or political circumstances, or inversely are forced to "travel" as refugees, through being removed from homeland, or as migrant workers sending remittances home to distant family. As Massey (1991) suggests, while some are "in-charge" of such time-space compression—"those who are both doing the moving and the communicating and who are in some way in a position of control in relation to it"—others are doing a lot of physical moving but are not in control of the process and rather are on the receiving end of time-space compression (p. 26).

Within a given place, there are also more localized asymmetries of power and privilege, for example, in who can walk or travel safely in particular places based on identifications of race, gender, or sexuality (e.g., Evans, 2002); who has access or 'ownership' and who does not; and who is disproportionately affected by environmental issues of water or air pollution (Lipsitz, 2011; LaDuke, 1999; Walker, 2012). As Cresswell (2004) suggests, "place does not have meanings not natural and obvious but ones that are created by some people with more power than others to define what is and is not appropriate" (p. 27). From religious institutions to schools to homes to the street to natural spaces, different types of locations have accepted members and norms that create and enforce boundaries and relative privileges. Likewise, urban, schooling, health, economic, and other policies operate through place to establish and reinforce inequities (Grande, 2004; Lipman, 2011; Peck, 2013).

Individual and collective histories and memories of place also contribute in powerful ways to what is possible or not. This operates in how people remember, experience, or imagine place, exemplified in June Jordan's (1989) *Poem about My Rights*. In this poem, Jordan writes about how being "the wrong age the wrong skin" can make it impossible to go down to the beach or into the woods alone to think about the world, God, "all of it disclosed by the stars and the silence" (p. 102). As Reed (2002) writes, Jordan is asserting, "with and against the Thoreauvian tradition, a 'right' to enter the literal and literary 'woods' of America as an equal partner, free from the fear of rape attendant upon her race, her class, her gender" (p. 155). In part asking how the nature of colonialism reinforces the colonization of nature, as well as how a privileged enjoyment of "wilderness" might obscure the nature of injustices experienced by the less privileged,

> Jordan reminds us throughout the poem that her 'natural' body is a colonized site, one colonized *with and as part of* the natural world, that the rape of an African country, an environment, an African American woman's body, are all entwined, that each violation of rights shapes each of the others, reinforcing mutually. (p. 155)

In addition to unequal access to place, some memoried accounts of place are explicitly impressed to the continued advantage of specific groups at the expense of others, for example, in the case of the principles and practices of Manifest Destiny in the United States, which gave and continues to give European populations justification for settling Indigenous land (McCoy 2014). As David Harvey (1996) writes, the "production of memory in place is no more than an element in the perpetuation of a particular social order which seeks to inscribe some memories at the expense of others. Places do not come with some memories attached as if by nature but rather they are the contested terrain of competing definitions" (p. 309). An excellent example of this is described in environmental historian William Cronon's (1992) essay "Kennecott Journey: The Paths out of Town." Tracing the history of the now ghost town, Kennecott, Alaska, Cronon describes the trade between the Indigenous population previously in the area and arriving settler populations, including in relation to other organisms, food importation after settlement via the railroad, the mining of copper, and other means through which people and goods came in and out of Kennecott. Describing the essay, Cresswell (2004) writes,

> In order for the new population to mine the copper they had to import new definitions of property—thus a legal landscape was imported along with the turnips. The native population had no concept of static property or place. They were nomadic and would move according to the availability of resources. This lifestyle, Cronon writes, "left them little concerned with drawing sharp property boundaries upon the landscape" [sic] the newcomers "had in mind a completely different way of owning and occupying the terrain. And therein lay the origin of the community of Kennecott" (Cronon, 1992, 42). So the irony of Kennecott—a place produced by its connections—was that the idea of

place itself was imported from outside. Place based on property and boundaries. (p. 42)

Concerned with the exclusions that are committed in the name of place, Harvey (1996) credits place-making with dominantly negative outcomes. However, others have suggested power can operate through and in relation to place and land also to unsettle, to create public space, and to otherwise work counter to oppressive understandings and practices of power (Sassen, 2006). Towards further expanding on the politics of place, we first need to extend our understanding of place beyond social relations and implications, to consider more deeply the land itself as well as nonhuman species that inhabit it. In other words, place has meanings and implications that extend beyond human considerations.

BEYOND THE SOCIAL

We are wary of approaches to place that seemingly collapse place to its social considerations, and in this section, we discuss some of the consequences of applying *only* social meanings to place. Instead we suggest we also need deeper consideration of the land itself and its nonhuman inhabitants and characteristics as they determine and manifest place. In earlier writing, Massey (e.g., 1991), for example, reduces place to its social (and thus human) contexts and considerations. Discussing each place as a meeting place or as a "particular constellation of social relations," she writes, "Instead then, of thinking of places as areas with boundaries around, they can be imagined as *articulated moments in networks of social relations*" (p. 28 emphasis ours). Going further in suggesting that place is a social construct, David Harvey (1996) proposes as a result that "the only interesting question that can be asked is: by what social process(es) is place constructed?" (p. 261).

Yet, in more recent writing, Massey (2005) suggests that the physical and land-based aspects of place do matter in what place is and can be for humans and beyond, such as her example of the rocks of Skiddaw discussed earlier in this chapter. However, these effects and considerations are not elaborated at depth, with most emphasis placed on the fact that physical aspects of place are, like the social aspects, open, in transition, or unfinished.

One way in which place is frequently collapsed into its social considerations is in a subset of place-based work on borders and border crossing. Borders are surely human constructions, represented in the imagination, on maps, and sometimes through walls and barbed wire. Yet there is a physicality to borders that makes them more than socially constructed, as anyone who has extralegally tried to cross them knows intimately. The physicality of borders does not just apply to humans—land animal migration patterns are disrupted by the enforcement of borders through structures, whereas fish contaminated by nuclear waste defy the borders that are imagined for them.

The language of borders and border transgression is commonplace in social science inquiry, even and especially outside of critical recognition of the significance of place. Part of a call towards critical place inquiry is to problematize the metaphorizing of borders and border crossing and transgressions in social science inquiry, not necessarily to curb such metaphorizing, but to call attention to the ways in which the figurative can eclipse the literal. We can forget that there are those who die every day because borders are not metaphors, but are very very real.

While contemporary border discourses within social theory find their roots in Gloria Anzaldúa's (1987) work *Borderlands/La Frontera: The New Mestiza*, some critical scholars seem to have (mis?)interpreted Anzaldúa's work, using it to call for a diminished significance of borders and boundaries. This interpretation of Anzaldúa's work sits uncomfortably aside the particular histories of Indigenous peoples and migrant peoples across the globe: histories of relationships of domination, dispossession, and appropriation. "A borderland," writes Anzaldúa, "is a vague and undetermined place, created by the emotional residue of an unnatural boundary. It is in a constant state of transition. The prohibited and forbidden are its inhabitants" (1987, p. 3). Contemporaneously, Donna Haraway writes, "Boundaries shift from within; boundaries are very tricky. What boundaries provisionally contain remains generative, productive of meaning and bodies" (1988, p. 595). In our view, Anzaldúa's work interrogates the depth of emotional conflict infused by desire in the borderland. Borderlands, like the invisible lines upon the earth's surface that separate Indigenous peoples from their ancestral land and arbitrarily enact nationhood, are locations of psychic, physical, and emotional conflict.

Part of what we see as the misinterpretation of Anzaldúa's work, then, is that the representations of borderlands in social science literatures are associated with individual and group identity, collapsed into the social—land is somewhat obfuscated, even when social identity comprises landed constructs, specifically the experiential knowledge of life shaped by borders. Another flawed interpretation is the presumption that because borders are crossable, they are less significant. "Boundary transgressions should be equated not with the dissolution of traversed boundaries (as some authors have suggested) but with the ongoing reconfiguring of boundaries" (Barad, 2007, p. 245, parenthesis original). Kevin Bruyneel's (2007) *The Third Space of Sovereignty* is an important exception to this problematic tendency in social science inquiry. Bruyneel's "boundary-focused approach" thoroughly attends to the spatial boundaries around territory and legal and political institutions and the temporal boundaries around the narratives of economic development, political development, cultural progress, and modernity (p. xiii) in order to analyze U.S.–Indigenous relationships.

The agency and interactions of materiality unto itself and including in relation to humans (e.g., the effects of different objects and species on one another) has been increasingly addressed in work in areas such as feminist theory, actor network theory, non-representational theory, speculative realism and other "objective oriented ontologies" (Barad, 2007; Bryant, Srnicek, & Harman, 2011). In fact much of this work breaks down the distinction between the social and material, turning and in some ways returning (Marx, 1969 (1888); Williams, 1961) to understandings of materiality as encompassing of, rather than singling out, social relations. Much of this new materialist work is theoretical and is only starting to make its way into the framings and methodologies of empirical studies; and in many cases still takes as a central focus the implications of such theorizing for understanding and practicing social life. In other words, and perhaps understandable given we are in social science terrain, the focus is more so on how other forms of materiality affect and interact with humans, versus emphasizing or examining, for example, land or other species in and of themselves. For example, Jane Bennett (2010a) writes,

> What would happen to our thinking about politics if we took more seriously the idea that technological and natural materialities were themselves actors alongside and within us—were vitalities, trajectories, or symbolic values humans invest in them? I'm in search of a materialism in which matter is an active principle and, though it inhabits us and our inventions, also acts as an outside or alien power. This new, "vital materialism" would run parallel to a historical materialism focused more exclusively upon economic structures of human power" [i.e., Marxism]. (p. 47)

Likewise Nayak and Jeffrey (2011) suggest the implications of non-representational theory (NRT) for understanding humans and social life (e.g., Anderson & Harrison, 2010; Thrift, 2008): "they [NRT] remind us that landscapes are not simply cultural texts but that their materiality must be understood through the body as we encounter these environments through sights, sounds, smells, tastes, touch and other sensual experiences" (Nayak & Jeffry, 2011, p. 293). This is important for critical place inquiry certainly, as we understand experiences of and in place as embodied and sensual: that it is not just *who* we 'meet' in place in terms of social and cultural influences, but also that who we are and how we are is influenced by land and the nonhuman.

Such relationships of and to place thus suggest a deepened understanding of materiality. Not as a static backdrop to human experience, this is rather a meshwork (Ingold, 2011) or entanglement (Barad, 2007) of life on the planet. In Indigenous cosmologies, land refers not just to the material aspects of places, but to its "spiritual, emotional, and intellectual aspects" (Styres, Haig-Brown, & Blimkie, 2013, p. 37). Signifying consideration of these aspects in the capitalization of Land, Styres and Zinga (2013) write:

> We have chosen to capitalize Land when we are referring to it as a proper name indicating a primary relationship rather than when used in a more

general sense. For us, land (the more general term) refers to landscapes as a fixed geographical and physical space that includes earth, rocks, and waterways; whereas, "Land" (the proper name) extends beyond a material fixed space. Land is a spiritually infused place grounded in interconnected and interdependent relationships, cultural positioning, and is highly contextualized. (pp. 300–301)

Returning Massey's (2005) lexicon, this suggests a meeting place, not only of human histories, spatial relations, and related social practices, but also of related histories and practices of land and other species. Mobile and practiced in a multitude of ways, including in and through the sedimentation and manifestation of power relations, what do such conceptualizations of place offer for critical politics of social change?

WHAT THEN FOR POLITICS?

Massey (2005) and others propose that conceptualizations of place that go beyond the social yield productive ways of interpreting multifaceted accumulations of human and nonhuman practices. Massey suggests how such interpretations also yield possibilities for politics. Instead of assumptions of a pre-given coherence or collective identity, Massey suggests that the multiplicity and mutability of place demands negotiation. She writes, "places as presented here in a sense necessitate invention; they pose a challenge. They implicate us, perforce, in the lives of human others, and in our relations with nonhumans" (Massey, 2005, p. 141). Likewise, in refusing binary categories of object versus subject, material versus cognitive, real versus imagined, and space versus place, Soja (2010) also suggests the importance of the practiced and lived for spatial justice. As Cresswell (2004) proposes, this provides a groundwork for thinking about a politics of place based on place as lived and inhabited. By these terms, "places are never established. They only operate through constant and reiterative practice" (Cresswell, 2004, p. 38).

Thus, to *practice* place or land productively towards versions of critical Indigenous and environmental politics will mean different things to different people and communities. Warning against the dangers of identification with place in terms of the creation of us/them categories in which the other is devalued, Cresswell (2004) also suggests the potential of forms of critical regionalism or militant particularism, in which the particularity of place is used as a platform for resistance. Sociologist Saskia Sassen (e.g., 2007, 2012) has examined the concept of territory in order to better understand how it is being mobilized to support the nation-state or new globalized forms of land-based colonization through practices such as land grabs. Advocating for the liberation of the notion of territory from these dominant uses, Sassen (2012) suggests the possibility of other place-based identifications that provide useful politics that go beyond place (Massey, 2009), such as the "global street" as mobilized in recent social movements such as Occupy, the Arab Spring, and Idle No More (discussed later). She asks,

> Do the powerless make history? They can, but there is a temporality that attaches to it and it can take many generations. It is a making that is easily rendered invisible. The actors are rendered invisible. So with the global street it makes it visible. This power of the powerless to make change is invisible to us and there's something about the global street that makes it visible." (Sassen, 2012, n.p.)

Elsewhere Sassen (2007) has written about how through focusing on local issues and linking with other places with related issues, this can enable a "multiscaler politics of the local" (p. 207).

Researchers on social and youth movements have documented the importance of social networks in organizing protests (Otero & Cammarota, 2011; Weiss, 2011; Yang, 2008). Social actions that appear to the media to be spontaneous, to spring up as if from nowhere, are made possible by rhizomes of communication facilitated by cell phones and social media. Recent uprisings in Tunisia, Egypt, Libya, and Palestine, massive student protests in Europe and Quebec, the Occupy movement in the United States and elsewhere, and youth protests against police violence draw our attention to the power of resistance networks but also the specificity of place of resistance (Tuck & Yang, 2014). In late 1998, students in Serbia formed *Otpor* (translation: Resistance), an anti-Milosevic-government movement starting with a small group of middle-class students that soon spread across the entire country. *Otpor* established a template that would be followed by *Kmara* (translation: Enough) in Georgia, and *Pora* (translation: It's time) in Ukraine— using similar branding, music, fashion, pranks, public performances, and sticker campaigns (Collin, 2007, pp. 3–5; see also Tuck & Yang, 2014). Organizers from one movement provided trainings to organizers in other movements in other places, understanding the need for meticulous strategic planning. Most striking about these movements was their wildfire reach and speed. Other movements were ignited in Kyrgyzstan, Azerbaijan, and Belarus, and inspired actions in 2005 in the Zvakwana/Sokwanele (translation: Enough) groups in Zimbabwe (where protesters distributed condoms with Bob Marley lyrics on them), Kefaya (translation: Enough) in Egypt (where protesters tried to prevent Mubarak from entering a fifth term), and in the Cedar Revolution of Lebanon (where protesters set up a camp in Martyrs Square in Beirut to protest the 15,000 Syrian troops stationed there) (Collin, 2007, p. 167).

As referred to earlier in this chapter, in late 2012, an Indigenous environmental and sovereignty movement, Idle No More, began in Saskatoon, Canada. It was started with a teach-in on the consequences of Prime Minister Stephen Harper's Budget Omnibus Bill's C-38 and C-45, which changed more than 130 federal Acts without proper Parliamentary debate, and without First Nations consultation, and greatly diminished environmental protection across the country (Land, 2013). Idle No More events and teach-ins spread throughout North America and across the globe, especially among Indigenous peoples in other settler colonial nation-states, including the United States, New Zealand, Australia, and Palestine/Israel. This was achieved through place-specific actions, such as round dances, protests, teach-ins, and other displays of resistance, images, and accounts, which were then shared through social media (Tuck & Yang, 2014).

In December 2012, Ogichidaakwe Theresa Spence went on a hunger strike consuming only fishbroth for six weeks. Inspired by Ogichidaakwe Spence's hunger strike, on January 17, 2013, six young people, including Travis George, Stanley George Jr., Raymond Bajo Kawapit, Johnny Abraham Kawapit, David Kawapit, and Geordie Rupert, from Whapmagoostui First Nation began a 1,600-kilometer walk from their homeland that would conclude on Parliament Hill. They called it the Journey of Nishiyuu (translation: Human beings). The youth were joined by about 200 others along their journey, and they were greeted by an estimated 5,000 people when they arrived in Ottawa more than two months later on March 25, 2013. Their walk was for recognition as sovereign peoples: "We just want to be equal, we just want Algonquin and Cree, all the reserves . . . to be known and to be treated equally," said Jordan Masty, who joined them on the walk (Barrera, 2013, n.p.). On May 22, 2013, at 5 pm, First Nations Peoples restored the peak of Mount Douglas to its original name, *PKOLS*. Tsawout, Songhees, and W̱SÁNEĆ nations participated in the reclaiming actions, including the installment of a new sign, a walk, and drumming. Participants held signs that said, "Reclaim, Rename, Reoccupy" (Lavoie, 2013, n.p.). These examples of movement building that are very much based on and in relation to land in specific places, but also connecting to people and places regionally and globally, exemplify a "politics of place beyond place" as theorized by Massey (2005, 2009).

In a study on the 2006 mobilizations for immigration rights through social networks and text messaging, K. Wayne Yang (2007) describes how what appears to be "fast organizing" or spontaneous is actually quite slow: "Youth fast organizing has been mistaken for ephemeral and spontaneous activity, rather than the outcomes of intentional and continuous organizing . . . spontaneity is an illusion generated by fast-technology, and can mask deeper structures of organized behavior" that took countless hours, days, or years of participation to develop (p. 19). The channels for collective resistance to flow are deepened over time, like trained neural pathways through which the repeated movements become body memory. Yang observes,

[V]irtual space provides otherwise un-propertied youth with a durable, malleable site of identity formation, social organization, and collective memory . . . That radicalizing moment of protest and crisis was preceded and succeeded by durable changes in ideology and social organizing—as remembered and lived through [social media]. These low-rent organizing halls and offices in virtual space can facilitate political activity, even formal political parties, that could mature into transformative urban movement. (p. 25)

Place itself, and our connections across place, can enable conceptualizations and practices of a "politics of place beyond place" (Massey, 2009). In accounts of social movements and political action, the role of place in shaping action can be obscured. Critical place inquiry seeks to make the influences of place on organizing and resistance more discernable and, thus, better able to be mobilized.

WHAT THEN FOR INQUIRY?

Toward the aims of this volume, the political implications of how place is conceptualized are also enacted in research itself; how we theorize place matters for how we do inquiry and research, but also what counts as evidence, as knowing, as legitimacy, as rigorous, as ethical, and as useful. Weighing the purposes of inquiry with regard to social change calls for not a small amount of cynicism. Policy, law, and public opinion have been disfigured by neoliberal market logics; as Elizabeth Povinelli (2011) observes, forms of life (and conceptualizations of land and life) that are not organized on the basis of market values are characterized as irrelevant, irrational, even as potential security risks (p. 22). Even if research determines a practice or intervention that "can be shown to lengthen life and increase health, but cannot at the same time be shown to produce a market value, this lengthened life and increased health is not a value to be capacitated" (Povinelli, 2011, p. 22).

Yet, neoliberalism (like development, like settler colonialism) is always uneven and incomplete, and there is hope in that (Peck, 2013). Although it is not always sequentially clear how inquiry can work to impact policy, pedagogy, or action (because channels between findings and applications can be convoluted or ideologically dismantled, as is often the case in fields like education and health), inquiry can have a meaningful role in maintaining, resisting, or mobilizing political trajectories with material outcomes. Chandra Mohanty (2003) observes that

> as we develop more complex, nuanced modes of asking questions and as scholarship in a number of relevant fields begins to address histories of colonialism, capitalism, race, and gender as inextricably interrelated, our very conceptual maps are redrawn and transformed. (p. 3)

Our hope is that the transformation of our very conceptual maps is informed by more deeply considered and more elaborately articulated theorizations of place and land. In our next chapter, we turn to decolonizing conceptualizations of place, attending to the latent assumptions of settler colonialism and encroachment of settler epistemologies on land and Indigenous life in social science research. Decolonizing conceptualizations of place, like the conceptualizations described in this chapter, yield implications for the ethics and protocols, topics, methodologies, and methods of research.

NOTES

1. To this point Chickasaw scholar Jodi Byrd wryly observes, "We are long-memoried peoples and we remember what happened last time the world was flat" (2011, p. xiv). Byrd insists that by making Indigenous peoples central to theorizations of globalization and postcoloniality, errors such as dismissing the continued significance of place can be avoided. This is discussed further in the opening of Chapter 3.
2. Part of N. Smith's project in *Uneven Development* is to disprove the assumption of nature as external object, tracing the assumption to the formulation of capitalism and its philosophical traditions (especially philosophies of Bacon and Newton, see 1984/2008, p. 15; see also Chapter 7 in this volume). New materialist scholar Manuel DeLanda insists,

   > Any materialist's philosophy takes as its point of departure the existence of a material world that is independent of our minds. But then it confronts the problem of the origin of enduring identity of the inhabitants of the world: if the mind is not what gives identity to the mountains and rivers, plants and animals, what does? . . . If one rejects essentialism then there is no choice but to answer the question like this: all objective entities are products of a historical process, that is, their identity is synthesized or produced as part of cosmological, geological, biological, or social history. (DeLanda in Dolphijn & van der Tuin, 2012, p. 39)

3. It is politically important to note that the "migration" referenced here is not the migration over a land bridge that is frequently/erroneously attributed to Indigenous peoples on the North American continent. Indigenous peoples in North America have cosmogony stories that refute the land bridge theory, and we defer to those stories.
4. It is interesting to consider this critique of mapping alongside Deleuze and Guattari's (1987) advocacy for making a map and not a tracing.

3   Decolonizing Perspectives on Place

Now the people spoke among themselves and agreed with what their leaders had said. They agreed to be known for the place where they first planted corn.

Charles Henry, as quoted in Keith Basso, 1996

Terra nullius, the colonizer's dream, is a sinister presupposition for social science. It is invoked every time we try to theorise the formation of social institutions and systems from scratch, in a blank space. Whenever we see the words "building block" in a treatise of social theory, we should be asking who used to occupy the land.

Raewyn Connell, 2007

Indigenous peoples have lived through environmental collapse on local and regional levels since the beginning of colonialism—the construction of the St. Lawrence Seaway, the extermination of the buffalo in Cree and Blackfoot territories and the extinction of salmon in Lake Ontario—these were unnecessary and devastating. At the same time, I know there are a lot of people within the indigenous community that are giving the economy, this system, 10 more years, 20 more years, that are saying "Yeah, we're going to see the collapse of this in our lifetimes."

Leanne Simpson in Klein and Simpson, 2013, n.p.

In this chapter, we zoom in our focus on decolonizing conceptualizations of place, which was discussed more generally alongside a variety of other conceptualizations in Chapter 2. Our aim here is to attend to decolonial and Indigenous renderings of place, and the ways in which they depart from (and collide with) conceptualizations of place that derive from Western philosophical frames. As we explain later, decolonizing perspectives and approaches are always spatially and temporally specific (Fanon, 1968; Tuck & Yang, 2012). The discussions in this volume are particularly concerned with decolonization away from settler colonialism, which projects those who already inhabited stolen land before settlers' arrival as "spatially, socially, and temporally before [the settler state] in the double sense of 'before'—before it in a temporal sequence and before it as a fact to be faced" (Povinelli, 2011, p. 36).

In Chapter 2, we began with a discussion on the competing conclusions about the saliency of place in a globalized context. Some scholars and popular media pundits have taken the increased mobility and technological connectivity of the world's populations to mean that place does not matter anymore. Others, especially Neil Smith (1984/2008) in his articulation of uneven development, insist that globalization means that place matters more. Chickasaw scholar Jodi Byrd (2011), in arguing that Indigenous peoples must be central to theorizations of the conditions of globalization and postcoloniality, offers this insertion to the debate: "For indigenous peoples, place, land, sovereignty, and memory matter. In a world growing increasingly enamored with faster, flatter, smooth, where positionality doesn't matter so much as how it is that we travel there, indigeneity matters" (p. xiii). Byrd's point is that mistakenly concluding that place no longer matters can be avoided if Indigeneity becomes a lens through which to view globalization and postcoloniality.

In most cases, decolonizing conceptualizations of place (and decolonization more broadly) draw upon Indigenous intellectualism and worldviews, which is why we discuss them together in this chapter. We agree that Indigenous perspectives must be at the center of decolonizing theories and practices (Tuck & Yang, 2012), and in this chapter we also note how decolonial perspectives on place might be informed by Southern theories (Connell, 2007) and theorizations of anti-Blackness in settler colonial nation-states.

Decolonizing conceptualizations of place confront, undermine, disavow, and unsettle understandings of place that emerge from what Mary Louise Pratt (1992) calls "Europe's planetary consciousness" (p. 15). The specific version of European planetary consciousness that Pratt describes arose in 1735, with the publication of Swedish naturalist Carl Linne's *The System of Nature,* a classification of all plant forms on the planet, and the launch of the La Condamine expedition, Europe's first formal pursuit of scientific evidence of the exact shape (a sphere or a spheroid?) of the planet. The classification system typified a European desire to order nature into hierarchies, whereas the expedition typified a European desire for not only wealth, but Science and scientific knowledge (capitalization intended) to enkindle colonial expansion. Constructed of the dual impulses toward interior exploration and constructions of global-scale meanings, this European planetary consciousness is the basic element of modern Eurocentrism (Pratt, 1992, p. 15).

Pratt (1992) explains that these two activities, classification and expedition, were primary activities of colonialism and the establishment of settler colonies. We note that both are concerned with place—the former with placing/emplacing various hierarchies, the latter with the accumulation of place. Seneca scholar Mishuana Goeman (2013) observes,

This 'planetary consciousness' [described by Pratt, 1992] which still largely orders the world, has had major implications for Native and non-Native communities alike . . . Colonization resulted in a sorting of space based on ideological premises of hierarchies and binaries. Settler colonialism continues to depend on imposing a "planetary consciousness" and naturalizing geographic concepts and sets of social relationships. (p. 2)

Quechua scholar Sandy Grande (2004) elaborates the "deep structures" of what she calls "colonialist consciousness," which closely corresponds to Pratt's term, *European planetary consciousness*. These are the animating beliefs that course through colonialist societies, hegemonic perspectives that serve as common sense. These deep structures involve five core beliefs:

1) Belief in progress as change and change as progress
2) Belief in the effective separateness of faith and reason
3) Belief in the essential quality of the universe and of "reality" as impersonal, secular, material, mechanistic, and relativistic
4) Subscription to ontological individualism
5) Belief in human beings as separate from and superior to the rest of nature (Grande, 2004, p. 69)

Grande posits that contemporary cultural and ecological crises can be credited to these deep structures—they both afford and justify environmental degradation, cultural domination, and the practices of "overdeveloped, overconsumptive, and overempowered first-world nations and their environmentally destructive ontological, axiological, and epistemological systems" (2004, p. 68).

Erstwhile, Indigenous philosophies of place predate and have co-developed alongside and in-spite of the deep structures of European planetary consciousness. Synthesizing the role of place in Indigenous philosophical frameworks, Vine Deloria, Jr. (Deloria & Wildcat, 2001) argues that,

> Power and place produce personality. This equation simply means that the universe is alive, but it also contains within it the very important suggestion that the universe is personal and, therefore, must be approached in a personal manner . . . The personal nature of the universe demands that each and every entity in it seek and sustain personal relationships . . . [Thus], the corresponding question faced by American Indians when contemplating action is whether or not the proposed action is appropriate. Appropriateness includes the moral dimension of respect for the part of nature that will be used or affected in our action. Thus, killing an animal or catching a fish involved paying respect to the species and the individual animal or fish that such action had disturbed. Harvesting plants also involved paying respect to the plants. These actions were necessary because of the recognition that the universe was built upon

constructive and cooperative relationships that had to be maintained. (Deloria in Deloria & Wildcat, 2001, pp. 23–24)

Indigenous philosophies of place represent significant epistemological and ontological departures from those that have emerged in Western frames.

Yet, in Indigenous worldviews, relationships to land are not overly romantic—it might be more accurate to say that they are familiar, and if sacred, sacred because they are familiar. Rarámuri ethnobotanist Enrique Salmón argues,

> When [Indigenous] people speak of the land, the religious and romantic overtones so prevalent in Western environmental conversation are absent. To us, the land exists in the same manner as do our families, chickens, the river, and the sky. No hierarchy of privilege places one above or below another. Everything is woven into a managed, interconnected tapestry. Within this web, there are particular ways that living things relate to one another. . . . One Raramuri elder mentioned to me that "It is the reason why people should collect plants in the same way that fish should breathe water, and birds eat seeds and bugs. These are things we are supposed to do." (Salmón, 2012, p. 27)

Salmón locates the tendency to romanticize Indigenous relationships to land inside the Western cultural tradition, a misunderstanding of the nexus of Indigenous identity and land.

Similarly, Seneca scholar Mishuana Goeman (2013) observes,

> Describing Native relationships to land is riddled with pitfalls and paradoxes, many of which are impossible to avoid given the nature of power and colonialism. I do not take the phrase "relationship to the land," as a given, unchanging, and naturalized part of Native American identities, especially as capitalism and colonization have produced new ways of experiencing time and space. . . . On one hand, Native relationships to land are presumed and oversimplified as natural, and even worse, romanticized . . . Respecting the environment is not encoded in the DNA. In fact, tribes have experience many travesties of justice in regard to environmental destruction. We also have a tendency to abstract space—that is to decorporealitize, commodify, or bureaucratize— when the legal ramifications of land or the political landscape are addressed: too often we forget that reserve/ations, resource exploitation, federal Indian law, and urbanization are relatively new phenomena. The stories that connect Native people to the land and form their relationships to the land and one another are much older than colonial governments . . . Stories create the relationships that have made communities strong even through numerous atrocities and injustices. (Goeman, 2013, p. 28)

DECOLONIZING CONCEPTUALIZATIONS DRAW
ON INDIGENOUS THEORIES

It seems self-evident that a discussion on decolonizing conceptualizations of land would primarily draw on conceptualizations by Indigenous peoples. Yet, as Eve Tuck and K. Wayne Yang (2012) have observed, the discourse of decolonization is frequently invoked without reference to the works and lives of Indigenous peoples:

> At a conference on educational research, it is not uncommon to hear speakers refer, almost casually, to the need to "decolonize our schools," or use "decolonizing methods," or, "decolonize student thinking." Yet, we have observed a startling number of these discussions make no mention of Indigenous peoples, our/their struggles for the recognition of our/their sovereignty, or the contributions of Indigenous intellectuals and activists to theories and frameworks of decolonization. Further, there is often little recognition given to the immediate context of settler colonialism on the North American lands where many of these conferences take place. (Tuck & Yang, 2012, pp. 2–3)

In these instances, the discourse of decolonization is epistemically severed from the specific colonial contexts from which it emerges. The result is the use of "decolonization" as a synonym for civil and human rights-based social justice projects. This is problematic because decolonization seeks something quite different than those forms of justice (Tuck & Yang, 2012, p. 2). The too-easy adoption of decolonizing discourse is a kind of inclusion that is also,

> a form of enclosure, dangerous in how it domesticates decolonization. It is also a foreclosure, limiting in how it recapitulates dominant theories of social change. (W)e wanted to be sure to clarify that decolonization is not a metaphor. When metaphor invades decolonization, it kills the very possibility of decolonization; it recenters whiteness, it resettles theory, it extends innocence to the settler, it entertains a settler future. Decolonize (a verb) and decolonization (a noun) cannot easily be grafted onto pre-existing discourses/frameworks, even if they are critical, even if they are anti-racist, even if they are justice frameworks. The easy absorption, adoption, and transposing of decolonization is yet another form of settler appropriation. When we write about decolonization, we are not offering it as a metaphor; it is not an approximation of other experiences of oppression. Decolonization is not a swappable term for other things we want to do to improve our societies and schools. Decolonization doesn't have a synonym. (Tuck & Yang, 2012, p. 3)

Decolonization within settler colonial nation-states is complicated because there is no spatial separation between empire, settlement, and colony/colonized.

When decolonization is allowed to stand as metaphor, it papers over this complexity, backing away from the very aspects of decolonization that are unsettling.

> Though the details are not fixed or agreed upon, in our view, decolonization in the settler colonial context must involve the repatriation of land simultaneous to the recognition of how land and relations to land have always already been differently understood and enacted; that is, all of the land, and not just symbolically. This is precisely why decolonization is necessarily unsettling, especially across lines of solidarity . . . Settler colonialism, and its decolonization, implicates and unsettles everyone. (Tuck & Yang, 2012, p. 7)

Thus, when we discuss decolonizing perspectives of place in this chapter, we are doing so with an understanding of decolonization that is purposefully informed by Indigenous analyses of colonization and theorizations of unsettlement. Further, we discuss decolonization as always involving recalibrations of human relationships to land.

"CONCEPTUALIZATION" IS NOT THE RIGHT WORD

In Western philosophical traditions, Descartes's *Cogito ergo sum* has sprouted a lexicon that links what humans do to/with ideas only to the mind, located in or near the brain in the human head. Intellect/ualization and concept/ualization are both nouns and activities that are thought or perceived to have a home in the mind, which is physically located, somehow, in the brain. Thoughts and perceptions, incidentally, also take place in/from the human head; so too with comprehension, cognition, theorizing, understanding, interpreting. This observation (again, the head) is not meant to be dense or obvious, but to draw attention to how the very words we use to describe how humans interact with ideas are over-coded by assumptions about where thinking comes from and goes to. This coding is perhaps a good match with Western common sense, which regards the mind as apart from the body, the self as apart from others, the body as apart from the rest of matter, and humans as perhaps part, but also discreet and unique from, the rest of the living world.[1] But, this coding is not a good match for how Indigenous philosophies engage questions of self, us, the (living) world, interactions with it, and interactions with ideas. As Gloria Anzaldúa (1987) says of the body, "We are taught that the body is an ignorant animal; intelligence dwells only in the head. But the body is smart. It does not discern between external stimuli and stimuli from the imagination" (p. 37).

In a discussion about decolonizing conceptualizations of place, it is necessary to remember that conceptualizations is not the right word. Theorizations is not quite right either, in this case not because Indigenous people do not position themselves as theorists, but because what counts as theorizing is often quite narrow in Western definitions. Maori scholar Leonie Pihama (2005) writes,

> Our histories remind us of many acts of resistance to colonial imperial-ism and struggles of resistance against the confiscation of our lands. In the history of Taranaki, where my own tribal links hold firmly, we have many examples of the approaches taken by our tupuna, our ances-tors, in the struggle against the confiscation of our land, the imprison-ment and death of many of our people, and the denial of our language, culture, and knowledge bases. As such our people have always been theorists. We have generations engaged with our world and constructed theories as a part of our own knowledge and ways of understanding our experiences. (p. 191)

In this excerpt, Pihama fuses together notions of resistance, ancestors, land, knowing, experience, and theory.

Thus, although we employ the word *conceptualizations* in the title of this chapter and throughout, we do so with the important acknowledg-ment that the epistemological and cosmological departures represented by Indigenous worldviews (especially when compared to Western perspectives) require an expansion to the connotative meanings of concept/ualization. "Interactions" and "relationships" are somewhat helpful words toward describing what we are getting at, but only if they are imbued with notions of intention, consideration, reflection, and iteration. Learning from Pihama (2005), "conceptualization," must connote resistance, land, knowing, and experience over generations.

PLACE IS NOT THE RIGHT WORD EITHER

As it becomes quite clear in reading Indigenous philosophy, "place" and "space" are not the right words either. Even when the term *place* is used, it is clear that it is a referent to something quite different than can be found in Western philosophical traditions. Vine Deloria, Jr. (Deloria & Wildcat, 2001), writing about American Indian [sic] metaphysics, observes,

> The best description of Indian metaphysics was the realization that the world, and all its possible experiences, constituted a social real-ity, a fabric of life in which everything had the possibility of intimate knowing relationships because, ultimately, everything was related. This world was a unified world, a far cry from the disjointed sterile and emotionless world painted by Western science. Even though we can translate the realities of the Indian social world into concepts famil-iar to us from the Western scientific context, such as space, time, and

energy, we must surrender most of the meaning in the world when we do so. The Indian world can be said to consist of two basic experiential dimensions that, taken together, provided a sufficient means of making sense of the world. These two concepts were place and power, the latter perhaps defined as a spiritual power or life force. Familiarity with the personality of objects and entities in the natural world enabled Indians to discern immediately where each living being had its proper place and what kinds of experiences that place allowed, encouraged, and suggested. And knowing places enabled people to relate to the living entities inhabiting it. (pp. 2–3)

For several reasons related to Deloria's observations, Indigenous authors have indicated preference for the term *land* over place. "Land" in these discussions is often shorthand for land, water, air, and subterranean earth—for example, in discussions of wetlands (Bang et al., 2014) and Sea Country (Whitehouse et al., 2014). As we discuss throughout this chapter, land is imbued with the experiential sense making invoked by Deloria in the previous passage.

Among Indigenous peoples, relationships to land and place are diverse, specific, and un-generalizable (Lowan, 2009):

> Every cultural group established relations to [their land] over time. Whether that place is in the desert, a mountain valley, or along a seashore, it is in the context of natural community, and through that understanding they established an educational process that was practical, ultimately ecological, and spiritual. In this way they sought and found their life. (Cajete, 1994, p. 113, as cited in Lowan, 2009, p. 47)

"Land" is imbued with these long relationships and, as we discuss in the following section, the practices and knowledges that have emerged from those relationships.

DIFFERENCES BETWEEN PLACE AND LAND[2]

Megan Bang et al. (2014) differentiate Western connotations of place from Indigenous connotations of land by invoking Brian Yazzie Burkhart's (2004) discussion of Descartes's aforementioned insistence. Burkhart revises Descartes statement, "I think, therefore I am," away from an individualist focus toward a more tribal understanding, "We are, therefore I am," to express the saliency of collectivity in Indigenous life and knowledge systems (Bang et al., 2014, p. 44). Bang et al. extend Burkhart's revision in order to compare notions of place to notions of land.

Similarly, we might imagine that ontology of place-based paradigms is something like "I am, therefore place is," in contrast, the ontology of land-based [paradigms] might be summarized as "Land is, therefore we are" (p. 45, insertion ours, original word was pedagogies). Bang et al. (2014) seem to be saying that the ontology of place prioritizes and centers the individual human, the surveyor or place, whereas an ontology of land prioritizes and centers land, which constitutes the life of a collective. This represents a profound distinction that cannot be overlooked. Understandings of collectivity and shared (although not necessarily synchronous) relations to land are core attributes of an ontology of land.

Further—and this is not a romantic point—the *land-we* ontology articulated by Bang et al. (2014) is incommensurable with anthropocentric notions of place. Daniel Wildcat (Deloria & Wildcat, 2001) insists that indigenous means "to be of a place," meaning that "Indigenous people represent a culture emergent from a place, and they actively draw on the power of that place physically and spiritually" (p. 32). This is why Eve Tuck has argued elsewhere that Indigenous peoples have creation stories, not colonization stories about how Indigenous people came to (be) a place (Tuck & Yang, 2012). In *Wisdom Sits in Places* (1996), Charles Henry, ethnographer Keith Basso's Apache host, tells Basso the following story about how one Apache community narrated their land:

> This is where our women first planted corn. They have planted it again and again. Each year we have harvested enough to roast and dry and store away. These fields look after us by helping our corn to grow. Our children eat it and become strong. We eat it and continue to live. Our corn draws life from this earth and we draw life from our corn. This earth is part of us! We are of this place . . . We should name ourselves for this place! (quoted in Basso, 1996, p. 21)

Henry continues, "You see, their names for themselves are really the names of their places. This is how they were known, to others and to themselves. They were known by their places. This is how they are still known" (p. 21). This narrative of being "known by their places" cannot be made compatible with flat world ontologies (e.g., Friedman, 2007) and other ontologies that put humans at the center of the universe, or conversely, as but small and simple cogs in a universal scheme (see N. Smith, 1984/2008, p. 7). This characteristic of Indigenous worldviews is derived in no small part from necessity. Yup'ik elder Oscar Kawagley wrote,

> The cold defines my place. Mamterilleq (now known as Bethel, Alaska) made me who I am. The cold made my language, my worldview, my culture, and my technology . . . I grew up as an inseparable part of Nature. It was not my place to "own" land, nor to domesticate plants or animals that often have more power than I as a human being. (Kawagley, 2010, p. xviii)

Finally, Bang et al.'s (2014) insistence on "Land is, therefore we are" is not an abstraction. Many Indigenous cultures refer to seascapes, mountains, and other land formations literally and not figuratively as ancestors. This is as true in Indigenous cosmogony as it is in contemporary accounts of Indigenous resistance, such as the October 2013 attack on Mi'kmaq anti-fracking protesters by Royal Canadian Mounted Police at Elsipogtog. Writing about the Mi'kmaq mothers, grandmothers, aunties, sisters, and daughters—armed with drums and feathers against the pointed rifles of the RCMP—and their choice to lay their bodies on their land to protest and protect their land from fracking, Leanne Simpson remarks, "Our bodies should be on the land so that our grandchildren have something left to stand upon" (Klein & Simpson, 2013, n.p.). This, like the notion of land as ancestor is simultaneously poetic and real; it is both a notion and an action.

Land

As Styres, Haig-Brown, and Blimkie (2013) recently articulated in discussing a "pedagogy of Land" (echoing Cajete [1994] and Lowan [2009]), "land" refers not just to the materiality of land, but also its "spiritual, emotional, and intellectual aspects" (p. 37). These scholars choose to signify consideration of these aspects in their capitalization of Land (as do Styres & Zinga, 2013; Korteweg & Oakley, 2014; and Engel, Mauro, & Carroll, 2014).

Land can be considered as a teacher and conduit of memory (Brooks, 2008; Wilson, 2008) in that it "both remembers life and its loss and serves itself as a mnemonic device that triggers the ethics of relationality with the sacred geographies that constitute Indigenous peoples' histories" (Byrd 2011, p. 118).

Relationships to land are familial, intimate, intergenerational, and instructive. For example, Manulani Aluli Meyer (2008) writes,

> Land is our mother. *This is not a metaphor.* For the Native Hawaiians speaking of knowledge, land was the central theme that drew forth all others. You came from a place, you grew in a place and you had a relationship with a place. This is an epistemological idea. . . . One does not simply learn about land, we learn best from land. (p. 219, italics original)

Land teaches and can be considered as first teacher (Styres et al., 2013). Yup'ik scholar Angayuqaq Oscar Kawagley (2010) writes that for Yupiaq people, land and nature are "metaphysic" and pedagogical:

> It is through direct interaction with the environment that the Yupiaq people learn. What they learn is mediated by the cultural cognitive map. The map consists of those "truths" that have been proven over a long period of time. As the Yupiaq people interact with nature, they carefully

observe to find pattern or order where there might otherwise appear to be chaos. (p. 88)

He continues, "It was meaningless for Yupiaq to count, measure, and weigh, for their wisdom transcended the quantification of things to recognize a qualitative level whereby the spiritual, natural, and human worlds were inextricably interconnected" (p. 90). Kawagley's rendering of Yupiaq relations to land braids together the cosmological, pedagogical, pragmatic, and spiritual.

Significantly, Indigenous and non-Indigenous scholars theorizing the connotative differences between land and place include the urban in their considerations. Land does not exclude the urban, to be relegated only to the "green spaces" outside and within the urban (Bang et al., 2014; Paperson, 2014).

Styres and colleagues (2013), Meyer (2008), Kawagley (2010), and others also warn against understandings of Indigenous knowledge of land as static or performable. Calderon (2014) emphasizes embracing protocols "that are mindful of how indigenous knowledge has been co-opted and omitted" (p. 6), including, for example, expectations that Indigenous peoples lead discussions on place. This mindfulness of co-option also entails an acknowledgement that Indigenous identities and knowledge are not static and that non-Indigenous desires for performances of "authentic" Indigeneity are also problematic. Friedel (2011) outlines this concern effectively in her paper on "urban Native youth's cultured responses to Western place-based learning" in western Canada. The youth in the study resisted the stereotypes and expectations of the White educators for them to "get back to nature," instead holding fast to their own desires for social experiences and connections, wanting to "to learn to be Aboriginal without being in the woods" (p. 535). Friedel (2011) writes,

Of the pernicious representations of Indigeneity today, none is more equivocal than the trope of 'the Ecological Indian'. Borne from nineteenth-century romantic primitivism, this White construction (Bird, 1996) has become a prevalent signifier in the environmental realm, an ideal to which Canadians and others look today for a critique of Western institutions. (p. 534)

As this suggests, mindfulness of non-Indigenous desires to access assumed Indigenous knowledge also needs to extend to a mindfulness of non-Indigenous desires to adopt or use such knowledge (e.g., critiques of the formulations and uses of "traditional ecological knowledge," as in Agrawal, 2002). This is difficult terrain in working both with Indigenous and non-Indigenous peoples: to acknowledge and include Indigenous knowledge and perspectives but in non-determined ways that do not stereotype Indigenous knowledge or identities.

THEORIZING COLONIALISM

Raewyn Connell (2007) observes,

> The most important erasure in globalization theory concerns colonialism. The fact that the majority world has deep prior experience of subjugation to globalizing powers is surely known to all the theorists. But this experience of subjugation does not surface as a central issue in any of the [major] theories of globalization." (p. 65)

Theories of colonialism have largely focused on what is sometimes called exogenous domination (Veracini, 2011), exploitation colonialism, or external colonialism—three names for the same form. In this form of colonization, small numbers of colonizers go to a new place in order to dominate a local labor force to harvest resources to send back to the metropole, for example, the spice trade that impelled the colonization of India by several different European empires. Exploitation colonialism, its nature, consequences, endgame, and post-possibilities, has been the focus of (what would become) the field of postcolonial studies for the past fifty years.

It has only been in the last two decades that settler colonialism has been more comprehensively theorized, mostly via the emergence of the field of settler colonial studies. Settler colonialism is a form of colonization in which outsiders come to land inhabited by Indigenous peoples and claim it as their own new home (see also Hinkinson, 2012). Subsequent generations of settlers come to the settler nation-state for many reasons, under many circumstances—but at the heart of all of those rationales is the need for space and land. This form is distinct from the exploitation colonialism that has been so deeply theorized in postcolonial studies because in settler colonialism, settlers come to the new land seeking land and resources, not (necessarily) labor (Wolfe, 2011). Put another way, in this version, the colonizers arrive at a place ("discovering" it) and attempt to make it a permanent home (claiming it). Settlers enforce their interpretations on everyone and everything in their new domain, and their new societies require corporeal and epistemic elimination of the Native (Wolfe, 1999, 2006; Veracini, 2011). Although there are many important parallels and connections between exploitation colonialism and settler colonialism, especially as settler colonial nation states also occupy and colonize other lands, there are important differences to be teased apart (see also Hinkinson, 2012). For example, Veracini (2011) observes that exploitation colonizers and settler colonizers want very different things: the exploitation colonizer says to the Indigenous person, "you, work for me," whereas the settler colonizer—because land is the primary pursuit—says to the Indigenous person, "you, go away" (p. 1). Of course, in reality, settler colonizers communicate an amalgamation of these messages to Indigenous peoples; Veracini observes that the accumulating sentiment may be more like, "you, work for me while we wait for you to disappear," or "you, move on so you can work for me," but the base intention of settlers has been to disappear Indigenous peoples from the land to make it available for settlement (p. 2).

One of the notable characteristics of settler colonial states is the refusal to recognize themselves as such, requiring a continual disavowal of history, Indigenous peoples' resistance to settlement, Indigenous peoples' claims to stolen land, and how settler colonialism is indeed ongoing, not an event contained in the past. Settler colonialism is made invisible within settler societies and uses institutional apparatuses to "cover its tracks" (Veracini, 2011). For example, most non-Indigenous people living in settler societies, if they think of colonizers and/or settlers at all, think of Captain James Cook, Christopher Columbus, colonies, and forts (Donald, 2012; see Hinkinson, 2012, for a discussion of the colonization of Australia). They think of colonization as something that happened in the distant past, as perhaps the unfortunate birthpangs of a new nation. They do not consider the fact that they live on land that has been stolen, or ceded through broken treaties, or to which Indigenous peoples claim a pre-existing ontological and cosmological relationship. They do not consider themselves to be implicated in the continued settlement and occupation of unceded Indigenous land. Indeed, settler colonial societies "cover" the "tracks" of settler colonialism by narrating colonization as temporally located elsewhere, not here and now (Veracini, 2011).

Another of the general characteristics of settler societies is that settlers are located at the top and at the center of all typologies—as simultaneously most superior and most normal (Tuck & Yang, 2012). These typologies include settler/Indigenous, but also the hegemony of settlers over non-Indigenous workers. These hierarchies are established through force, policy, law, and ideology and are so embedded that they become naturalized.

The hegemony of the hierarchy of settlers over Indigenous peoples was already well established and thriving before Captain Cook left England to "discover" lands in the South (Moreton-Robinson, 2009). A letter from the President of the Royal Society documents full knowledge of the presence of Indigenous peoples on (what is now) Australia, but also their existing proprietary rights (which Cook was further instructed to ignore to claim possession of the land for the king) (Moreton-Robinson, 2009, p. 30). From Cook's notes, the Natives he encountered in Australia did not value the possessions he and his men offered them, nor would they be willing to part with their possessions or land in exchange for what Cook could provide—this was the rationale for claiming land without consent.

> To be able to assert "this is mine" requires a subject to internalize the idea that one has proprietary rights that are part of normative behaviour, rules of interaction and social engagement. Thus possession which constitutes part of the ontological structure of white subjectivity is

also constituted socio-discursively. For Cook to be able to take possession of the east coast of Australia without the consent of the 'natives' means he had to position Aboriginal people as will-less things in order to take their land in the name of the King. Thus Cook's white possessiveness operated ontologically and epistemologically by willing away Indigenous people's sovereignty in order to make them appear will-less. (Moreton-Robinson, 2009, p. 32)

Cook's idea of possession was informed by the logic of capital according to which possessions are those things having an exchange value when they are sold or otherwise traded, usually man made material objects or other things occurring naturally and taken without constraint. This logic underpins Cook's perception of Indigenous people as property-less and living in a state of nature whose possessions do not go beyond satisfying their immediate needs. Being perceived as living in a state of nature relegates one's existence to being an inseparable part of nature and therefore incapable of possessing it. (Moreton-Robinson, 2009, p. 34)

Scott Lauria Morgensen (2011) theorizes settler colonialism as a form of biopower, observing that "the biopolitics of settler colonialism arose in the Americas by perpetuating African diasporic subjugation and Indigenous elimination simultaneously" (p. 57). Thus, in several contexts, settler colonialism has simultaneously taken form as "Slave estates" (Spillers, 2003; Wilderson, 2010), requiring the forced labor of stolen peoples on stolen land. In these cases, settlement required/s the labor of chattel slaves and guest workers, who must be kept landless and estranged from their homelands. For example, as Kate McCoy (2014) has detailed, Tsenecommacah peoples were killed, displaced, and otherwise removed from areas surrounding colonies in Virginia, as Black men and women were brought from Africa to be bought and sold to labor the land. This same "triad" dynamic continues to operate in North America and elsewhere in the working and living conditions of migrant workers (Byrd, 2011; Patel, 2012).

A final, general characteristic of settler colonialism is its attempt (and failure) to contain Indigenous agency and resistance. Indigenous peoples have refused settler encroachment, even while losing their lives and homelands. Writing about Aotearoa/New Zealand, Jo Smith (2011) cites the long history of Maori resistance to settler invasion, describing the settler nation's need to "continually code, decode, and recode social norms and social spaces so as to secure a meaningful (read: proprietary) relationship to the territories and resources at stake" (p. 112, parentheses original). Thus, when we theorize settler colonialism, we must attend to it as both an ongoing and incomplete project, with internal contradictions, cracks, and fissures through which Indigenous life and knowledge have persisted and thrived despite settlement.

DECOLONIZING POSSESSION AND PROPERTY

One of the false but widely circulated narratives that has justified steal-ing Indigenous land in the United States and Canada has always been that Indigenous people traded land for beads and baubles because they lacked a serious understanding of buying and owning land. This story is featured in public school textbooks and is used to both pity and romanticize Indigenous peoples, while still explaining away settler complicity in living on ill-gotten land.

For example, countless websites, children's books, and posters feature the words of a fictional 1854 Chief Seattle (Suquamish) speech, which sup-posedly asked,

> The President in Washington sends word that he wishes to buy our land. But how can you buy or sell the sky? the land? The idea is strange to us. If we do not own the freshness of the air and the sparkle of the water, how can you buy them? (Perry, 1972, n.p.)

The fictional speech continues,

> If we sell you our land, remember that the air is precious to us, that the air shares its spirit with all the life that it supports. The wind that gave our grandfather his first breath also received his last sigh. The wind also gives our children the spirit of life. So if we sell our land, you must keep it apart and sacred, as a place where man can go to taste the wind that is sweetened by the meadow flowers. (Perry, 1972, n.p.)

The fictional speech concludes,

> As we are part of the land, you too are part of the land. This earth is precious to us. It is also precious to you. (Perry, 1972, n.p.)

In reading these lines, it is easy to see how they became a sort of anthem for environmental movements, including the establishment of Earth Day, New Age Indians, and others. The words echo something that settler children learn about Indigenous peoples: that they enjoy a more simple and noble relation to the environment and are ignorant of more sophisticated aspects of civil life.

Seattle was a real Suquamish leader, and he did make a speech directed to U.S. President Franklin Pierce in the 1850s. The original speech was in response to the reach of the U.S. Government onto Suquamish land and to protest removal of Suquamish people from their homelands. However—as, hopefully, is now widely known—the previous words that are regularly attributed to Seattle were fictionalized for an eco-awareness film, called *Home*, by filmmaker Ted Perry, a white Southern Baptist, in 1971. Perry appropriated and co-opted the original speech by Seattle to amplify his film's message of Judeo-Christian stewardship of the planet (Black, 2012, p. 635). Perry's fictionalized version seems to loosely be based on what Seattle actually said, but he amplified themes of simplistic understandings of land ownership, inserted environmental themes, and completely ignored Seattle's message of resistance and refusal. Perry's reasons were strategic, in order to build upon existing tropes of Indigenous peoples in order to redirect them toward an environmental movement supposedly rooted in "so-called Native connections to the earth" (Black, 2012, p. 635).

The problem, of course, is that Perry's bogus speech was widely and wrongly attributed to Chief Seattle, recirculated by the National Wildlife Federation, then later by Joseph Campbell and Spokane's 1974 World's Fair (p. 636). Black (2012) observes,

> The Eurocentric pursuit of authenticity, in particular, is problematic because it punctuates a Western obsession with attributing essentialized genuineness to key Native agents. This pursuit denies a Native oral tradition that puts stock in individual tribal lifeways . . . The way fragmented discourse circulates says much about a public that interprets it and the ideologies that underscore that particular public's civic imaginary. (p. 636)

Although there is no surely accurate record of Chief Seattle's actual speech directed at Franklin Pierce, several historians support that the speech more likely contained lines like the following (also a fictionalization):

> The young men, the mothers, the girls, the little children who once lived and were happy here [on Suquamish land], still love these lonely places. And at evening the forests are dark with the presence of the dead. When the last red man has vanished from this earth, and his memory is only a story among the whites, these shores will still swarm with the invisible dead of my people. And when your children's children think they are alone in the fields, the forests, the shops, the highways, or the quiet of the woods, they will not be alone. There is no place in this country where a man can be alone. At night when the streets of your town and cities are quiet, and you think they are empty, they will throng with the returning spirits that once thronged them, and that still love those places. The white man will never be alone.
>
> So let him be just and deal kindly with my people. The dead have power too. (Liberation Theology and Land Reform website, n.d., n.p.)

The foreboding quality to these words reveals a different strategy of resistance, not one confused by "white man's" ways, but surely certain of their consequences.

We elaborate this point to be sure to avoid well-worn traps in circulations of discourse about Indigenous peoples. There is indeed a problem with

Western conflations of place and property, but not because Indigenous peoples were/are too pre-modern to understand property. New interpretations of historical accounts argue that Native people engaged in heated debates over notions of colonial property and extensively used legal arguments to oppose European dispossession from the very outset of colonial occupation (Belmessous, 2012, p. 3). Although Indigenous resistance to colonization is widely known, Indigenous resistance through legal counter-claims and arguments with regard to property and making-property is less commonly discussed. This history confounds descriptions of Native legal resistance as a more recent phenomenon—Native people fought colonization with legal resistance immediately (Belmessous, 2012). Further,

> Cultural boundaries were porous, allowing Indigenous and European peoples to translate each other's legal documents, to draw parallels, and to understand what kind of titles they could use to make recognizable and valid claims to land. Europeans often, although not always, understood the nature of the claims put forward by their Native competitors: they understood that when Indigenous communities made claims to ownership (hence British insistence, for example, upon purchasing the land), they were distinct from when they made claims that resembled sovereignty: that is, when they made claims to a particular territory with delimited borders and upon which they had established the law of the land, determining, for example, who could come and live on that territory. (Belmessous, 2012, p. 5)

Although violence was an important aspect of establishing and enacting land claims, claims were also negotiated nation-to-nation between tribes and Europeans. The status of claims acquired through conquest were more clear than the status of claims acquired through purchase, possession, or occupation (p. 12). The connotation of claim is/was not just about requesting or demanding land, but more an appeal to justice with the promise of force as a consequence (pp. 10–11).

SETTLER COLONIALISM MAKES PROPERTY AND UNMAKES INDIGENOUS LAND

Through the process and structuring of settler colonialism, land is remade into property, and human relationships to land are redefined/reduced to the relationship of owner to his property. When land is recast as property, place becomes exchangeable, saleable, and steal-able. The most important aim of recasting land as property is to make it ahistorical in order to hack away the narratives that invoke prior claims and thus reaffirm the myth of terra nullius. Existing epistemological, ontological, and cosmological relationships to land are interred, indeed made pre-modern and backward (Tuck & Yang,

2012). Conceptualizations of land as property are enmeshed in the ideologies of settler colonialism, reliant upon constructions of land as extractable capital, the structural denial of indigenous sovereignty, the fantasy of discovery, and the naturalization of heteropatriarchal nation-state (Arvin, Tuck, & Morrill, 2013).

Thus, from the perspective of Indigenous scholars and writers, Western notions of place have been compromised by an over-reliance on the European, colonial notion of property (see Barker, 2005; Grande, 2004; Belmessous, 2012, for elaborations on this point). But, as Indigenous philosophers and elders remind us, there are more complex and meaningful relationships to land that humans have always enacted. For example, Chamberlin (2001, 2004) tells the story of a meeting between Canadian government foresters and Gitskan elders and leaders.

> The meeting was about jurisdiction over the woodlands. The foresters claimed the land for the government. The Indians were astonished by the claim—they couldn't understand what the relative newcomers were talking about. Finally, one of them put what was bothering them in the form of a question. "If this is your land," he asked, "where are your stories?" (2001, p. 127)

This question reveals the interwoven aspects of land (origin) stories, claims, and identity that comprise Gitskan and other Indigenous peoples' relationships to place. This, Chamberlin continues, "was a revelation not about ownership in any simple-minded sense, because these stories didn't establish possession of the place. On the contrary, they showed how people were possessed by it—owned and occupied as it were, and answerable to it by means of their stories and songs" (p. 127).

Again, it is the *structure* of settler colonialism that has reduced human relationships to land to relationships to property, making property ownership the primary vehicle to civil rights in most settler colonial nation-states. In the United States and other slave estates, the remaking of land into property was/is accompanied by the remaking of (African) persons into property, into chattel (Wilderson, 2010; Spillers, 2003; Tuck & Yang, 2012). The remaking of land and bodies into property is necessary for settlement onto other people's land.

These manifestations of materiality as property suggest multiscalar discourses of ownership (McKittrick, 2006). These include discourses of "having 'things,' owning lands, invading territories, possessing someone," all "narratives of displacement that reward and value particular forms of conquest" (McKittrick, 2006, p. 3). McKittrick observes,

> (This) reward system repetitively returns us to the body, black subjecthood, and the where of blackness, not just as it is owned, bit as black subjects participate in ownership. Black diasporic struggles can

also be read, then, as geographic contests of discourses of ownership. Ownership of the body, individual and community voices, bus seats, women, "Africa," feminisms, history, homes, record labels, money, cars, these are recurring positionalities, written and articulated through protest, musics, feminist theory, fiction, the everyday. These positionalities and struggles over the meaning of place add a geographic dimension to practices of black reclamation. Yet they also illustrated the ways in which the legacy of racial dispossession underwrites how we have come to know space and place, and that the connections between what are considered "real" or valuable forms of ownership are buttressed through racial codes that mark the body as ungeographic. (pp. 3–4)

Thus, discourses and practices of property are also central to the hegemonic relations of colonialism and slavery. As Wilderson (2010) observes about the United States, there are three structuring positions that converge to typify relationships of power and place, ultimately remaking land into property. Each of the three structuring positions ("Savage," Slave, and Human in Wilderson's analysis) are "elaborated by a rubric of three demands: the (White) demand for expansion, the (Indian) demand for return of the land, and the (Black) demand for 'flesh' reparation" (p. 29). Here, we briefly sketch these structured antagonisms:

Indigenous Erasure

Settler colonialism wants Indigenous land, not Indigenous peoples, so Indigenous peoples are cleared out of the way of colonial expansion, first via genocide and destruction, and later through incorporation and assimilation (Wolfe, 2006). The settler colonial discourse turns Indigenous peoples into savages, unhumans, and eventually, ghosts. As a structure and not a past event, settler colonialism circulates stories of Indigenous peoples as extinct, disappeared, or maybe as never having existed at all. The goal of settler colonialism is to erase Indigenous peoples from valuable land (see McCoy, 2014; Paperson, 2014). Indigenous peoples, by their survivance and persistence, disprove the completeness, cohesiveness, civility, and ultimately the presumed permanence of the settler nation-state (see Bang et al., 2014).

Black Containment

"Chattel" means property of the owner. In the United States, Africans were stolen, enslaved, and brought by force to colonies as chattel, and kept from owning land (see McCoy, 2014). "The slave has no socially recognized existence outside of his master, he became a social nonperson . . . the definition of the slave, however recruited, [is] a socially dead person" (Patterson, 1982, p. 10, as quoted in Wilderson, 2010, p. 51). In chattel slavery, it is the body that is valuable, not the person. The person is seen as in excess of the body; the person is ownable, punishable, murderable (Tuck & Yang, 2012). Settler colonialism structures anti-blackness by circulating stories of (the descendents of) chattel slaves as monsters, as requiring containment; we can understand the contemporary prison industrial complex in the United States as an extension of chattel slavery, in which Black and brown bodies are contained to build the wealth of mostly white towns relying financially on incarceration centers.

Settler Ascendancy

Settlers are defined by their actions. " 'Settler' is a way to describe colonizers that highlights their desires to be emplaced on Indigenous land" (Morgensen, 2009, p. 157). Settler emplacement, in Morgensen's analysis, is concerned with settlers' attempts to live on stolen land and make it their home. The desire to emplace is a desire to resolve the experience of dis-location implicit in living on stolen land. A core strategy of emplacement is the discursive and literal replacement of the Native by the settler, evident in laws and policies of eminent domain, Manifest Destiny, property rights, and removals. Settlers are not immigrants who come expecting to become part of existing communities and cultures; they implement their own laws and understandings of the world onto stolen land.[3] Settler emplacement is incommensurable with Indigenous life insofar as it requires erasure of Indigenous life and ontologies. Thus, settlers engage a range of settler moves to innocence (Tuck & Yang, 2012) to relieve themselves of the discomfort of dis-location, and to further emplacement/replacement.

There are important variations to the settler colonial triad, specifically Jodi Byrd's borrowing of the word arrivants from African Caribbean poet Kamau Brathwaite in place of "chattel slave" to refer broadly to people forced into the Americas "through the violence of European and Anglo-American colonialism and imperialism around the globe" (2011, p. xix). This nomenclature is a recognition of the ways in which arrivants both resist and participate as settlers in the historical project of settler colonialism. Settler colonialism "requires settlers and arrivants to cathect the space of the native as their home" (Byrd, 2011, p. xxxix).

IMPLICATIONS OF THE STRUCTURED ANTAGONISMS OF SETTLER COLONIALISM

It cannot be emphasized enough that settler colonialism wants Indigenous land. In a 2013 interview between Naomi Klein and Leanne Simpson (2013) about the Indigenous movement Idle No More, Simpson observes,

> Extraction and assimilation go together. Colonialism and capitalism are based on extracting and assimilating. My land is seen as a resource. My

relatives in the plant and animal worlds are seen as resources. My culture and knowledge is a resource. My body is a resource and my children are a resource because they are the potential to grow, maintain, and uphold the extraction-assimilation system. The act of extraction removes all of the relationships that give whatever is being extracted meaning. Extracting is taking. Actually, extracting is stealing—it is taking without consent, without thought, care or even knowledge of the impacts that extraction has on the other living things in that environment. That's always been a part of colonialism and conquest. Colonialism has always extracted the indigenous—extraction of indigenous knowledge, indigenous women, indigenous peoples . . . Children from parents. Children from families. Children from the land. Children from our political system and our system of governance. Children—our most precious gift. In this kind of thinking, every part of our culture that is seemingly useful to the extractivist mindset gets extracted. The canoe, the kayak, any technology that we had that was useful was extracted and assimilated into the culture of the settlers without regard for the people and the knowledge that created it. (Simpson, in Klein & Simpson, 2013, n.p.)

The problems of invasion and settlement include the ways in which settler colonialism turns Indigenous land into property by destroying Indigenous peoples, and turns humans into chattel/property by destroying their humanity. In order for the settlers to make a place their home, they must destroy and disappear the Indigenous peoples that live there. For the settlers, Indigenous peoples are in the way, and, in the destruction of Indigenous peoples, Indigenous communities, and over time and through law and policy, Indigenous peoples' claims to land, land under settler regimes, is recast as property and as a resource. Indigenous peoples must be erased, must be made into ghosts (Tuck & Ree, 2013).

At the same time, settler colonialism involves the subjugation and forced labor of chattel slaves[4] whose bodies and lives become the property, and who are kept landless. Slavery in settler colonial contexts is distinct from other forms of indenture whereby excess labor is extracted from persons. First, chattels are commodities of labor, and therefore it is the slave's person that is the excess. Second, unlike workers who may aspire to own land, the slave's very presence on the land is already an excess that must be dislocated. Thus, the slave is a desirable commodity, but the person underneath is imprisonable, punishable, murderable.

Drawing out the problems of settlement is an important distinction to make, especially when considering the strategies of ecological and environmental justice; justice efforts that aim to disentangle from capitalism, for example, may in effect reinforce settlement. As Patrick Wolfe (2006) insists, "Settler colonialism destroys to replace" (p. 388). Frequently it does so by denying the existence of Indigenous peoples and the legitimacy of claims to land. It denies the long-lasting impacts of slavery. It continues to dispossess

Indigenous peoples and Black peoples, promoting white supremacy. It requires arrivants to participate as settlers. Settler colonialism implicates everyone (Tuck & Yang, 2012).

SETTLER EMPLACEMENT

One of the ways in which current theories of space and place that emerge from Western philosophical frames are incommensurable to Indigenous and decolonizing conceptualizations involves the degree to which Western theories enable or are agnostic towards settler emplacement. Settler emplacement, in Morgensen's analysis, is the desire of settlers to resolve the experience of dis-location implicit in living on stolen land. A core strategy of emplacement is the discursive and literal replacement of the Native by the settler, evident in laws and policies such as eminent domain (and similar constructs), Manifest Destiny, property rights, and removals, but also in boarding schools, sustained and broken treaties, adoptions, and resulting "apologies" (see Coulthard, 2007, for a discussion on the politics of recognition in Canada). "Historically, a desire to live on Indigenous land and to feel connected to it—bodily, emotionally, spiritually—has been the normative formation of settlers," writes settler-scholar Scott Morgensen (2009, p. 157; see also Korteweg & Oakley, 2014).

Here, we wish to differentiate the goal of settler emplacement, which is one way of resolving the colonial situation, from decolonization, which is another way. Settler emplacement, according to Morgensen (2009), can never lead to decolonization.

> Decolonization does not follow if settlers simply study and emulate the lives of Indigenous people on Indigenous land . . . [this] is relevant in particular to those for whom anarchism links them to communalism and counterculturalism, such as in rural communes, permaculture, squatting, hoboing, foraging, and neo-pagan, earth-based, and New Age spirituality. These "alternative" settler cultures formed by occupying and traversing stolen Indigenous land and often by practicing cultural and spiritual appropriation . . . They must ask, then, if their interest to support Indigenous people arose not from an investment in decolonization, but in recolonization. (p. 157)

Settler emplacement is incommensurable with decolonization because at its basis is a drive to replace the Native as the rightful claimant of the land. Replacement relies on fantasies of the extinct or becoming-extinct Indian as natural, forgone, and inevitable, indeed, evolutionary (see Tuck & Gaztambide-Fernández, 2013). Replacement is invested in settler futurity; in our use, futurity is more than the future, it is how human narratives and perceptions of the past, future, and present inform current practices and framings in a way that (over)determines what registers as the (possible) future. Settler futurity, then, refers to what Andrew Baldwin calls the "permanent virtuality" (2012, p. 173) of the settler on stolen land. Theorizing the significance of futurity for researching whiteness and geography, Baldwin (2012) examines whether a history-centered analysis paves the way for the faulty,

> teleological assumption that [settler colonialism] can be modernized away. Such an assumption privileges an ontology of linear causality in which the past is thought to act on the present and the present is said to be an effect of whatever came before . . . According to this kind of temporality, the future is the terrain upon or through which [settler colonialism] will get resolved. It cleaves the future from the present and, thus, gives the future discrete ontological form. (p. 174)

Replacement and emplacement, to be clear, are entirely concerned with settler futurity, which always indivisibly means the disruption of Indigenous life to aid settlement. Any form of place or space theory that seeks to recuperate and not interrupt settler colonialism, to reform the settlement and incorporate Indigenous peoples into the multicultural settler colonial nation state, is invested in settler futurity. In contrast, Indigenous futurity forecloses settler colonialism and settler epistemologies. This does not mean that Indigenous futurity forecloses living on Indigenous land by non-Indigenous peoples. That is to say that Indigenous futurity does not require the erasure of now-settlers in the ways that settler futurity requires of Indigenous peoples (see also Tuck & Gaztambide-Fernández, 2013).

DECOLONIZATION AND COLLAPSE

Indigenous peoples have predicted the collapse of settler societies since contact, all the while building and articulating viable alternative epistemologies and ontologies. That theories of decolonization have been taken up across disciplines in academe now rather than in prior generations is evidence of the more widely held recognition among settlers of impending environmental and economic collapse. Nishnaabeg writer Leanne Simpson tells Naomi Klein in a 2013 interview,

> Our elders have been warning us about this for generations now—they saw the unsustainability of settler society immediately. Societies based on conquest cannot be sustained, so yes, I do think we're getting closer to that breaking point for sure. We're running out of time. We're losing the opportunity to turn this thing around. We don't have time for this massive slow transformation into something that's sustainable and alternative. I do feel like I'm getting pushed up against the wall. Maybe my ancestors felt that 200 years ago or 400 years ago. But I don't think

it matters. I think that the impetus to act and to change and to transform, for me, exists whether or not this is the end of the world. If a river is threatened, it's the end of the world for those fish. It's been the end of the world for somebody all along. And I think the sadness and the trauma of that is reason enough for me to act. (Simpson in Klein & Simpson, 2013, n.p.)

Simpson's words speak to both the urgency and undeniability of the need for decolonization. They also hint at the inevitability of decolonization (see also Fanon, 1968). To say that decolonization is inevitable is not to say that it is guaranteed or that it does not require human agency. Just as Indigenous youth learned from elders in Chicago when they saw tobacco growing in the cracks in the concrete, decolonization is not just something that humans (may) do; it is (primarily) something that the land does on its own behalf. Whether or not humans can survive this latter form of decolonization can't be known.

NOTES

1. As an aside, this coding is not a good match for the most recent science (see, for example, studies on proliferation of brain cell in the human stomach).
2. Parts of this section and the following section draw from Tuck, McKenzie, and McCoy, 2014.
3. Settlers are not a particular racial group. Settler pursuits of valuable land are the context for the invention of race in the United States—race, almost two hundred years after plantation colonies were established, became the justification for the ways in which settlers made Indigenous peoples and slaves inhuman to get land and labor (Tuck & Yang, 2012).
4. As observed by Erica Neeganagwedgin (2012), these two groups are not always distinct.

Part II

4 Methodologies of Critical Place Inquiry

In the first part of the book we introduced the need to (re)examine how we research place in the social sciences, and we provided a discussion of some of the inspiring critical theories taken up in such research. In Chapter 2 we engaged current approaches to conceptualizing place, mostly from Anglo-American and Continental frameworks, but also from Indigenous worldviews. In Chapter 3 we discussed approaches that theorize and practice place as *land*, which have emerged from the fields of settler colonial studies and Indigenous studies. In this second part of the book, we move from a discussion of theory to a discussion of related practices of doing research on place: we focus on research methodologies and methods of data collection and analysis.

In this chapter, we overview some of the most compelling methodologies that meaningfully address or engage place. As discussed in the introduction, in examining critical place inquiry we are referring to research that takes up critical questions and develops corresponding methodological approaches that are informed by the embeddedness of social life in and with places, and that seeks to be a form of action in responding to critical place issues such as those of globalization and neoliberalism, settler colonialism, and environmental degradation. The focus on place includes not only social science research that uses this term, but a range of work that uses different terms to talk about the materiality of the world, including its physical characteristics and related historical, social, and cultural dimensions, as well as its both localized and interconnected aspects. This includes a broad spectrum of research across a range of disciplines and interdisciplinary areas in the social sciences, such as geography, anthropology, area studies, sociology, psychology, history, education, policy studies, environmental studies, Indigenous studies, and methodological studies. As signaled already, our aim is not the task of chronicling in detail all existing and emerging research approaches to place across these and other domains. Rather we survey a variety of approaches currently being engaged as a heuristic to assist researchers in determining which type of approach or approaches may be the best fit for a given research question or scope and particular place.

By *methodology* we mean the epistemological, ontological, and axiological assumptions guiding the research, or in other words, the ways in which the researcher's explicit or implicit assumptions are at work in the selection of research focus, problem, and approach. These explicit or implicit assumptions have also been termed one's paradigm or worldview (Kuhn, 1970; Wilson, 2008). Table 4.1 offers a heuristic for thinking through an underlying paradigm in relation to its epistemological, ontological, and axiological assumptions, as well as suggesting the types of theories, methodologies, and methods that are more commonly used in relation to particular paradigmatic orientations. This table is not intended to be static or to fix research approaches: we invite readers to make additions and adjustments, or to build their own heuristics for thinking through how one's theory, methodology, and methods of research align with or are influenced by their epistemological, ontological, and axiological assumptions. In terms of the approaches included in Table 4.1, we draw on categorizations used elsewhere (e.g., Lather, 2006) and have added in categories of "new materialist" and "Indigenous." We also recognize that postmodern, materialist, or Indigenous approaches are often also "critical" and that approaches can be mixed together or taken up at different times by the same researcher with strategic aims of having the research "be of use" in particular settings or times (Fine & Barreras, 2001; McKenzie, 2009).

Others have offered different, although related, typologies of research in the human disciplines; for example, Denzin and Lincoln's (2000, 2005, 2011) sketches of at least eight "moments" of research in North America: the traditional (1900–1950); the modernist or golden age (1950–1970); blurred genres (1970–1986); the crisis of representation (1986–1990); the post-modern, a period of experimental and new ethnographies (1990–1995); postexperimental inquiry (1995–2000), the methodologically contested present (2000–2010), and the future (2010–), which is now. As these authors suggest, "These moments overlap and simultaneously operate in the present" (p. 3). We join others in being wary of assumptions that newer necessarily means better in terms of paradigmatic or methodological approach (Greene, 2013; Merriman, 2013). Instead, we seek to provide descriptions and heuristics for researchers to better consider which approaches may be the best fit given their underlying commitments, intentions, and audiences.

That said, we also focus more on the paradigmatic approaches and the associated theories, methodologies, and methods included in Table 4.1 from the "Critical" to "Indigenous" columns. The reason for this is twofold: it is these domains in which more critical approaches to place have been engaged, and also where there is more recent theorizing and consideration of place and associated concepts in social science research. We also recognize that at one level, all of the approaches other than Indigenous share certain assumptions at a more macro scale, for example, of the secular nature of knowledge and social science research, and can therefore all be understood as sharing a Western or Eurocentric framework or meta-paradigm.

Table 4.1 Paradigms and Their Epistemological, Ontological, Axiological, and Methodological Orientations to Research

Paradigm:[1]	Positivism	Postpositivism/ Interpretivism	Critical	Postmodernism/ Spatial turn	New Materialism[2]	Indigenous
Epistemology (Understanding of Knowledge):	Knowledge is based on observable and verifiable experience.	Knowledge is influenced by our perceptions.	Knowledge is influenced by power.	Knowledge is situational, partial, and incomplete; influenced by temporal, spatial, and social contexts	No separation between epistemology, ontology, and ethics.	Knowledge is holistic, cyclic, and relational. Knowledge is not just mental, but emotional, spiritual.
Ontology (Understanding of Being/ Reality):	There is one Truth or reality.	The truth is seen through a variety of lenses. Our subjective experience affects our perception of the truth of reality.	The truth is that reality is structured by arrangements of power that require social change.	There are no grand narratives ("Truths"), but action is still possible.	Matter and meaning are entangled. Materiality is a dynamism.	Reality is relational and holistic.
Axiology (Understanding of Ethics/ Values):	Knowledge is objective and value-free.	The ability to know is affected by one's perceptions and values. By bracketing these out, it may be possible to determine the truth.	Knowledge and values are inextricably linked.	Knowledge is subjective and value-laden.	Ethics is not responsibly responding to the other, but responding to an entanglement of which we are part.	Knowledge and values are one and the same.

(Continued)

Table 4.1 (Continued)

Paradigm:[1]	Positivism	Postpositivism/ Interpretivism	Critical	Postmodernism/ Spatial turn	New Materialism[2]	Indigenous
Methodologies Frequently Used:	Usually none stated	E.g., general inductive qualitative research, ethnography, grounded theory, narrative inquiry, phenomenology	E.g., critical ethnography, participatory research, action research	E.g., narrative approaches, arts-based research, experimental research, spatial ethnography	E.g., following objects, network analysis, diffraction analyses	E.g., modified cultural practices, Decolonizing methodologies, methodologies modeled after Indigenous cosmology and understandings of ecology
Methods Frequently Used:	quantitative (e.g., surveys) and qualitative (e.g., interviews)	qualitative (e.g., observation, interviews, focus groups, visual methods)	quantitative and qualitative (e.g., surveys, observation, interviews, focus groups, visual methods)	qualitative (e.g., observation, interviews, focus groups, visual methods, mobile methods); Experimental	qualitative (e.g., interviews, visual methods, sensory methods, mobile methods)	Storywork, mappings and remappings

[1] The organization and inspiration of this table is from Lather, 2006, pp. 37–39.
[2] From Dolphijn & van der Tuin with Barad, 2012.

In the past (and still in some approaches and fields), the language of "methodology" has been used interchangeably with "methods" to mean empirical data collection and analyses methods (e.g., survey, interviews, photovoice, etc.). However, as social science research has expanded over the past half century, increasingly researchers are using the language of methodology to name the assumptions embedded in their study about knowledge, reality, and the role of research in society, and retaining the language of methods to talk about specific methods of data collection or analysis (Wilson, 2008). In many cases, similar methods of data collection (e.g., survey, observation, interview, etc.) and analysis may be used across methodologies, and it is the methodology that drives and informs how those methods are used, and with and by whom. In this chapter we focus on methodologies, and on those we see being taken up most prevalently or in emerging ways in research on place.

Finally, we also want to draw attention to ways in which the methodologies we present in this chapter are conceptual and/or empirical. This distinction has become less useful in the social sciences as researchers have become more aware of how all research is unavoidably embedded within the researcher's worldview and associated assumptions (Clifford & Marcus, 1986) and, thus, that all inquiry carries *theory* within it to some degree. Likewise, a researcher's experience, or the "empirical," can be considered to inform all research, including the development of theory or conceptual research. Nonetheless, we find *empirical* to be a useful term to indicate when research involves the collection and analysis of quantitative or qualitative data. Likewise, the term *conceptual* is useful to prioritize the use and development of ideas in addition to and beyond what can be collected through empirical research (Jackson & Mazzei, 2012). Thus, while all approaches can be considered to be conceptual and empirical on one level, we focus in this chapter on methodologies that involve some quantitative or qualitative data collection and analysis.

The remainder of the chapter is divided up into sections discussing the following methodologies used in researching place: archival research; narrative research; phenomenology; ethnography; participatory, action, and community-based research; mixed, "post," and strategic methodologies; and Indigenous methodologies. We note again that these methodologies are not necessarily exclusive and that more than one may be used in combination by some researchers. We also recognize "suspicions of efforts to codify and discipline" approaches to research (Lather, 2013, p. 242), and this is not our intention. We appreciate the call toward transversality,[1] the cutting across of dual oppositions, offered by new materialist approaches (Dolphijn & van der Tuin, 2012). Rather, we want to examine a range of methodological approaches currently being used in ways that explicitly attend to place in order to contribute to the future depth and diversity of means of engaging place in research.

ARCHIVAL RESEARCH AND PLACE

Archival research includes studies that rely on archival content for their data, such as previously existing photography collections, newspaper reports, historical accounts, policy documents, legal cases, and online repositories. We list the study of such materials as a methodology because of the epistemological, ontological, and axiological assumptions that underlie these approaches to inquiry. Detailed later in this chapter in relation to examples of archival research, these physical materials are viewed by researchers as representing particular understandings of place, time, and subjects and are analyzed in various ways to elicit and elaborate those understandings.

Writing in 2009, L'Eplattenier remarks that when she and a colleague tried to find examples of "practical articles to orient and guide people new to archival work, articles that described the methods of historical research," few were to be found (p. 67). While she observes that concerns about organizing and using sources, verifying information, and methods of archival research—or in other words, a methodology of archival research—have been posed at important moments throughout the field's history, she contends that a methodology must be more comprehensively articulated so that archival research is understood as work engaged systematically and incrementally, in a way "that both highlights the uniqueness of archival study and creates the depth and breadth of knowledge required to begin generalizing about the tools our discipline needs and uses" (L'Eplattenier, 2009, p. 68). In many ways, L'Eplattenier is arguing that existing articulations of archival methodology are thin because they do not adequately discuss the methods of archival research. Indeed, she contends that an appropriate methods section would address the name and location of the archives, finding aids, amount of time spent in archives, number of linear feet in a collection, amount of collection examined, the provenance of the artifacts, physical state of the artifacts, problems with materials, missing materials, and specificity of the materials (p. 72). A methods section might also discuss elements of the archive that puzzled the researcher or were of special note, or other surrounding facts, in order to "destabilize the story presented" by the archive and by the researcher's use of the archive (p. 73).

Terrance (2011) uses Native feminist theory to "refuse" the archive, telling and not-telling an account of finding an autograph journal of a young Indigenous woman who attended a boarding school in the early twentieth century. In her analysis, Terrance will not reveal the location of the archive, the journal, or even the specific identifying information of its author. Terrance believes it is not her right to reveal these details, or the personal reflections of a young Indigenous woman in a colonial space.

> The journal's very designation as an archival object demonstrates the relationship between the state's colonial project/objectives and its production of indigenous peoples as "objects-of-knowledge" (Spivak, 1999),

specimens for study, primitive and historical, forever vanishing as a result of the pathology that defines their communities. Moreover, it reinforces the conception of social hierarchies as inevitable and natural: some populations are to be investigated, scrutinized and objectified by those who are able to cogitate and analyze. Refusing to reify the narrative of colonization and the naturalization of colonial structures necessitates a re-evaluation of what constitutes "legitimate" research material. (2011, p. 625)

Terrance interrogates the colonial gaze of archival research, its voyeurism and seduction towards believing that the dead can have no secrets. For the most part, Terrance's refusal is concerned with not telling/not selling (Tuck & Yang, 2014) the place-based details that would authenticate her research.

In our discussion of Terrance and L'Eplattenier's contrasting arguments, we draw attention to the material-spatial components of what comprises the methods, and ultimately the methodology of archival research. The methodology hinges on the specificity, materiality, physicality, and location of the archive and how much of the archive was examined. Parrish (2010) has described the human-physical aspects of engaging the archive as prompting nausea and motion sickness, both because "the backlit small white curving shapes [cascading] in a vertical loop" made the author "dizzy to the point of queasiness" and because of the "deeper sense of motion sickness . . . somewhere between boredom and hopelessness" (p. 289). She writes,

> The motion is historical and spatial, and the sense of sickness comes from the experience of not being able to make the crossing into other worlds of signification. Sometimes you worry that you have crossed into their world, and frankly, it was not worth the trouble. (p. 289)

The work of archival research is spatial in concept and in practice. Its rigor and refusal (Terrance, 2011) is related to its location in place, or in ether space.

With regard to representations of place within the archive, much of the archive includes photos of places, maps, and historical accounts of places. Thomas (2009) theorizes the use of photographs by historians and readers' ability to interpret photographs, even when seen as discursive objects. Stewart (2008) engages oral stories as archival data in order to "read the landscape" for its relationships between cultures, communities, and geographical places. Van Wyck (2008) pursued his research in the Mackenzie River basin with the typewritten field journals of Harold Innis as his companion; his goal was to render a North that was much more than an empty space and passage to elsewhere.

As an example of the representation of place through archival analysis, in research on the history of education, O'Donoghue (2010) sought to learn what understandings emerge when considering classrooms as installations.

He applied the tenets of installation art practice in analyzing archival classroom photographs, including the tenets that objects always signal something beyond themselves and that meaning resides in the study of objects.

> These spaces, entered and inhabited by students and teachers, are structured in accordance with a set of particular ideas about what constitutes teaching, learning, and the teacher and learner. Then layout, designed, and associated disciplinary and spatial practices of this space, to a large degree, determine the types of engagement students will have here. (p. 402)

O'Donoghue posits that educational historians might think of classroom photographs as photographs of installations in order to "imagine what it might possibly mean to inhabit this space" (p. 411).

NARRATIVE, STORYTELLING, AND PLACE

> Here speaks the storyteller, telling by voice what was learned by ear. Here speaks a poet who did not learn language structure from one teacher and language meaning from another, nor plot structure from one and characterization from another, but always heard all these things working together in the stories of other storytellers. (Tedlock, 1983, p. 3)

Narrative researchers examine narratives of any kind, including personal experience stories, ethnographic and historical stories, individual stories, shared stories, written texts, and oral stories, in order to "understand how individuals and groups of people construct reality" (Bird, 2002, p. 521). Narrative and storytelling methodologies hold that narratives are how humans come to know, understand, and make meaning in the social world, while also making ourselves known, understood, and meaningful in the world (Bird, 2002).

Clandinin and Rosiek (2007) remark that narrative inquiry is an old practice, engaged by humans through storytelling practices since humans could speak. Yet, the methodology feels new as it has gained prominence in social science inquiry. This emergence has been accompanied by "intensified talk about our stories, their function in our lives, and their place in composing our collective affairs" (p. 36). Clandinin and Rosiek use a cartographic lexicon to situate narrative inquiry on the conceptual borders (and in the composite borderlands) of post-positivism, Marxism and critical theory, and poststructuralism; the trajectories and travels away and toward these borderlands are defined only by their shared effort to study experience as it is lived through questions of temporality, sociality, and place (p. 69). Concerns of place are central to narrative inquiry because all inquiry and events occur in some specific place, the specificity of which is important (p. 70).

In *Reflections in Place: Connected Lives of Navajo Women* (2009), Donna Deyhle uses ethnography and narrative methodology to bring together the already interconnected place-based stories of three women. The research, which took place over twenty-five years, tells stories told over time, in interviews, at community gatherings and cultural events, interfaced with ethnographic portraits compiled by the author. Deyhle insists upon the centrality of place in the very definition of community—which is "not a uniform group of people, but rather a location or place" (2009, p. xvii). As a white woman researching the lives of Navajo women, Deyhle took careful steps not to reinscribe the discourse of "manifest manners" into her telling of the women and her interpretations of the tellings they offered of themselves (p. xxi). This dilemma, or tension, was not one that Deyhle attempted to resolve or overcome; instead, her research and emphasis on the narratives shared by research participants engaged these tensions as the ethical context of the relationships that formed.

Attending to shared narratives, Bird (2002) has sought to understand how Western cultures (not just Indigenous and non-Western cultures) "re-create place through historic reconstructions . . . to tell stories to locate us where we feel we should be" (p. 523). Bird and undergraduate students collected stories, folktales, and narratives related to a variety of places throughout the state of Minnesota. These places, sometimes only made significant through the stories told and re-told about them, are what Bakhtin (1981) called "chronotypes," locations in which "time and space intersect and fuse," standing "as monuments to the community itself, as symbols of it, as forces operating to shape its members' images of themselves" (p. 7 as quoted in Bird, 2002, p. 544). Stories, Bird concludes, are opportunities for people to make sense of place while also making those spaces meaningful in their own cultural contexts.

In another example of critical place narrative inquiry, Myers (2010) considers three artist-guided walks that engaged participants in order to bring attention to the landscape. The walks, conducted using a variety of approaches including recordings, live voices, and whispers, were forms of what Myers came to call "conversive wayfinding," allowing for "patterns, paces and paths of walking as experienced in the breath, rhythm, sweat and memory of the walker" (p. 59). Invoking Lavery's (2005) premise that walking is "an ideal strategy for witnessing," involving what Miller (2003) calls a "sense of relinquishing ourselves to a rhythmic state of being (n.p.), Myers (2010) posits that walking-narrative methodology or conversive wayfinding methodology involve

> embodied, participatory, and spontaneous modes of responsiveness and communicability. Furthermore, they are conversive, activating and inviting modes of participation that generate places and knowledge of places through a conversational and convivial activity of wayfinding, where a percipient becomes more a wayfarer than a map reader, a mode

of travel that encourages convivial and social interaction with inhabitants of places. (p. 67)

Myers emphasizes the combining of narrative and wayfinding methodologies as fertile for coming to know (more about) place.

Recent textual analyses also make place more significant in their methodologies. Lee's (2009) dissertation documented the thriving community meanings attributed to urban sites disregarded as placeless—commercial districts in Gwangbok-dong and Nampo-dong in Busan, South Korea. The sites of anonymous commercialization (the author's words) almost erase the powerful social history of those places—almost. Lee's methodology put textual interpretive analysis in relation to mapping and narratives as research participants narrate the connections they saw between maps and newspaper clippings. Lee finds that personal meanings and renderings of place persist and outlast corporate insertions of function and meaning.

PHENOMENOLOGY AND PLACE RESEARCH

Phenomenology literally means the study ("logos") of that which appears ("phenomena") and can be understood as attempting the objective study of topics that are usually regarded as subjective, such as perceptions and emotions. Husserl (1913/1982) was central to the early development of phenomenology as a methodology of inquiry, or "the reflective study of the essence of consciousness as experienced from the first-person point of view" (Smith, 2007). Merleau-Ponty (1945/2002) is another particular central figure in the development of phenomenology. In the words of David Seamon (1980), a phenomenologist concerned with the role of place in people's everyday lived experience:

> Phenomenology . . . asks if from the variety of ways which men and women behave in and experience their everyday world there are particular patterns which transcend specific empirical contexts and point to the essential human condition—the irreducible crux of people's life-situations, which remains when all non-essentials—cultural context, historical era, personal idiosyncrasies—are stripped bare through phenomenological procedures. (in Creswell, 1994, p. 33)

Such reflective attentiveness to "lived experience" has been taken up in relation to place in various trajectories of phenomenological scholarship (e.g., Heidegger, 1971; Malpas, 1999; Relph, 1976; Tuan, 1974, 1977). This scholarship ranges from a focus on the conditions of "dwelling" in a place; to experiences of movement between places (or of experiences in "non-places"; Augé, 1995); to relationships or attachments between people and places/the natural world (including considerable work on "place attachment" in psychology and related disciplines, e.g., Chawla, 2007). It also varies in the extent to which it is conceptual and/or empirical. While the diversity of phenomenological approaches to place in research prevents easy summary (see Cresswell, 2003, 2004, for more extensive overviews), we point to a few examples to indicate some of the ways in which researchers are engaging place in phenomenological research.

The work of David Seamon (e.g., 1979, 1980) is one example that has been influential within cultural geography over the last several decades. In *Geography of the Lifeworld* (1979), Seamon focuses on "everyday environmental experience," which is defined as people's "experiential involvement in their everyday geographical world" (p. 17). Seamon examines research participants' emotions and practices in relation to their movement and lives in an American city. He (1980) introduces a specific vocabulary to discuss the role of place or environment in research participants' bodily, and thus, human experience. For example, a sequence of preconscious actions used to complete a particular task are termed a "body-ballet," and when sustained over a considerable period of time become a "time-space routine." Other researchers have drawn on Seamon's work to support phenomenological analysis of people's experiences in and across other places. For example, Moores and Metykova (2009) examine young Eastern Europeans' experiences following migration to the UK, illuminating the "close connection between matters of migration and those of place-making in daily living" (p. 185). They discuss how factors such as physical movement in the new locations (e.g., driving, public transportation, walking) facilitated the "formation of particular affective attachments and they can contribute, in turn, to complex rearrangements of at-homeness" (pp. 178–179).

Another recent example of phenomenological research on place can be found in a study by Worster and Abrams (2005) on New England commercial fisherman and organic farmers. Responding to the lack of empirical research on "the conceptual framework of sense of place," the researchers undertook phenomenological interviewing (Seidman, 1998) to gather qualitative data to address the following "essential questions regarding sense of place" (p. 527):

- How do the people in these communities perceive the place in which they work?
- Who and what do they speak of when discussing their livelihood?
- How do they speak of the land or ocean?
- How were these views formed? How are they sustained?

Reporting some of the analysis from a larger study on the same topic, Worster and Abrams (2005), like the study by Moores and Metykova (2009) discussed previously, include quite extensive selections of quotations from participants. The excerpts suggest how participants' experiences with place have both influenced, and been influenced by, their worldviews, choice of occupation, "spiritually perceived relationship with the ecological content" (p. 530), and other factors. Seeking to better understand the phenomena of social and ecological knowledge and experience in relationship to participants' identities, the researchers suggest broader implications in the development of sense of place.

ETHNOGRAPHY AND PLACE

Ethnography literally means "the study of culture," with this methodology having its roots in the field of anthropology in the early study of various cultures around the world. This legacy was critiqued in the 1980s and '90s, both over concerns with the Western academic studying and "writing" culture that is not their own, as well as due to recognition of the subjectivity of the researcher more broadly and how their experiences and assumptions influence the accounts that are provided (Clifford & Marcus, 1986). Through the development of post-positivism and later research paradigms, increasing numbers of researchers came to view "the study of culture" as always occurring through the lenses that the researcher brings to the inquiry, and also questioned the appropriateness and protocols of research conducted across cultures (L. T. Smith, 1999/2012). More recently, the methodology of ethnography has been mobilized to study one's own culture, or sub-cultural groupings within it, including in relation to place. The term *ethnography* is used by some researchers as synonymous with "qualitative research"; however, more usually it is still used to connote a fine-grained qualitative analysis of "culture," understood here as "ordinary," or as all forms of social activity that comprise a way of life (Williams, 1958).

Since its beginnings as a methodology, ethnography has been concerned with place, or with the physical settings of the ordinary and their relationships to other material aspects of people's lives, such as household objects, animals, institutions, and technologies. Ethnographers have explored how such material aspects of people's lives are bound up, for example, with social practices and customs (Bourdieu, 1990), emotion or affect (Pain, 2009; Stewart, 2007), the senses (Pink, 2009), movement (Ingold & Vergunst, 2008), or spirituality (Dillard, 2000; Meyer, 2008). A range of adjectival descriptors are used to indicate ethnography with various foci. These include "critical ethnography" as engagement in ethnographic study, not only to understand or describe, but with aim of contributing to social change (e.g., Carspecken, 1995). "Autoethnography" is used to refer to diverse forms of self narrative in which the ethnographic focus is one's self in relation to social context (e.g., Ellis, 2004). "Digital ethnography" is used to refer to ethnographies of digital environments as well as the use of digital tools for data collection and representation (e.g., ethnographies of YouTube or social networking sites, and the use of web-based surveys, social media sites, video, blogs, etc. in ethnographic research; see Murthy, 2008). Likewise, terms like "visual ethnography" are used to describe the use of visual methods in ethnographic practice (Pink, 2007), whereas "sensory ethnography" refers to topical and/ or data collection focus on the senses (Pink, 2009; Stoller, 1986). Across these and other subareas of ethnography, fieldwork (in physical settings and now online) has been central to this methodology, with common methods of data collection including extensive participant observation and interviews and, more recently, the use of photography, video, or the internet to collect or represent ethnographic research.

While difficult to generalize across this rich diversity of approaches, ethnography's general strength as a methodological approach to the consideration and study of place is in its fine-grained descriptive focus. Through chronicling lives lived in relationship to place through multiple methods, ethnographies can offer a sense of showing versus telling, bringing alive for the reader socially embedded qualities of particular places in relation to their historical, spatial, and political contexts. From classic anthropological studies that detail the interwoven aspects of physical locations and social practice in village life (e.g., Rosaldo, 1993), to sociological research that connects the reader to the particularities of social life in specific temporal and spatial locales in intimate detail (e.g., Willis's 1977 study of working class "lads" in England), the research literature is abundant with ethnographies that recognize the role of place and associated materialities (built environment, climate, living conditions, etc.) in the constitution and manifestations of social life. While the postmodern turn of the last several decades of the twentieth century emphasized dispersed and shifting social identities and a focus on the role of language in social constitution, ethnographers such as Nayak (2003) have re-established a focus place and materiality in ethnographic analysis. In contrast to suggestions that youth lifestyles had become de-territorialized or placeless in the face of globalization and technologized lives, Nayak's "place-based study" of youth subcultural groupings of "Real Geordies," "Carvers," and "B-Boyz" in northeastern English shows the ways in which youth identifies are still place-bound, or in other words, specific to the histories and geographies of local place.

As another contemporary example, a book edited by Ingold and Vergunst (2008) provides a sort of collective ethnography of "ways of walking." Chapters span research on walking with hunter-gatherers in Malaysia, on walking with goat herds, and on the road-based marches of colonizers versus the land-based walks of human and non-human inhabitants. The collection suggests the ways that knowledge is forged, both by the researched and the researcher, through the performances and habits of walking, as well as its embodied memories. As the editors write, "the movement of walking is itself a way of knowing" (p. 8), as well as a way through which traces are left on the world.

A final example of the ways in which contemporary ethnographers are focusing on place-based data and topics is the digital ethnography of Michael Wesch and his students at Kansas State University on mediated cultures. Functioning as participatory ethnographies in that the research is undertaken with groups of students as part of their course learning, topics have included virtual and physical settings such as the YouTube community, university classrooms, and a retirement center in which Wesch's students lived while filming a documentary ethnography. These examples of digital ethnographies, which can be watched at www.mediatedcultures.net, are emotional, exploratory looks at various cultures/places using digital tools and modes of representation (e.g., Wesch's video work has millions of hits on YouTube, with few written publications or citations to his name).

PARTICIPATORY, ACTION, COMMUNITY-BASED RESEARCH AND PLACE

Participatory action research (PAR) has long been practiced all over the globe, in at least 2,500 universities in 61 countries (Fals-Borda, 2006, p. 353). In participatory action research, those who would be the subjects of research—community members, young people, Indigenous peoples, people with disabilities, people in prison, migrants, and countless other groups—are instead engaged as co-researchers. As co-researchers, everyday people collaborate with (professional) researchers to identify research questions, select methods and design data collection instruments, collect and analyze data, interpret results and determine findings, and communicate findings to diverse audiences. Many have insisted that participatory action research is not a method or set of methods (Tuck & Fine, 2007). We categorize it as a methodology in this discussion because of the way we have been using the term throughout this chapter, to signal an approach to gathering and validating information, making decisions, and beliefs about knowledge and knowing. Certainly, PAR is an ethical framework in which exploitation is consciously theorized and avoided, people and their ideas are valued, and collaboration and mutual benefit are highly prized. Participatory action researchers engage in this approach because of its ethical touchstones, but also because they see it as resulting in richly textured, accurate, and useful data.

The "action" in PAR refers to the aims of change that PAR studies hold central. This is shared with other forms of research that are not participatory in terms of involving research participants in research design, data collection, or data analysis, but similarly aim to effect learning and change through the research (e.g., Carr & Kemmis, 1986). Community-based participatory research (CBPR) refers to participatory action research that is centered on issues of broad interest to community and often entails forms of community consultation, for example, in relation to land use, public health, or other policy-related issues.

Writing in 2006, Orlando Fals-Borda reflected on his 30 years of involvement in PAR in order to determine the contributions of PAR to theory and practice. Fals-Borda (2006) identified five key contributions, including (2) the building up of useful knowledge toward achieving social justice; (3) the development of techniques that facilitate collective search, recovery, and sharing of knowledge; (4) mutual respect for academic and popular knowledge; and (5) transformation of participating researchers in the struggle for radical change (p. 354).

At the top of Fals-Borda's (2006) list of contributions of PAR to theory and practice is the generation of "an interdisciplinary science or body of knowledge, contexts, and problems of a particular setting, such as the tropics or subtropics" (p. 354). Participatory action research and community-based participatory research, indeed because they are participatory and involve the efforts of real people in real places, are methodologies that can yield real and useful knowledge about place and places. Although this aspect of PAR and CBPR is not always highlighted in the field, it is an important characteristic that we attend to here. PAR and CBPR have utilized methods that are also associated with several other methodologies and that offer place-related data, including visual methods (especially photovoice and fotonovella and videography), participatory Geographic Information Systems (GIS) and other forms of participatory mapping or diagramming, web-based participatory discussion, and others.

The 1979 Appalachian Land Ownership Study is one of the earliest examples of comprehensive multi-site participatory action research, conducted by a task force on land ownership and taxation across Kentucky, West Virginia, Tennessee, Virginia, North Carolina, and Alabama (Scott, 2009). The task force comprised members of citizen groups and faculty, staff, and graduate students of local universities, and it convened at the Highland Research and Education center in the summer of 1978 (p. 187). The 1983 report written by the task force indicated that land ownership was concentrated among corporate and absentee owners who were relieved of fair tax burdens and that this arrangement limited the economic development of surrounding communities (p. 186). Few of the recommendations from the report were implemented, but the study is still viewed as an important early example of the promises of PAR (Scott, 2009).

Scott argues that many of the challenges inlaid in the study would also become challenges for the larger field of participatory research, particularly post-positivist approaches. Debates about the validity of "local perceptions" in the face of "hard" and "objective" quantitative data circled, and the task force concluded (too quickly, says Scott) that qualitative data could not be generalizable (p. 197). Yet, the study was a harbinger of many of the attributes that would go on to define participatory action research: participants interviewed 30 years later described their involvement as individually and collectively transformative, and the study built participants' capacities to actively engage in public discourse and policy-making. The study also provides a clear instance of the importance of "clarifying epistemological assumptions, justifying participatory research design, and asserting the validity of both participatory practices and everyday knowledge throughout all phases of our research" (p. 200).

Asking whether CBPR is "a good fit" for their study with newly arrived Mexican migrants to the Rocky Mountain West, Letiecq and Schmalzbauer (2012) found the methodology to be "riddled with challenges" (p. 257) but, ultimately, to hold "great possibilities to support community organizing, to build mutually rewarding relationships with community partners, to empower migrant community members, and to utilize research for both public health and social justice aims" (p. 257). Their study sought to learn from newly arrived Mexican migrants about the specificity of their experiences in their "new rural destination" (p. 244). Montana, the site of their research, is described in terms of both political and geographical terrain: the state has expanses of "rugged" "undeveloped" land, fewer than a million residents, and is experiencing a 121 percent population growth, in part due to migrants and immigrants (p. 244). Migrants encounter language barriers, racial homogeneity, cultural and political resistance to their presence, and few public transportation, housing, and social services. The presence of Immigration and Customs Enforcement is prominent.

Letiecq and Schmalzbauer provide a step-by-step account of their approach, including (1) establishing a community advisory board, (2) establishing partnerships, (3) collaborating with community partners in research, and (4) implementing action. However, with each of these steps came significant methodological challenges, which they identify as challenges of doing CBPR "on the margins" (p. 251). Among those challenges are issues concerned with identifying "community," selecting research questions and methods, negotiating power—particularly in partnership with undocumented migrants—negotiating university-installed barriers to collaboration and activism, and negotiating the spoken and unsaid concerns, fears, ambivalence, and resistance of participants and partners (pp. 251–254).

Also working with recent migrants, Kwok and Ku (2008) brought together a collective of university researchers, an anthropologist, an urban planner, and migrant women from China to Hong Kong to research migrant women's experiences of environmental stress, housing, and neighborhood planning needs. The goal of this PAR study was to document experiences in order to inform urban planning and design. In the discussion of the study, design, and findings, the authors emphasize the physical environment of Hong Kong and the material and lived aspects of "socio-spatial exclusion" (p. 262). In this study, a pilot study was conducted in which recently arrived mothers were interviewed to help shape research questions and methods. Later phases of the study included photovoice and a participatory design process in which participants used modeling kits to construct ideal furnished interiors and public spaces (p. 270). Finally, the participants all worked together (in focus group settings) to analyze data from the photovoice and modeling exercises. In their reflections on the strengths and weaknesses of the methodology of the project, the authors observed that the methodology helped to foster relationships among the newly arrived women and that project activities prompted sharing of information and mutual support (p. 279). However, the authors did not always feel that they were successful in transferring feelings of ownership to the migrant women. The authors conclude that this approach held important insights for urban planners and policy-makers.

Intersecting participatory research and mapping methods, community mapping is a participatory approach that emphasizes "openness and inclusiveness of the mapmaking process" (Amsden & VanWynsberghe, 2005, p. 361). Community mapping invites participants to map places and locations that matter to them, in whichever language or symbols is most meaningful to them. The results are often layered, textured, and far from static, conveying relationships, movement, trajectories, and multiplicities (Krueger, 2011). In one approach to community mapping known as bioregional mapping, participants create maps to marcate the relationships and "processes" of nearby natural systems (Krueger, 2011; see also Aberley, 1993). In another approach of capacity-focused development, participants construct maps of their neighborhoods and communities, pertaining to assets, capacities, and abilities (Amsden & VanWynsberghe, 2005; Kretzmann & McKnight, 1993). Thus, community mapping can document not only physical, geographical elements of place, but also other components imbued with human meaning.

MIXED, POST, AND STRATEGIC METHODOLOGIES

In this section we discuss methodological approaches to research being used in many studies that can be considered postmodern or new materialist in theoretical orientation. Over the past several decades, it has become common in these domains to not align with an identified methodology and instead to be strongly guided by a theoretical approach in the uptake and development of research methods. For example, in a recent book on *Emerging approaches to educational research: Tracing the sociomaterial*, Fenwick, Edwards, and Sawchuck (2011) write,

> Sociomaterial approaches to research to date more often appear to suggest a sensibility, rather than a specified set of methods for conducting research. . . . As Law (2004b: 195) writes of ANT, the question is of "method assemblage," which is not quite a method but a "resonance": "a continual process of crafting." (p. 177)

They suggest that such research begins from the local and singular, focusing on everyday interactions, and can draw upon, for example, "fine-fined ethnographic tracings," ethnomethodological studies, engaging groups in analyzing their own practices (participatory approaches), visual narratives (e.g., photography and film), cartographic methods (e.g., mapping social relations and resource flows), and/or using theory "as an analytical tool rather than a series of particular methods" (p. 177).

Such approaches to "socio-material" empirical research share characteristics with earlier attempts to "work the ruins" of social science research after postmodernism (Lather, 1991b; Scheurich, 1997; St. Pierre & Pillow, 2000) and more recent discussions of "post-qualitative research" (e.g., Lather, 2013; MacLure, 2013; St. Pierre, 2011). Offering a typology of approaches to qualitative research, Lather (2013) suggests that "QUAL 3.0 . . . begins to use postmodern theories to open up concepts associated with qualitative inquiry," such as validity, voice, data, reflexivity, and so forth, whereas "QUAL 4.0 . . . cannot be tidily described in textbooks or handbooks. There is no methodological instrumentality to be unproblematically learned. In this methodology-to-come, we begin to do it differently wherever we are in our projects" (p. 635). Working to articulate what "no methodological a priori" (Marcus, 2009) looks like in practice, Lather points to several exemplars, including a book by Margaret Somerville (2013) focused on a study on drought in Australia undertaken by a team of Indigenous and non-Indigenous researchers. Suggesting the book provides a "radical alternative methodology across worlds that cannot know one another," Lather (2013) outlines how Somerville mobilizes " 'a methodology of lemons' of entanglement and reflexivity out of bodywork" through artwork and stories that were then shaped into a series of public exhibitions of artworks and texts (p. 641).

The directions described previously could be understood as a movement away from "methodology," or perhaps more accurately, as mixing and experimenting with methodology (for example, Somerville's (2013) study is variously described as "a collaborative (auto) ethnographic study," as "arts-based methodology," as "a methodology of lemons"). In any case, many researchers working in postmodern and materialist theoretical domains are emphasizing invention in drawing upon familiar and new methodologies and methods to address the questions identified through their theoretical orientations (Greene, 2013; Merriman, 2013). Common to these approaches is a theoretical loss of confidence in the ability of research to "see" or accurately represent what is occurring in a research setting, and instead emphases on the identities and lenses of researchers (in earlier postmodern work; see Lather, 1991b) and on viewing research as a performance or enactment of relational and material conditions (Anderson & Harrison, 2010; MacLure, 2013). As Fenwick and colleagues (2011) write, "The question of producing knowledge and learning shifts from a representational idiom, mapping and understanding a world that is out there, to a view that the world is doing things, full of agency. Not only humans act, because non-humans act on and with humans" (p. 3).

With this book's emphasis on critical place inquiry, whether research captures reality in some ways and/or is a performance or product of the world is overshadowed by what it is that the research itself *does*. In this vein, there have been critiques of the emphasis on novelty and invention in the previously described approaches at the expense of a focus on the research's impact on social and broader material conditions (Greene, 2013). In contrast, some researchers have suggested that what matters in terms of choosing methods of data analysis and representation is how the research can best "be of use," or in other words, determining which methodologies and methods may be most effective towards particular ends (Fine & Barreras, 2001). As discussed by Marcia McKenzie (2009), from a large scale quantitative study, to court testimony, to participatory art as public pedagogy, framings and methods of research are designed to maximize the potential to act as a form of intervention, or as public scholarship. This type of orientation could perhaps be considered a strategic methodological approach, which involves selecting the methodology and methods of research best suited to the type of data and analysis most likely to critically inform the decision-making and conditions surrounding a particular issue. This is one of the methodological approaches with which we align, and it informs our motivations for writing a book discussing the range of theories, methodologies, and methods of research that can be mobilized in critical research on and in place.

Table 4.2   The Things We Do with Research*

Addressing wider audiences through media, op-ed articles, and other popular forms
Policy-making and engagement
Active participant in struggles and campaigns
Collaborating with community-based organizations
Participatory research with students, educators, community-members, policy-makers
Constituency building: creating social science 'literate' and activist communities
Workshops on the critical use of research and policy
Constructing curriculum documents or guidelines
Creating public service announcements from social science research
Translating research into practice
Theoretical contributions that shift thinking
Social criticism
Testimony in court
Political satire
Public art, museums, parks, photo exhibits, as venues for presenting research

---

Note: Adapted from McKenzie, 2009 (with original references to Fine & Barreras, 2001; Massey, 2008; Posner, 2001)

INDIGENOUS METHODOLOGIES AND LAND

Gregory Cajete (2000) writes that Indigenous languages have no words for "science," "psychology," or "philosophy," or any attempts to know more about life and nature (p. 2). What Cajete terms "Native science," then,

> is a metaphor for a wide range of tribal processes of perceiving, thinking, acting, and "coming to know" that have evolved through human experience with the natural world. Native science is born of a lived and storied participation with the natural landscape. To gain a sense of Native science one must *participate* with the natural world. (p. 2, italics original)

Cajete's definition of Native science, part of what we refer to more broadly in this book as Indigenous methodologies, makes clear the deep connections between Indigenous knowledge and land. As discussed in Chapter 3, Indigenous conceptualizations of land can be teased apart from European conceptualizations of place as property (see pages 89–100). We show examples of how these differences play out later in Chapter 6. This section, then, is dedicated to drawing out the significance of land and place within Indigenous methodologies.

Cajete (2000) argues that there have always been Indigenous methodologies, or processes for gathering and interpreting knowledge. Much of Angayuqaq Oscar Kawagley's work over the course of his career was dedicated to documenting Indigenous knowledge processes (2006, 2010). However, the need to bring Indigenous knowledges into professional research practice and the academy as a more cogent body of approaches and ideas emerged in response to generations of exploitation and abuse of Indigenous communities at the hands of academic researchers (L. T. Smith, 1999/2012; Kovach, 2009). Kovach emphasizes that Indigenous methodologies spring from tribal epistemologies, not Western philosophy (2009, p. 36).

Reading across several book-length articulations of Indigenous methodologies (L. T. Smith, 1999/2012; Cajete, 2000; Wilson, 2008; Kovach, 2009; and Chilisa, 2011), there are several epistemic touchstones. At the base of each of these touchstones is a rootedness on and in relationship to land. The first has to do with relationships, especially because "all relationships are related to other relationships" (Cajete, 2000, p. 41). Indigenous methodologies both are enacted by and seek to study relationships, rather than object-based studies that typify Western sciences. Among the most primary relationships, upon which all other relationships are configured, are relationships to land and place (L. T Smith, 1999/2012), or what sometimes gets called the natural world in the literature (Cajete, 2000; Kovach, 2009; see also the discussion in Chapter 3 of this volume on Indigenous conceptualizations of land). Bang et al. (2014) write,

> Indigenous scholars have focused much attention on relationships between land, epistemology and importantly, ontology. Places produce

and teach particular ways of thinking about and being in the world. They tell us the way things are, even when they operate pedagogically beneath a conscious level. (p. 44)

For example, Vine Deloria, Jr. (1991) has referenced Seneca planting practices of the three Sisters of the Earth crops—corn, squash, and beans—to describe the relational integrity with which Indigenous peoples in North America planted and harvested plants for food and medicine: Seneca planted three Sisters together because they grew well together, because they helped to deter one another's potential predators, and because they had compatible spirits. Many years later, laboratory science confirmed that the plants, together, create a complementary nitrogen cycle that promotes fertility and productivity of the soil (Deloria & Wildcat, 2001, p. 25).

Indigenous knowledges emerge and exist within a universe that is relational and responsive. Thus, another epistemic touchstone of Indigenous methodologies is reciprocity (Kovach, 2009; L. T. Smith, 1999/2012; Cajete, 2000; Wilson, 2008). Kovach (2009) explains that reciprocity is the ethical starting place of Indigenous methodologies. "Because of the interconnection between all entities, seeking information ought not to be extractive but reciprocal, to ensure an ecological and cosmological balance" (p. 57). Reciprocity, of course, is not a touchstone observed only within Indigenous methodologies—many other methodologies emphasize reciprocity, especially participatory methodologies. However, reciprocity in Indigenous methodologies takes a different tenor because of its cosmological connotation, concerned with maintaining balance not just between humans, but with energies that connect and thread through all entities in the universe. This is not a mystical statement, but one that is grounded in Indigenous metaphysics (Deloria & Wildcat, 2001; Kawagley, 2010), which, as has been previously noted, is regarded within Indigenous worldviews as simultaneously sacred and mundane.

A third epistemic touchstone of Indigenous methodologies is a notion of something like *the long view* (Cajete, 2000; Kawagley, 2006; Wilson, 2008). In no small part due to the thousands of years that Indigenous peoples have known their homelands, Indigenous research methodologies often emphasize the wisdom and catalytic validity (Lather, 1991a) of the long view (see Chapter 7, this volume, for a discussion on catalytic validity). By the long view, we mean the centuries-long, or millennia-long sense of time that allows a vision of land and place as animated, formed and unformed, mountains growing at the same speed of fingernails, and oceans and ice flows shaping the coasts. It is the long view that shows what is so alarming about rapid human-induced climate change, and it is the long view that might guide decisions related to energy and fuel sources, human migration, the whole of social life, and the necrophilic logics of late capitalism and neoliberalism (Povinelli, 2011).

A final epistemic touchstone of Indigenous methodologies is concerned with decolonization. In Chapter 3, we are careful to differentiate Indigenous conceptualizations from decolonizing perspectives; although there are frequent overlaps, it is important to not collapse them. However, decolonization is still an epistemic touchstone by sheer example of Indigenous methodologies as a viable alternative ontological frame that has persisted and resisted neoliberalism and market logics. "Indigenous methodologies do not merely model Indigenous research," writes Scott Morgensen (2012). "By exposing normative knowledge production as being not only non-Indigenous but colonial, they denaturalize power within settler societies and ground knowledge production in decolonization" (p. 805). We discuss more of the decolonial possibilities made available through Indigenous methods in Chapter 6.

FROM METHODOLOGY TO METHODS

In this chapter we have outlined some of the possible methodologies that researchers are using to engage in critical place research. This is not an exhaustive or exclusive list, and as we have indicated, researchers are employing mixed methodologies together or varied methodologies at different times based on the particular topic, audience, and place of inquiry. We have discussed archival, narrative, phenomenological, ethnographic, participatory, mixed, post, strategic, as well as Indigenous methodologies of research. In providing a sense of these varied methodologies, we have briefly discussed some of the specific methods they typically employ, and in the next chapter we offer further discussions of how researchers are using particular research methods to gather, analyze, and mobilize place-based data.

NOTE

1. Guattari coined the term *transversality* in 1964 to refer to means that search for the new not by critiquing the old but by radically questioning all the barriers that supported this logic (Dolphijn & van der Tuin, 2012, p. 100).

5 Methods of Critical Place Inquiry

Standing on the street in an urban downtown on Treaty 6 territory in the Canadian prairies, a group of teachers and soon to be teachers summarize their understanding of Guy Débord's description of the technique of dérive (Débord, 1958). More than half the students are white, multi-generation European settlers, with some Indigenous students and several recent immigrants and international students from Puerto Rico, China, and England. The students are enrolled in an intensive summer urban education course on "Place and socio-ecological experience" and are about to head off on half-day "dérives."

Vincent Kaufman (2006) writes in a biography of Débord, "the dérive is an art of detour," or of tactically reworking the structures and institutional intentions of the urban environment as well as of self, a reworking that occurs through "movement, mobility, and drift." Traveling in small groups for up to several days through the streets of the city, Débord and other Situationists developed the dérive in France in the 1950s and '60s as "the projection onto space of a temporal experience, and vice versa" (Kaufman, 2006, p. 109). As with de Certeau (1984) as discussed in chapter 2, the Situationists were concerned with the potential politics in practices of walking the structures of the city.

In the urban education class, educators engage in urban walking as a critical pedagogical/research method on one morning of their six-day course. After three hours of unstructured walking and exploring in small groups, students reflect on the experience, including in relation to their broader course on critical anti-oppressive pedagogies of place:

> *A Dérive is an experience of 'letting go' and becoming 'drawn by the attractions of the terrain and the encounters' (Débord, 1958). What an unusual thing for our structured world. This contradiction was an amazing experience being totally aware of my surroundings, the new classmates I was with, and sharing stories of Saskatoon. This wandering we did created what it was supposed to: wonderment. (Kellie, 2011)*

Another student writes of committing to the experience:

> *In the next moment or two I was totally caught off guard by the amazing green growth going on between two buildings not more than 12 inches apart. The natural growth had decided, in spite of human intervention, that this was where it was going to flourish. I began to notice more and more of this. (Julie, 2011)*

Students discussed seeing the racialized history and locations of the city through the layering and juxtaposition of critical readings and differing stories of parents, communities, peers, and people and places encountered and discussed while walking. This collective urban walking experiment/exercise "really highlighted how our past experiences shape our present perceptions of place and space" (Katie, 2011). These and other data from student course journals were later collected as one part of a participatory research project on teachers' experiences of learning to teach for social and ecological justice undertaken by Marcia McKenzie and colleagues (2013).

This example of urban walking as teaching and research method suggests several of the key issues we will focus on in this chapter. Having discussed theorizations (Chapters 2 & 3, this volume) and methodologies (Chapter 4, this volume) of critical place inquiry, we turn our attention to methods of critical place inquiry in this chapter and in Chapter 6. Issues discussed include the "where" of methods, or how data collection takes place in relation to land and place, and in stationary and/or mobile locations; other embodied aspects of data and data collection and analysis processes; and the productivity of methods. The latter includes the participatory and performative aspects of methods and of what is learned and done through the research process. Like developing work in "ecology of place" or "place-based research" in the sciences (Billick & Price, 2010), here we highlight social science research that assigns place "a central and creative role in its design and interpretation," rather than considering it "a problem to be circumvented" (p. 5).

In Chapter 6, we specifically discuss Indigenous methods of critical place inquiry. As you will see, this does not mean that we do not discuss Indigenous methods in this chapter; our intention is not at all to install a barrier between methods of critical place inquiry writ large and Indigenous methods of critical place inquiry. Instead, after the broader discussion of the current chapter, our aim in Chapter 6 is to determine some of the considerations and commitments that may be specific to Indigenous methods. In Chapter 7, we address how the larger project of critical place inquiry might be more accountable to people *across* places.

EMPLACED AND LAND-BASED DATA

> When it comes to research approaches, geographers have largely failed to take the difference that place makes to methodology seriously. While social science has done much to demonstrate the significance of social relationships in methodology (through, for example, processes of researcher reflexivity), the influence of the 'where of method' has received less attention. (Anderson & Jones, 2009, p. 292)

With places "partially responsible for how knowledge is formulated, accessed and articulated," Anderson and Jones (2009) suggest that researchers ought to pay more attention to "the where of the research encounter" (p. 293). We agree and also expand consideration beyond the where of data collection (or what McKittrick [2006] calls the "where of subjectivity") to other ways that various methods "get at" the influence of place in the broader understandings and practices that the research may be examining or furthering. This suggests the importance of how various methods and the data they elicit may be responsive to or indicative of various "emplaced" understandings/ practices, not only through the location of data collection, but also more broadly in the type of data collected or created.

Sofia Cele (2006) elaborates on this through use of a typology of "concrete" and "abstract" aspects of place. Concrete aspects of places are defined as including the physical characteristics and objects present in a place, as well as how humans interact with these places and objects through their senses. The category of abstract aspects of place is used to refer to inner processes that places evoke, including dreams, imagination, memory, and feelings as they relate to people's understandings and connections to place. Trell and van Hoven (2010) suggest that various research methods offer insight into these different aspects of place (see Table 5.1). For example, they propose that visual methods that include seeing places with participants (walks), or are created with or by participants (photos or video), enable more insight into the concrete aspects of place that may be affecting understandings and actions. Oral data collection methods, including interviews, on the other hand, are suggested to provide data on abstract orientations to place through information on participants' thoughts, memories, and feelings as they relate to place.

This typology can be helpful in understanding the value of different types of methods for eliciting qualitative data on place and people's relationships with place. Perhaps most importantly, it suggests the value of going beyond oral or written methods to include visual and sensory modes of data collection (Pink, 2007, 2009). As Anderson and Jones (2009) suggest, changing the location of oral methods such as interviews to familiar places, or through walking interviews or video "go alongs," can enable the elicitation

Table 5.1   Themes and Aspects of Place Revealed with Different Research Methods

Method	Themes/Aspects of Places Revealed
Interviews	Abstract aspects (i.e., thoughts, memories, feelings towards places)
Walks	Concrete aspects (birds, tractor, dogs, sounds, smell-appearance of place); abstract aspects (memories, activities, opinions, interaction with each other and place)
Mental Maps (& Discussion)	Location of places in relation to each other; relative importance of places; shared and individual key places; information about past experiences, opinions, future plans, interests, and hobbies
Video & Photography	Concrete aspects (appearance, sounds, smells); written explanations behind photos revealed use of places, information about friends and favorite places; narration of video revealed emotions, personal meanings, use of place

Note: Adapted from Trell & van Hoven, 2010, p. 101

of "data" of both the concrete and abstract varieties (Cele, 2006): for example, as we see the grass sprouting up between buildings and hear a research participant's reflections in relation to this same experience.

However, a typology of concrete and abstract aspects of place also assumes these considerations can be separated—that objects and physical characteristics are merely physical without human abstraction; and likewise that human thoughts and feelings do not have concrete or material qualities such as manifestations in the body. In contrast, a number of different approaches emphasize the liveliness or agency of the land and materiality, and/or the embodied and emplaced aspects of human thoughts, memories, or feelings. As discussed in earlier chapters, when we stop viewing place as a static backdrop for social life and research, and instead consider more fully how place and materiality more broadly are mutually constitutive with the social, it changes the research frame. We become interested not only in how humans perceive or understand places, but also how various aspects of places themselves are manifested as well as influenced through human practices.

In Chapter 2 we discussed conceptualizations that understand and practice place as mobile, as mutually constitutive with the social through practice, as manifesting and perpetuating power relations including those of colonization, as emphasizing land and the non-human in addition to social considerations of place, and as perpetuating and enabling of politics. To undertake empirical research with this kind of contextual and active orientation to place suggests the need to go beyond collecting data from and with human research participants on and in place, to also examining place itself in its social and material manifestations. See Table 5.2 on pp. 119 and 120 for an overview of possible methods for engaging with place. What this can look like in terms of research methods is a matter of imagination. In what follows we discuss four interwoven areas of consideration in selecting or developing methods for critical place research. These include:

- land and materiality
- embodied and emplaced data
- memory and historical data
- location and mobility
- accountability to community

LAND AND MATERIALITY IN DATA

In the book *Power and Place* Daniel Wildcat explains, "You see and hear things by being in a forest, on a river, or at an ocean coastline; you gain real experiential knowledge that you cannot see by looking at the beings that live in those environments under a microscope or in a laboratory experiment" (Deloria & Wildcat, 2001, p. 36). Researching the material aspects of place itself has been the domain of the sciences for several centuries but is also an increasing focus in social science research. Here we draw on Indigenous methodologies' relational approaches to research, as well as interdisciplinary "new materialist" or sociomaterial approaches to researching the nonhuman, to highlight potentially fruitful research methods for better considering land and materiality in critical place research.

Writing about centering tribal epistemologies in Indigenous research frameworks, Margaret Kovach (2009) outlines how because Indigenous knowledge is specific to people and place, likewise Indigenous research approaches are specific to place and local knowledge. She writes:

> As tribal people, there is an understanding of how to proceed based upon a long history of interrelationship with a particular territory. Place is what differentiates us from other tribal peoples, and what differentiates us from settler societies . . . What we know flows through us from the "echo of generations," and our knowledges cannot be universalized because they arise from our experience with our places. (p. 61)

Turning to Nêhiýaw (Plains Cree) knowledge to illustrate how such understandings are manifested in specific ways with one tribal epistemology, Kovach (2009) discusses the "historic practice emerging from place" of the buffalo hunt (p. 64). After describing the practices and history of the hunt, Kovach writes:

> In many ways, the story of the buffalo hunt is a research teaching story, an allegory for a Plains Cree conceptual framework for research— preparation for the research, preparation of the researcher, recognition of protocol (cultural and ethical), respectfulness, and sharing the

knowledge (reciprocity). The buffalo hunt provides an epistemological teaching, a reference point for how to do things in a good way born of place and context specific to Plains tribes. (p. 65)

This suggests the place-specific aspects of methods, including the importance of place-specific protocols, relationships, and accountabilities in designing and conducting empirical research by and with Indigenous peoples (L. T. Smith, 1999/2012).

Discussing how "the epistemological interrelationship between people, place, language, and animals" influence "coming to know," Kovach (2009) outlines how specific knowledge of and with place is held in storied practice: For example, "This is why name-place stories matter: they are repositories of science, they tell of relationship, they reveal history, and they hold our identity" (pp. 61–62). The interweaving of place and story yields knowledge not only about social life, but of the embedded understandings of other beings and land. Or as Mishuana Goeman (2008) writes,

What continues to endure and "reinforce connections" are stories and our "appropriate action or relationship[s]" to each other. Knowledge of where to collect grasses for basket weaving or the best hunting spots continue to be passed on and used for cultural survival, though fences mark private property and the government punishes transgressions. (p. 32)

For Indigenous scholars undertaking research on and with place, data may be gathered through a wide range of methods, including protocols, narratives and storytelling, dreams, sharing circles, walking, mapping, or other methods (Bang et al., 2014; Kovach, 2009; Meyer, 2003). Advocating for Indigenous peoples to mobilize narrative orientations to land instead of abstract and state-based conceptualizations of territory, Goeman (2008, 2013), for example, discusses how community projects are engaging Indigenous mappings that relate a storied land. She writes,

These maps serve multiple functions: they teach the future generations about their peoples intimate relationship to the land, they act as a mnemonic device in which a past story, memory, or communal memories are recalled, and they are important to political processes. The importance of naming the land from a tribal collective memory is one of the most important political and social tools to tie people together in a shared story. (2008, pp. 24–25; see also Basso, 1996; Brooks, 2008, for examples of the mappings and namings)

As Shawn Wilson (2008) documents, central to this and other research is approaching methods as ceremony, within an Indigenous paradigm of relationality, and as undertaken by Indigenous people. We elaborate further the ways in which Indigenous research methods suggest both how social life can be better understood through place and vice versa in Chapter 6.

In discussing emerging sociomaterial approaches to research, Fenwick, Edwards, and Sawchuck (2011) suggest they share an understanding of the performativity of materiality, including of human beings and social relations. Thus, as discussed in Chapter 4, instead of a focus on distinct objects with properties (human or nonhuman), the emphasis is on "the relations and forms of connections/disconnections among things, where things are taken to be gatherings rather than existing as foundational objects with properties" (pp. 2–3). Or in the words of Jane Bennett (2010b), this is a focus on the "force of things" or the "vitality of materiality." Fenwick et al. (2011) draw specifically on research in the areas of complexity theory, cultural historical activity theory, actor-network theory, and spatiality theories and suggest that, despite their differences in trajectory and premises, they share important characteristics in how they take up the socio-material as research focus. They outline these as follows:

1) They take whole systems into account, regardless of the scope of the material or activity that has been chosen as research focus.
2) They trace interactions among human and non-human parts of the systems, emphasizing heterogeneity of system elements and the need to focus on "relations and mediations, not separate things or separate individuals."
3) They understand human knowledge to be embedded in material action and interaction, or in other words, they do not privilege human intention or consciousness but rather trace how "knowledge, knowers and known (representations, subjects and objects)" emerge together through activity. (p. 6)

These epistemological and ontological, and thus methodological, orientations in turn affect the research methods engaged. While Fenwick and colleagues (2011) suggest that this type of sensibility does not entail a specific set of methods, they indicate a common focus in such studies on the local and singular and on everyday interactions. Given the emphasis on tracing interactions in order to better understand systems and their material components, an increasing number of projects are using analysis and representation methods that map in various ways everyday sociomaterial interactions within a particular scope of setting. An example that explicitly addresses place in relation to other material objects is a study by Nissa Ramsay (2009). In research "following" tourist souvenirs made and purchased in Swaziland, she adapts early ethnographic approaches to following objects (e.g., Appadurai, 1986; Marcus, 1995), but with an aim of going beyond creating biographies for objects. She uses Bennett's (2001) concept of object agency, or the capacity for everyday objects to influence social life, to consider the internal qualities of liveliness in objects, in this case souvenirs, external to enlivenment by human subjects. Interested in how objects forge connections with place, Ramsey's analysis suggests the ways in which souvenirs manifest qualities of place (for example, the different colors of soapstone from which carvings are made), which then act on potential purchasers. With a central focus on the social and affective associations with the materiality of the objects she is following, Ramsey's study is one example of emerging work that considers the inter-relations among land, material objects, and humans. As suggested in Chapter 4, to date much empirical sociomaterial research has a relatively narrow and depoliticized research gaze. We anticipate a growing number of empirical studies that use similar theoretical frames to take up critical questions of place and materiality. For example, a conceptual collection on *Political Matter: Technoscience, Democracy, and Public Life*, edited by Bruce Braun and Sarah Whatmore (2010), discusses the role of the "thing power" of plastic bags in ethical reasoning about the environment (Hawkins, 2010), as well as the role of thermostats and lightbulbs as "technologies of citizenship" (Rose, 1999) and as potential mediators of public involvement in environmental issues (Marres, 2010).

In considering how the liveliness of objects also affects the operationalization of research methods, Kim Kullman (2012) suggests how this kind of "thing power" or object agency (Bennett, 2001) necessitates openness and experimentation. In the example of her own digital picture-making research with children in Helsinki, Kullman suggests the ways that visual research extends beyond the production and interpretation of images "to all kinds of performances: running with cameras, sharing them with friends, even using the equipment as play objects" (p. 2). Embedded within these performances are not only engagements with the objects at hand (in the case of Kullman's research, a camera), but also "sensations and movements of the body as it engages with the material environment" (p. 6). In one data excerpt on walking home from school with four girls between the ages of 10 and 12, Kullman writes:

> My initial attempts to engage them in picture-making are met by reluctant looks. However, after we leave the pavements, zebra crossings and traffic lights behind us and enter a nearby park, events take a new turn: Niia announces that she wants to photograph and grabs the camera from my hand. Suddenly, the girls start making pictures of each other at an intensive pace, circulating the camera from hand to hand as if keeping it in constant motion is of utmost importance. (p. 9, see Figure 5.1)

Kullman (2012) analyzes the way in which the digital camera went beyond being a representational tool to being an artifact circulated as part of play. As is discussed further in later sections, the sensory experiences and mobility partly produced by the object can also be part of data collection and analysis. Kullman argues that this necessitates an experimental attitude to research methods in an attempt to open more space for "eventful" ways of doing research.

Figure 5.1   "Photographs taken collectively by Miia, Alma, Ida and Aino during our walk from school" (Kullman, 2012, p. 9).

EMBODIED AND EMPLACED DATA

Other trajectories of research focus in particular on the relationships between human bodies and places in developing and approaching research methods. While the language of "embodiment" implies the integration of mind and body, "the emergent paradigm of emplacement suggest the sensuous interrelationships of body-mind-environment" (Howes, 2005, p. 7, in Pink, 2009, p. 25). As Pink (2009) suggests, it is now commonly recognized that we need to investigate the emplacement of research participants, and it is equally important for researchers to acknowledge their own emplacement as part of research contexts. Further, emplaced embodied methods of critical place inquiry are perhaps better poised to acknowledge the theoretical contributions of scholars on Black geographies that emphasize the ways in which the production of space has required bodies, Black bodies in particular, as landscapes of domination (Gilmore, 2002; McKittrick, 2006. See Chapter 2, this volume, for more on this point).

Considering embodied methods more broadly, phenomenology is one methodological frame that entails methods of seeking to elaborate and understand embodied relationships to place (see also Chapter 4, this volume). For example, in a study that draws on David Seamon's (1979) work on people's everyday experiences in the world, Worster and Abrams (2005) use interviews to attempt to get at fishermen's and farmers' lived experiences in place, including in relation to environmental impacts on their livelihood practices. In talking about composting, one farmer suggests a relationship between place and embodied understandings and emotions:

> Just making it, all the layers of dead rotting, strange things, old moldy hay, whatever you have, putting it all in there. Then a month or two later it is just ground soil. I just love that regeneration aspect of it. The property has been farmed for hundreds of years. Hundreds of years of cow manure being spread on the land, and things being turned under,

the soil is really nice. There was already a high productivity in that soil and I've only just added to it. (p. 530)

While this description provides a sense of how body and emotion and social practice are woven together with place, in other instances language is less able to convey embodied experiences of place. For example, one New England fisherman says, "The feeling sometimes to be out there, morning especially, 'Wow.' There is something . . . Pacifying effect I guess I don't know" (p. 532).

Responding to concerns about the ability of language or the discursive, to represent embodied experiences, increasingly researchers have turned to additional methods to examine, represent, or mobilize embodied understandings of and in place. As Anderson and Jones (2009) write, "Taking the 'sensuous, embodied, creativeness of social practice seriously' thus requires a focus on experiences, practices and feelings that are *before or beyond* conventional linguistic representation" (p. 294). Methods engaged to attempt this range from ethnographic observations of participant interactions with place (McKay, 2005; Nayak, 2003) to historical photo analysis (Thomas, 2009), mental mapping (Brennan-Horley, Luckman, Gibson, & Willoughby-Smith, 2010; Kayira, 2013; Krueger-Henney, forthcoming), or participatory video (Threadgold, 2000). Visual methods have especially become more common, particularly photography, video, mapping, and drawing, but also visual arts more broadly as well as web-based representation. Drawing on interdisciplinary histories of visual methods and advocating for a multi-sensory ethnography, Pink (2007) suggests that particular visual methods must be developed and determined as appropriate to diverse research sites.

One visual method in researching embodied relationships to place involves what researchers call mental mapping or cognitive mapping. Patricia Krueger-Henney (forthcoming) has used mental mapping in her participatory action research with New York City youth to research their experiences within public schools typified by neoliberal dispossession marked by mayoral control, shrinking curriculum, high stakes testing, intensified police presence and surveillance, school closures and rapid openings of charters schools, and hyperbolic philanthropic influence. She writes,

Mental mapping as a research methodology invites both the mental mapper and the viewer into naming often under-acknowledged mundane spaces, including as schooling. Unlike colonial and colonizing traditions of cartography that are anchored in calculations of scales (and) precision . . . mental maps do not position the mapmaker as outsider to the documented lifeworld. Neither do mental maps frame the spaces under investigation as stagnant or homogenized. Instead, mental maps are extremely personal, subjective and intimate, and hold "promise for understanding how space and place are internalized, interpreted, embodied and revised within individual-level experiences" (Futch &

Fine, 2014). Further, mental maps show how the physical, remembered, and imagined spaces intersect in production of place and thus trace "a narrative or history of an individual or group via the discussion and/or portrayal of materialities such as spaces, bodies, or life events" (Gieseking, 2008). Most noteworthy, mental maps work from the scale of the body and move beyond location to levels of meaning of the intimate (i.e. "disposable"). Hence the numerous details on mental maps reflect a high level of meaning and personal connections the mapmaker has with his or her depicted lifeworld. (forthcoming, shared through personal communication, 11/22/13)

This approach generated "kaleidoscopic" views of young people's experiences in public schools as sites of learning, but also social control discipline and neoliberal disinvestment.

In another dynamic example of mental mapping, Jean Kayira (2013) uses the method in research with youth in Chiduzi, Malawi, on their identities in relation to local and globalized places and (un)sustainable agricultural practices. After being asked to draw her favorite place in the village, one of the youth, Thandizo, explains that she has drawn an image of place that includes conditions not currently a part of the village (for example, a chimney despite the fact that none of the houses in the village have a chimney, see Figure 5.2). Belaying the effects of real and imagined embodied circumstances, as well as the tension between traditional and Western practices, the drawing and accompanying description suggest the additional layers of data that can be enabled through visual methods.

> *Thandizo: Ine malo amene ndimakonda ndi omwe pali nyumba yamakono, maluwa, komanso amayi atabvala zobvala zamakono zachizungu, handibagi yokongola. Komanso mtsuko wabwino wotungila madzi. Komanso pakhale ng'ombe za mkaka, galimoto monga iyi, munda wa chimanga wothila feteleza.* (My favourite place is one with a modern house, flowers; the lady of the house dresses in fashionable, Western-style clothes with a beautiful handbag. Also a good clay pot for drawing water [top right]. In addition, the place should have milk-producing cows [second row, middle], a car like this one [second row, right], a maize garden to which fertilizer has been applied [second row, left of cow] . . .
>
> *Jean: Kodi malo okhala ngati amenewa alipo ku Chinduzi?* (Does such a place exist in Chinduzi?)
>
> *Thandizo: Ayi, koma ndi malo omwe ndimala-laka nditakhala nawo mmudzi muno.* (No, but I aspire to have such a place in this village) (Third youth focus group discussion).

In other studies, similar types of data are linked with geographic information system (GIS) coordinates, which can be mapped to link drawings and interview responses to actual locations on a map, collating and displaying the data in meaningful ways (Brennan-Horley et al., 2010).

Figure 5.2   "Thandizo's favourite place representing hope (e.g., house with iron roof, chimney; lady in fashionable clothes; truck; girl milking cow) and despair (deforestation)" (Kayira, 2013, p. 139).

However, engaging diverse methods focused on embodied and emplaced understandings and practices also extends beyond the visual, and oral representations of the visual. Paul Stollers (1989) discusses realizing in his decade-long research with the Songhay of Niger that "taste, smell, and hearing are often more important for the Songhay than sight, the privileged sense of the West. In Songhay one can taste kinship, smell witches, and hear the ancestors" (p. 5). In part building on Stollers's work, sensory ethnography, as Sarah Pink (2009) writes, "is trying to access areas of embodied, emplaced knowing and to use these as a basis from which to understand human perception, experience, action and meaning and to situate this culturally and biographically" (p. 47). Drawing on understandings that the senses are not separate activities but different facets of the same activity (Ingold, 2000), attending to these varied facets can provide richer data. Drawing on the work of Ingold, Pink (2009) suggests it is essential that sensory research appreciate the cultural and biographical specificity of sensory meanings and "the sets of discourses through which they mobilise embodied ways of knowing in social contexts" (p. 28). Also important are the ways in which the senses play a role in how cultures and places are constituted and changed. Linked to this is how the senses are connected to memory, as is discussed further in the next section. If we understand memories as sedimented in the body, it suggests that memories are bound up in the sensory and "are an inextricable element of how we know in practice." These considerations extend to how cultural, gendered, racialized, class-based, generational, and other experiences and identities influence the meanings and memories imbued into sensory encounters.

In addition to a reflexivity about how the sensory experiences of the researcher and participants are produced through and influence the research encounter, considering emplaced understandings in research entails selecting methods that are aligned with the research questions and setting of focus. For example, Howes and Classen (1991) suggest, "If one's field research involves participant observation, then the question to be addressed is this: Which senses are emphasized or repressed, and by *what means and to which ends?*" (p. 259, original italics). Stollers's (1989) research offers a well-known example of this in him realizing he needed to attend to the knowledge embedded in a broader range of sensory data. As a result, his participant observation practices extended, for example, to the meanings contained in the intended taste of food (e.g., anger intentionally contained in the taste of food prepared as a gift). The location of observation, as well as other research methods such as interviews, can also influence the ability to attend to embodied and emplaced data—for example, in eating or walking with participants or interviewing or working together in different locations.

In a collaborative study by Anglo-European Australian women of the experiences of Vietnamese women who have migrated to Australia, Threadgold (2000) discusses the challenges of understanding the women's experiences without common language or experience. She narrates how, as a result, the Vietnamese women initiated sharing their knowledge through embodied practices of space and food instead of primarily through focus group discussions. For example, writing about the early stages of the research meetings with the women participants, Threadgold states,

> they chattered among themselves while we were talking and then listened to the interpreter, that they would get up in the middle of one another's stories and leave the room to make coffee—all of these things were their ways of translating us into their space, of domesticating us, of training us into the bodily habitus and the geography of their spatial habitus and bodily and cultural rhythms. (p. 197)

Later, food became a form of research method, able to translate understandings in ways that the hired translator was not able to convey:

> Food became here a complex intermediary in this network of actors, a way of translating what they could not tell us in English about who

they were, what they knew and why it mattered. It had ceased, in other words, to be no more than an empty sign of cosmo-multiculturalism and become an intermediary of crosscultural translation. It mattered what colour foods were, how they smelled, what you did with them. We would be taken physically by the hand to see and be shown. (p. 203)

Other methods, such as narrated videos made by the women and a shared visit to a local Vietnamese market, provided other multi-sensory types of data, demonstrating various forms of emplaced knowledge. The ways in which these sensory data share embodied and emplaced experiences that crisscross locations in Australia, Vietnam, and elsewhere, and through time and memory, provide a richness of data that forecloses any one analysis. For this reason, Threadgold ends the discussion of the research with descriptions of the images contained in the women's films, writing, "Such are some of the alternative visual narratives that might translate elderly Vietnamese women's lives into different realities for those who make policy and for those who enact it" (2010, p. 212).

MEMORY AND HISTORICAL DATA

This section interfaces with earlier sections on land and material data, and embodied and emplaced data, and focuses in on the temporal dimensions of research methods concerned with place and social life. Specifically, it highlights the use of historical data in studying past, present, and future conditions, including in the ways in which research methods address memory in social science research on and in place.

As oral historian Lynn Abrams (2010) writes,

Memory is not just the recall of past events and experiences in an unproblematic and untainted way. It is rather a process of remembering: the calling up of images, stories, experiences and emotions from our past life, ordering them, placing them within a narrative or story and then telling them in a way that is shaped at least in part by our social and cultural context . . . Memory (and remembering) for the oral historian is not an abstract concept but a practical and active process of reconstruction whereby traces of the past are placed in conjunction with one another to tell a story. Memory is not just about the individual; it is also about the community, the collective, and the nation. (pp. 78–79)

Given that individual and collective memory exist in a symbiotic relationship with the public memorialization of the past, Abrams (2010) thus suggests that memories expressed via interviews are situated within a field of memory work that operates at many levels in society, including family, community, and public representations (also true for other research methods we would add).

Likewise, place has been shown to have a significant influence in the shaping and recalling of memory (Striffler, 2007). Places can function intentionally or implicitly as "sites of memory," or as locations "where both formal and popular memories are produced, negotiated and take root" (Sarmento, 2011, p. 1). For example, public memorials, historical sites, and tourist destinations are types of sites where memory is intentionally attached to place.

Studies from different disciplines thus suggest the ways that memories are actively constructed and reconstructed in relationships of family, community, and nation-state, including in relationship to land and place. This implies, as Tamboukou (2008) suggests, that researchers, in considering their methods, need to ask why specific stories are told in particular ways and in particular locations, and how individual and collective memories are constituted and shifted through various manifestations of memories, whether in place sites, individual stories, or collective narratives. For example, although recollection and memory are otherwise considered valuable within many Indigenous epistemologies, some Indigenous researchers have pushed back against the (apparent) twin project of recovery to some illusory pure point in the past (see Goeman, 2013; Byrd, 2011).

The narratives or stories constructed in relation to individual and collective memories and through and in place are central to a range of research methodologies. In a book on the temporal and social science research, McLeod and Thomson (2009) discuss six methodological traditions that explicitly engage the temporal, including memory-work, oral/life history, qualitative longitudinal research, ethnography, intergenerational, and follow-up studies. We would add to this list a broad range of narrative and storytelling approaches, including Indigenous methodologies, as discussed in Chapter 4. However, memory is a central aspect of social life and thus can also be considered implicit in all methodologies and methods. Researchers have taken up a focus on the role of the temporal in relation to place and social life, by engaging in multiple interviews and in different locations, in relation to historical documentary sources, in genealogies of specific practices, through participatory methods, and by many other means, in order to attempt to consider memory and the temporal in relation to place in research, including in circumstances of privilege and injustice (McLeod, 2003; Radstone, 2000).

In some research the focus is on examining the construction of memories through place, such as João Sarmento's (2009) research on postcolonial landscapes and memory making in Cape Verde off the coast of West Africa. Studying three sites on the island of Santiago—an old fort and historical town, a concentration camp, and a global resort—the research seeks to "reveal the connections and flows that constituted history in Cape Verde, while destabilising the process of privileging a singular version of heritage and eliding other stories" (p. 524). Offering a critical historical narrative mixed with stark photos depicting landscapes in which histories of colonialism, slavery and "development" have been cast in consumptive orientations to place, Sarmento suggests how "the presence and absence of the representation of the past" is at work on Santiago (p. 541). As he observes, the past also has a pressing contemporary relevance, as divergent understandings of the past become political sites with which communities can "cultivate identity and invoke claims to socio-economic resources" (p. 541).

Various kinds of texts about places can also be examined for the histories and social and environmental conditions perpetuated therein, including in maps (Brooks, 2008; Gieseking, 2013a, 2013b), policy documents (Gulson & Parkes, 2009), school textbooks (Calderon, 2014), or analyses of oil industry advertising (Friedel, 2008). Maps, for example, are social texts that perpetuate power through representations of history and the future, and as such can be productively deconstructed (Winlow, 2009). While some work in critical cartography has read maps as claims for power and over territory, Wallach (2011) suggests alternative readings of political maps as "empty signifiers" capable of multiple interpretations of history and memory. Maps have also been used productively as tactics in shifting power, for example, in the early twentieth century to show the spread of women's suffrage in the United States. Displayed on posters and pamphlets, the map was used as a means of claiming public space through rewriting history and public memory. Dando (2010) argues that such use of mapping demonstrated the molding of masculine ways of knowing to advance the suffrage cause, although simultaneously marginalizing women of color. As discussed earlier, Goeman (2008) also outlines how the formalized mapping of Indigenous land can act as a mnemonic device that recalls communal memories and can be mobilized in political processes.

In a study of urban youth identity in the "global cities" of Toronto and Vancouver, Dillabough and Kennelly (2010) combine youth interview transcripts, photo-taking, and journaling with historical images of past youth in these same locations. In some cases asking present-day youth to narrate these archival and media images, the researchers attempt to intersect historical time with the present "as a way of signalling the importance of the temporal to present-day youth cultural configurations" (p. 52). Indicating that too often methodological engagement with the role of historical knowledge is missing in the making of contemporary representations of young people, Dillabough and Kennelly suggest that the use of archival materials enabled them to better critique the institutional practices (of policy, media, education) that sustain sedimented experiences of youth in relation to place, such as poverty, gender, and racialization. Anoop Nayak's (2003) work similarly layers past and present in ethnographic accounts of the lives of working class white youth in Northeastern England. Bringing historical research and data to bear on analyses of interviews with, and observation of, contemporary youth, Nayak is able to offer an analysis that spans beyond the individual memories or narrations of the youth to the longer narratives and practices of place-bound social life that continue to constitute their identities. In this way, the research offers insight into the ways in which collective memory of and in place is sedimented in contemporary youth bodies and practices, often unbeknownst to them.

Rather than examining social history in relation to place in a given location, other studies research the role of memory across locations, for example, in wide ranging studies on the experiences of diasporic and immigrant communities in relation to place. We discuss one of many possible examples to highlight how researchers are studying the role of memory and nostalgia in new immigrant experiences of places. Building on research on the role of physical environment in culture shock and the role of material objects and homemaking in adjusting to a new culture, Rishbeth and Finney (2006) worked with asylum seekers and refugees from Asia and Africa in greenspaces in Sheffield, England. Using various photo techniques such as photo-elicitation and photo journals, the participants visited 10 greenspace sites over 12 weeks. In addition to novel aspects of the places visited, participants identified nostalgic elements in the locations and the photos of locations. With landscapes and plants becoming the starting point for stories about participants' home lives and outings before moving to England, the research provided insight into both participants' relationships with places in the UK as well as in their countries of origin. The researchers also suggest the ways that multi-sensory experiences of place were important in linking to past memories. As one participant said of a plant encountered in a greenspace, "'The smell is very nice . . . I don't know how I can explain it . . . when I found this it reminded me of my home country. It's good, it's nice' (Firmina, 25, from Rwanda, in the UK for two years)" (p. 288). Drawing on Boym's (2001) work on nostalgia, the researchers suggests that the methods engaged enabled participants both an opportunity for looking back (reflective nostalgia) as well as a means of integrating their pasts within a new future (restorative nostalgia).

Linked to this focus on the effects of research on participants, we also want to highlight the ways in which memory and history are engaged in participatory and action research methods. These engagements range from the specifics of "memory-work" undertaken by groups of researchers to examine their own constitution within dominant social values (Kaufman, Ewing, Hyle, Montgomery, & Self, 2006; McLeod & Thomson, 2009), to participatory mapping and/or photovoice projects in which participants map and thus affirm or reshape memory and historical events (e.g., Gieseking, 2013b; McIntyre, 2003). Through the examination and in some cases reframing of individual and collective histories, memory proves to be an important, although often implicit, aspect of participatory work. An example of participatory research that explicitly takes up memory in relation to place is Jen Jack Gieseking's (2013b) research as part of the Our Queer Lives and Spaces Project, a project "dedicated to affording lgbtqtstsiq people a place to map and record their stories in their own words and images" (http://jgieseking.org/research-writing-projects/oqls/). Concerned about the invisibility of "all lesbians and queer women—broadly-defined and self-defined," the project aims to record spatial memories in order to build a more visible history for those who identify as queer. Using vojo.com technology, the project centers on an interactive online map in which participants can post and view favorite memories in relation to places in New York City (Gieseking, 2013b).

Finally, sometimes the best way to consider the role of time in social and place-based practice is over time. McLeod and Yates's (2006) longitudinal research on class-based youth identity followed 26 young Australians over 7 years. Undertaking research that considers the effects of the temporal in "real time" enables insights on the impacts, for example, of policy effects manifested in schools, as well as of the influences on the formation of youth identities. The researchers suggest there are two forms of temporality built into their study: historical specificity and the timescape of the adolescent years, which they sought to bridge through a qualitative longitudinal design involving interviews with the youth twice a year during and a year after high school. Through their analysis, they attempt to show how "history is manifest in lives as well as demonstrating that the abstract and normative 'ages and stages' approach of developmental psychology is challenged by a recognition that nothing is inevitable in concrete times and places" (McLeod & Thomson, 2009, p. 66).

LOCATION AND MOBILITY

Discussions of location and mobility in relation to research methods have permeated the previous sections of this chapter. We draw this focus out as a distinct section to highlight its importance in relation to previous discussions of land and material data, embodied and emplaced data, and memory and historical data. As we have suggested in each of these proceeding discussions and as somewhat self-evident in a book on place, location matters in considering and operationalizing research methods. We have discussed methods such as mental mapping, digital mapping, taking photos and videos in different locations, as well as how objects in different locations and the land itself can be considered actors in the research process. Here we elaborate further, in particular on how the location of the implementation of methods may matter for the data collected or created, including via mobile methods such as walking interviews or video go alongs, as well as how particular methods and technologies, such as social network analysis (SNA) and global positioning systems (GPS), are being used to map and analyze data in relation to location and mobility.

Certain methodologies of research, such as ethnographic and participatory or community-based approaches, originated with a focus on attention to the location of data collection. Going to "the field" or "the community" to undertake participant observation or meet with community members recognizes that the "where" of the research matters for what is observed or undertaken. However, more generally, as Anderson and Jones (2009) suggest, "The role that place plays in influencing the knowledge produced during the research encounter (see Preston 2003), or how place could be harnessed to elicit information on identities, emotions, and power relationships, is often overlooked (Elwood and Martin 2000)" (p. 292). More specifically, Anderson and Jones

(2009) focus on the location of data collection and how different locations may elicit different data. Following Sin (2003), who suggested that "Despite the plethora of spatial metaphors, the theorization of space in the setting of an interview has been curiously abstracted and removed from the concrete 'place' in which an interview takes place" (p. 306), they discuss how different interview locations may influence the type of information shared by participants. In Jones's doctoral research (e.g., Jones, 2008), she undertook interviews with youth in a school storecupboard as well as in their social settings after classroom-based interviews suggested youth were withholding information in the formal and surveilled classroom site. She writes,

> The storecupboard was (unsurprisingly) not a place pupils usually inhabited. It therefore provided an alternative space in contrast to the previous classroom location. The storecupboard had a positive impact on the research process, facilitating a different type of knowledge than was obtainable through interviews in a classroom context. The storecupboard represented a liminal space, in-between the formal and informal worlds of the school talked about by Valentine (2000). (p. 329)

Because individual and group identities and roles are tied to places, what is or is not possible in an interview or other research activity may be dependent on the location of the research (see also J. M. Smith, 2008).

These considerations also extend to the possibilities of mobile methods of data collection. Researchers are increasingly exploring the use of walking interviews, video "go alongs," and other means of collecting data while traveling with participants (Fincham, McGuinness, & Murray, 2010). However, despite this mobility focus in data collection, Jones et al. (2008) suggest that still few researchers have attempted to connect what participants say with where they say it. As a result, techniques such as linking GPS data to walking interview, photo, or video data are being used to situate gathered data physically. Evans and Jones (2011) warn that focusing on GPS data risks emphasizing a technocentric analysis that may prioritize locational above other narrative and affective elements. Other research has begun to explore mobile phone and social media produced data, however little of this research to date has a critical and/or place focus. We anticipate an increasing number of studies that use mobile data generated through Twitter or Facebook posts, for example, to trace the origins and mobilities of place-based social movements (Tuck & Yang, 2014).

Additional interesting methods are being used to track and map the spread of social policy or other place-based and networked aspects of social life, such as organizational or activist networks. As one of these methods, social network analysis (SNA) can be understood as an approach used to analyze the patterns of networks and develop theoretical perspectives of these relations (Fuhse & Mützel, 2011). SNA is being used to identify relationships between network members in order to compare, understand, and potentially enhance those relationships. Identified relational ties may be those that persist over time (for example, those of family, friends, or knowledge), or discrete ties that change over time (such as events or correspondence) (Borgatti & Halgin, 2011). Relationships, ties, and flows are typically examined through quantitative data collection methods such as surveys, structured interviews, or archival documents. Data are assigned measures, which are then organized in matrices to represent the presence, type, and quality of ties, and/or used to create network diagrams (sociograms) to map the various components of networks (McRuer, in press). While SNA is a quantitative approach to data collection and analysis, related qualitative approaches to network analysis are also being developed, such as the sociomaterial analyses of object effects as discussed in an earlier section of this chapter (Ramsay, 2009), or through more ethnographic approaches to mapping networks that also consider the role of place/space in networks (e.g., Ball, 2012). Newly developing technology linking social media to place also offers new possibilities for developing methods for studying place-based methods (e.g., Jones & Grandhi, 2005).

Related to the study of networks is newly developing work in policy mobility studies (Peck & Theodore, 2010; Temenos & McCann, 2013). Building on earlier studies of policy diffusion that traced social policy development from a particular place to locations elsewhere, mobilities approaches also understand policy creation and mobilization as more dispersed due to globalized networks and actors, and as not necessarily having a clear center or point of origin. However, McCann (2011) emphasizes that such an approach builds on longer trajectories in geography (for example, the work of David Harvey and Doreen Massey) that have understood place "in terms of fixity *and* mobility; relationality *and* territoriality" (p. 15, emphasis in original). Much of the existing research on policy mobilities focuses on unique urban planning, social, or health policy initiatives that can be traced in their uptake across different locales—for example, workfare policies in the United States (Peck & Theodore, 2010) or urban design policies such as smart growth or business improvement districts as they have spread globally (McCann & Ward, 2012). Temenos and McCann (2013) suggest that most policy mobilities work to date has mostly employed "'standard' qualitative case study methods" (p. 351) and that there is additional need for more detailed empirical research. Elsewhere, McCann (2011) also advocates for analyzing policy documents and websites to better understand the structural and historical contexts within which policy mobilities have emerged and are active, as well as the potential of quantitative methods in examining some data.

ACCOUNTABILITY WITH COMMUNITY

Finally, we also want to draw attention to the role of accountability to and with community in critical research on and in place. As discussed in earlier chapters, the focus in this book is on research concerned with critical questions of place—of Indigenous sovereignty, climate change and climate injustice, the spatialization and institutionalization of racism and colonization, urban food access, global neoliberalization, and the localized effects of policy mobility, youth identity, and agency in an era of potential human extinction. Central to research on such questions of Indigenous, social, and environmental justice is how the research contributes to interventions in such conditions. Rather than attempting axiological neutrality, critical place research is conceived, designed, and undertaken with aims of being of use (Fine & Barreras, 2001). The methodology and methods mobilized to such aims will depend on the social location and skills of the researcher, the audience and intended outcomes of the proposed research, what is feasible logistically and within given timeframes, and other considerations. However, deciding what approach to research is in the best interests of a given issue or context necessitates the input or participation of those potentially affected by the research or the issues it seeks to address.

We recognize the obstacles associated with conceptualizations and practices of community accountability. "Community" as a concept has been critiqued for its assumptions of shared understandings, for the ways it establishes insiders and outsiders, and for glossing over differences in power and participation (Cooke & Kothari, 2001; Ellsworth, 1989). As Gayatri Spivak writes in her introduction to the English translation of Derrida's *De la Grammatologie*, we suggest "both that the concept is inaccurate and that it is necessary" (Derrida, 1976). A politics of difference, while important, cannot be at the expense of enabling the realities of common experience and solidarities (Grande, 2004). Yet, we are also moved by Donna Deyhle's (2009) observation in *Reflections in Place: Connected Lives of Navajo Women*,

> A community is made up of many different stories, sometimes speaking to each other, sometimes speaking past each other, sometimes invisible to each other, and sometimes ignored by each other. In this sense, a community is not a uniform group of people, but rather a location or place. (p. xvii)

Thus, the following conversation about methods of critical place inquiry and accountability to community is imbued with Deyhle's characterization of community *as place.*

As discussed in Chapter 3, Linda Tuhiwai Smith's (1999/2012) book on *Decolonizing Methodologies* was groundbreaking in articulating the harm done to Indigenous peoples through research as part of European imperialism and colonialism. Smith proposes an Indigenous research agenda that has Self-determination at its center. More than a political aim, self-determination is also a social justice goal (pp. 116–117). In terms of research methods, Smith articulates the implications for protocols as methods. Instead of Western conceptions of research ethics "framed in ways which contain the Western sense of the individual and of individualized property—for example, the right of an individual to give his or her own knowledge, or the right to give informed consent" (p. 118), there needs to be recognition and respect for community and Indigenous rights and views. She writes, "Indigenous peoples have attempted through the development of instruments such as treaties, charters and declarations to send clear signals to the world's scientific and research communities that open-cast mining approaches to research (see, take and destroy) are absolutely unacceptable" (p. 118). Other researchers continue to build on the implications of Self-determination for research methods, including through emphasizing researcher responsibility for following local protocols, using methods epistemologically appropriate to the communities involved in the research, and ensuring the research gives back in concrete ways furthering the priorities of Indigenous peoples involved in the research (Kovach, 2009; Wilson, 2008).

Related principles of ethics and accountability are also relevant to other communities, where past research experiences have served to marginalize or pathologize, and where research ethics are laced with assumptions about the naïvete and vulnerability of the researched (Tuck & Guishard, 2013). Writing of how the stories told or left untold in research can do further harm rather than good, Michelle Fine and colleagues (Fine, Weis, Weseen, & Wong, 2000) emphasize the importance of working "with—not on or despite—local community efforts" (p. 125). This involves contributing to conversations about researcher responsibility, recognizing that "questions of responsibility—for whom, will, and should, forever be paramount—because the 'whom' is not a coherent whole . . . and because the context in which we write will change tomorrow, and so too will the readings of this text" (p. 125).

Responding to these concerns, many researchers and communities have turned to participatory forms of research that, rather than research "on" or "for," entail research "with" and "by" community (Fine, 1994). Eve Tuck and Monique Guishard (2013) outline an ethical framework for decolonial participatory action research, which involves considerations of reflexivity, expertise, humility, dignity, action, and relationality: this is "research that is conducted in and with community, not on communities, and in ways that are anti-colonial, not imperialistic" (Tuck & Guishard, 2013, p. 16). To touch on some of the implications for research methods, such an ethical approach suggests highlighting researcher "blind-spots and biases" in as much detail as "the seeming contradictions and inconsistencies of the people with whom we conduct research" (p. 23). Engaging explicitly with settler colonialism in considering research methods and ethics, this indicates how "participation" needs to go beyond merely including more people in the data collection and/or analysis processes.

In earlier sections of the chapter we have shared examples of the many research methods engaged in participatory and action research. All of the methods outlined in Table 5.2 can in fact be engaged in participatory projects in certain circumstances as deemed appropriate by the involved research participants. We want to close this section by emphasizing the importance

Table 5.2 Examples of Social Science Data Collection Methods and Sample Works

Type of Method	Place-Related Data	Sample Works
Written Methods		
Survey	Connections to places; Time spent in places; Locations of places	Maneja Zaragoza et al., 2009
Audits	Connections to places; Time spent in places; Locations of places; Relationships among places	Opondo et al., 2007
Narrative/(Auto)biography	Place-based stories and memories, Recountings, Journals	Deyhle, 2009
Textual/Document analysis	Connections to place (historical and/or current); Analysis of social inequities in relation to place	Gulson & Parkes (2009)
Oral Methods		
Protocols	Ethics of places	Kovach, 2009; Wilson, 2008
Storytelling/Storywork/ Interviews	Historical meanings and uses of place contained in story variations; Instructions on carrying forth the story; Origin stories; Connections to places	Archibald, 2008; Kovach, 2009; Worster & Abrams, 2005
Narrative/(Auto)biography	Historical and current meanings of place through variations of stories, songs, and other narrative forms; Connections to places	Kaufman et al., 2006
Focus Groups/Sharing Circles	Historical and current meanings and memories of place; Connections to place; Decolonizing analyses of place	Kovach, 2009
Dream Data	Connections to places; Meanings of place	Dé Ishtar, 2005

(*Continued*)

Table 5.2 (Continued)

Type of Method	Place-Related Data	Sample Works
Visual Methods		
Historical Map Analysis	Historical meanings and uses of places; Decolonizing analyses of mappings	Wallach, 2011
GPS/GIS Mapping	Current and historical meanings and uses of places; Linking other data to specific places	Brennan et al., 2010; Evans & Jones, 2011; Maneja Zaragoza et al., 2009
Diagramming/Mental Mapping	Connections to places; Time spent in places; Understandings of places; Practices in places	Brennan et al., 2010; Gieseking, 2013b; Trell & van Hoven, 2010; Krueger-Henney, forthcoming
Drawing	Representations of place; Connections to place	Béneker, Sanders, Tani, & Taylor, 2010
Network Analysis	Analyses of social networks in relation to places	Ball, 2012
Photo Analysis	Connections to places; Understandings of places; Analysis of place-related issues	Larsen et al., 2007; Mitchell, 2008; O'Donoghue, 2010
FotoDialogo	Connections to places; Understandings of places; Analysis of place-related issues	Ramos, 2007
Photovoice	Connections to places; Time spent in places; Narratives of places; Narratives of place-related issues; Participants speaking out on place-related issues	Hergenrather et al., 2009 (review paper); McIntyre, 2003
Video/Digital Storytelling	Connections to places; Time spent in places; Narratives of places; Narratives of place-related issues; Participants speaking out on place-related issues	Sandercock & Attili, 2010; Threadgold, 2000

Type of Method	Place-Related Data	Sample Works
Mobile Methods		
Walking Interviews/ Go Alongs	Connections to places; Time spent in places; Narratives of places; Narratives of place-related issues	Evans & Jones, 2011; Middleton, 2010
Object Following	Analysis of movement of objects in and across places	Ramsay, 2009
Policy Mobility Analysis	Analysis of uptake and movement of policy in and across places	Peck & Theodore, 2010; Temenos & McCann, 2013
Arts & Social Media Methods		
Visual Art	Connections to places; Understandings/ practices of places; Expressions of place-related issues; Participants speaking out on place-related issues	Irwin et al., 2009; Huss, 2008; Tolia-Kelly, 2007
Theatre	Connections to places; Understandings/practices of places; Expressions of place-related issues; Participants speaking out on place-related issues	Cieri & McCauley, 2007
Spoken Word & Music	Connections to places; Understandings/practices of places; Expressions of place-related issues; Participants speaking out on place-related issues	Lashua & Fox, 2007
Social Media & Web-based	Connections to places; Understandings/practices of places; Expressions of place-related issues; Participants speaking out on place-related issues	Tuck & Yang, 2014

of collaborative decision-making to determine data collection and analysis methods that match the knowledge and aims research participants are prioritizing. For example, in a photovoice project with youth and adults on neighborhood violence, at the suggestion of community members, Wang, Morrel-Samuels, Hutchison, Bell, and Pestronk (2004) recruited a group of policy-makers and community leaders to provide support and political will for implementing the participants' policy and program recommendations.

Working with nomadic Bedouin women in Israel, Ephrat Huss (2008) describes a participatory art-based methods through which participants shared the shifting inside and outside, sedentary and mobile spaces in which they live. Huss suggests that by using a method appropriate to their own experiences, women were able to articulate those experiences according to their own categories and epistemological understandings (see Figure 5.3; see also Cahill, 2004). An edited collection on participatory action research methods as they connect "people, participation, and place" (Kindon, Pain, & Kesby, 2007) provides a range of other helpful examples of how researchers are undertaking critical participatory research in relation to place and in ways that address accountability with community: for example, through participatory diagramming and mapping (Alexander et al., 2007; Sanderson, with Holy Family Settlement Research Team, Newport, & Umaki Research

Figure 5.3 "My drawing gives me a feeling of my life: I am standing, thank God, and I am like the tree because I am trying to be strong and connected to the ground although my branches feel the wind" (Huss, 2008, p. 66).

Participants, 2007), participatory auditing (Opondo, Dolan, Wendoh, & Kathuri, 2007), participatory theatre (Cieri & McCauley, 2007), participatory art (Tolia-Kelly, 2007), participatory photography (Krieg & Roberts, 2007), participatory video (Hume-Cook et al., 2007), and participatory GIS (Elwood et al., 2007).

DATA ANALYSIS: REPRESENTATION AND PERFORMATIVITY IN METHODS

Data analysis is often embedded within "data collection": for example, in selecting which photos to take or include in formal analysis (Pink, 2007), or in reflexive and collaborative discussions through participatory research processes (Cahill, 2007). It also occurs "after" data collection in determining how to make sense of, organize, present, and mobilize the data collected or produced. The specifics of what analysis can look like in relation to a particular data collection method ought to be determined in alignment with a study's methodological underpinnings, as described in Chapter 4. What we want to focus on here are understandings of analysis broadly and in relation to critical place research.

Specifically, we want to focus on the ways in which analysis functions to represent and produce research. As Cele (2006) writes of her research on children and place,

> The subjective experience of place is difficult for others to understand and even more difficult to capture and reflect in research. Our everyday interactions with our surroundings and the communication our bodies and minds have with place is both subjective and volatile and, hence, difficult to mediate and communicate . . . Research on the experience of place may be seen as a contradiction since these experiences are processes based on individuals' perceptions and inner lives. The research I present here is, of course, not on the experiences of place, even if this is the vocabulary I use: it is rather on the narratives of these experiences and perceptions. These narratives, though, are not necessarily verbal but may take different forms depending on the individuals involved and the contexts they derive from. (p. 14)

Here Cele remarks on the mediating effects of language and narration in research on experiences of place, suggesting that it is not possible to access experiences of place in unmediated ways. This inevitability of the mediation of experience by language (or of reality by culture) was at the heart of the "crisis of representation" that took center stage in much of social science research in the 1990s and 2000s. As researchers grappled with this, they responded through advocating increased reflexivity of the researcher and on the part of research participants, they diversified methods to see from multiple angles in ways that might refract different understandings, they juxtaposed and cobbled, broke down divisions between art and social science, and otherwise emphasized a stance of openness and creativity in methods in ways that hoped to at least shed some light on these mediating influences (Lather & Smithies, 1997; Richardson, 2000; St. Pierre & Pillow, 2000).

More recently there is a renewed interest in related questions of representation regarding research methods. In a recent paper on "Methodology-21: what we do in the afterward?" Patti Lather (2013) suggests a "post-qualitative" research era. She proposes this as entailing "no methodological a priori" and rather that the design and practice of research "are up for grabs" (p. 638). She writes, "'What is usually thought of as method' (p. 6) shifts to a sort of 'running away' from traditional models" (p. 638). While Lather wants to continue to complicate representational methods and texts, in her paper in the same special issue Maggie MacLure (2013) argues for "non- or post-representational thought and methods" (p. 658). Drawing on new materialist work, MacLure suggests how a flattened logic "where discourse and matter are mutually implicated in the unfolding emergence of the world" (p. 660) can enable researchers to consider their research as a material-discursive assemblage rather than through a representational logic. Redefining analysis as "alertness," MacLure suggests focus on the material-discursive elements of events. This seems to suggest that rather than distinguishing between language and experience, they are considered in interaction. The research act itself becomes part of those interactions so that research is understood as performative rather than representational, or what Jensen (2010) characterizes as "from epistemology and representation to practical ontology and performativity" (in Fenwick et al., 2011, p. 3).

However, we worry that a narrowed focus on the inventiveness of methods understood as performative misses the point of what types of interactivity are performed/represented and to what ends (Greene, 2013). As Nayak and Jeffrey (2011) suggest, such emerging materialist and non-representational approaches to research methods ask us to consider the "'what elseness' of human experience and look further than talk and text . . . This does not mean forgoing representation altogether but involves a concerted opening-out towards a performative methodology that engages with events, practices and activities as they occur" (p. 291). Proposing that representation and presentation are linked, Nayak and Jeffrey (2011) suggest that "more-than-representational" might be a more fitting descriptor. In any case, research can be considered a "messy and fragile practice that inescapably mingles with the phenomena it studies, both shaping and becoming shaped by them in unexpected ways" (Kullman, 2012, p. 5). According to John Law (2004),

the challenge is not to take the improvisatory and uncertain quality of research as a methodological failure, but as an inspiration to think about method more inclusively by considering all modes of relating to the world as potentially suitable methods. Research entails finding new ways of engaging with daily life as it unfolds, whether these are verbal, pictorial, gestural, or affective. This realisation invites us to direct more attention to 'method-in-practice' (Law 2004, p. 45) and the opportunities to think differently about research that encounters between methods and the world bring out. (Kullman, 2012, p. 5)

We would add, it also requires an ethical responsibility to consider the impacts of the means and ends of the methods engaged.

6 Indigenous Methods of Critical Place Inquiry

Indian tribes combine history and geography so that they have a "sacred geography," that is to say, every location within their original homeland has a multitude of stories that recount the migrations, revelations, and particularly historical incidents that cumulatively produced the tribe in its current condition.

Vine Deloria, Jr., 1973/2003

If the goals of decolonization are justice and peace, as is often stated by governments and people in Native politics, then the process to achieve these goals must reflect a basic covenant on the part of both Onkwehonwe and Settlers to honour each others' existences. This honouring cannot happen when one partner in the relationship is asked to sacrifice their heritage and identity in exchange for peace.

Taiaiake Alfred, 2013

In this chapter, we discuss Indigenous methods of critical place inquiry. This discussion follows the more comprehensive description of methods of critical place inquiry arising from across intellectual traditions in Chapter 5. Our goal is not to set up a false binary between Indigenous and non-Indigenous methods of critical place inquiry, which is why Indigenous methods are discussed alongside others in Chapter 5. Yet, while not at all mutually exclusive, there are specific features of Indigenous methods of critical place inquiry that set them apart from methods that emerge from other intellectual traditions. Our work in this chapter is to try to understand these specific features, and how they might be refracted back to inform our broader description and definition of critical place inquiry.

Although we have referred to Indigenous peoples throughout this volume, it always makes sense to clarify whom we mean by using that term. *Indigenous*, especially in settler colonial nation-states such as Canada, the United States, Australia, and New Zealand, is a racialized category, but more importantly, Indigenous is a collectivized political identity. Many Indigenous peoples in settler colonial nation-states make prior claims to unceded land and to ceded land now occupied by settlers. Writing about Indigenous peoples in the United States, Kim Tallbear (2013) states,

> We Native Americans have been racialized as such with the broader American cultural milieu. We privilege our rights and identities as citizens of tribal nations for good reason: citizenship is key to sovereignty, which is key to maintaining our land bases. But race has also been imposed on us. Race politics over the centuries in both Europe and the United States have conditioned our experiences and opportunities, including the federal-tribal relationship. (p. 33)

Designations of who may be called Indigenous are powerfully complex, especially because such designations are precursors for making claims to land. We defer to the sovereign power of each tribe, Nation, or tribal community to determine membership, but as Tallbear explains, such determinations have at times been informed by problematic assumptions about blood, and more recently, DNA. We adhere to definitions of Indigeneity that recognize the power of long-held relationships to land, the role of other tribal members in conferring belonging, and tribe-specific understandings of kinship and responsibilities related to kinship.

Our emphasis in this chapter is on methods that have been developed by Indigenous scholars or in collaboration with Indigenous people to reflect Indigenous ways of knowing and articulating knowledge. Indigenous methods are Indigenous because they take inspiration from practices in tribal communities, because they are designed to be meaningful for Indigenous participants, and because they work to gather information that is useful to tribal communities. And, as we discuss in the conclusion of this chapter, what we have learned from looking deeply across several exemplars, there are theoretical commitments that differentiate Indigenous research methods from non-Indigenous methods of critical place inquiry.

THE NEED FOR INDIGENOUS METHODS OF SOCIAL SCIENCE

Many Indigenous scholars have shared accounts of their first forays into social science inquiry, journeys that were made complicated by the history of unethical research conducted on Indigenous people and land (Archibald, 2008; L. T. Smith, 1999/2012; Wilson, 2008). Of her attempts to develop an Indigenous research method, Stó:lō scholar Jo-ann Archibald (2008) writes,

> I started with the principles of respect for cultural knowledge in the stories and respect for the people who owned the stories as an ethical guide. Like Old Man Coyote I wanted the (re)search to be easy. I didn't really want to deal with colonial history, and I did not want to

question my motives and methods. But unlike Old Man Coyote, I knew that I had to venture to the unfamiliar territory of decolonization by questioning my motives and methods and ensuring that the negative legacy of research history was addressed . . . Going away from the fire and finding ways to move beyond the history of colonization is hard but necessary work. Staying near the fire and trying to adapt qualitative methodology to fit an Indigenous oral tradition is also problematic because Indigenous theory does not drive the methodology. Finally, I figured out . . . that I needed to go back to the Elders. (p. 36)

In *Research as Ceremony*, Shawn Wilson (2008) describes his personal motivations for writing about Indigenous research paradigms in the context of a letter he writes to his sons:

An Indigenous research paradigm is made up of an Indigenous ontology, epistemology, axiology, and methodology. These beliefs influence the tools we as researchers use in finding out more about the cosmos. Like myself, other Indigenous scholars have in the past tried to use the dominant research paradigms. We have tried to adapt dominant system research tools by including our perspective into their views. We have tried to include our cultures, traditional protocols and practices into the research process through adapting and adopting suitable methods. The problem with that is that we can never really remove the tools from their underlying beliefs. Since these beliefs are not always compatible with our own, we will always face problems in trying to adapt dominant system tools to our use. (p. 13)

Clearly, Audre Lorde's (1984) often-quoted sentiment/essay, "The master's tools will never dismantle the master's house" (p. 110), is relevant to Archibald and Wilson's discussions. Speaking back to the proclivity of feminist theory to ignore or exclude the theories and experiences of poor women, Black women, Third World women, and lesbians, Lorde's essay was delivered at a conference attended by mostly white feminist academics. Lorde's rejoinders, that racism and homophobia are conditions that cannot be overlooked and suggestions that every conference participant/reader "reach down into that deep place of knowledge inside herself and touch that terror and loathing of any difference that lives there" (p. 114), still have resonance for the academy. Lorde's essay expresses an abiding doubt that those white feminists promising solidarity will ever do the self-education required to break cycles of racist patriarchal thought.

Wilson's (2008) discussion in particular, offered to his children, references a related doubt and weariness in attempting to use dominant research paradigms and methods. Like Lorde, for Wilson the trouble is in the ways those dominant paradigms and tools exhibit underlying beliefs of dominant settler colonial society. Another way to understand this may be to return to Patrick Wolfe's (1999) insistence that settler colonialism is a structure and not (just) an event. Settler colonialism, as scalular structure, is evident in every aspect of a settler colonial society, from broad ideologies to the research instruments used to collect data and information (see also Tuck & Guishard, 2013, and Chapter 7, this volume).

This is why, in *Decolonizing Methodologies* (1999/2012), Linda Tuhiwai Smith discusses Indigenous and decolonizing research methods in the context of "researching back." Smith locates researching back within the same critical research legacy that enables the "writing back" or "talking back" that is so central to postcolonial, feminist, queer, and ethnic studies literatures (see Cahill, 2004, on speaking back). Researching back and "theorizing back" (Tuck, 2009c) engage everyday people in rejecting and reclaiming theories that have been used to disempower them: "theories that we have mis/believed about ourselves, that have fed our own self abnegation, theories that have made us rely upon, cater to, offer gratitude to, and even congratulate the colonizer" (Tuck, 2009c, p. 120). Researching back and theorizing back shifts the gaze of research on to the institutions and structures that maintain settler colonialism (Tuck & Guishard, 2013, p. 20).

THE IMPORTANCE OF SURVIVANCE

Indigenous methods of critical place inquiry are designed to engage the survivance of Indigenous peoples (Vizenor, 1994, 1998; Vizenor, Tuck, & Yang, 2014). *Survivance* refers to ontologies directly connected to the ways that Indigenous peoples have always engaged the world and rights to who Indigenous peoples have always been (Castagno & Brayboy, 2008). Anishinaabe scholar Gerald Vizenor observes that storytelling that emphasizes survivance is an "active repudiation of dominance, tragedy, and victimry," and these survivance stories "are the creases of transmotion and sovereignty" (1998, p. 15). Vizenor's concept of survivance is distinct from survival; it is a "moving beyond our basic survival in the face of overwhelming cultural genocide to create spaces of synthesis and renewal" (1994, p. 53). Elsewhere Vizenor writes, "Survivance, in my use of the word, means a native sense of presence, the motion of sovereignty and the will to resist dominance. Survivance is not just survival but also resistance, not heroic or tragic, but the tease of tradition, and my sense of survivance outwits dominance and victimry" (1999, p. 93; see also Tuck, 2009b).

Although previously avoiding a firm definition of survivance (Vizenor, Tuck, & Yang, 2014), more recently, Vizenor has further elaborated on the concept:

> Survivance is an intergenerational connection to an individual and collective sense of presence and resistance in personal experience and the word, or language, and particularly through stories. Intergenerational

communication looks different in other communities, passing on a business, trade, or profession, but in Native communities on this continent the knowledge of survivance is shared through stories. (Vizenor, Tuck, & Yang, 2014, p. 107)

More,

> There is no way to know the outcome of survivance. It is a spirited resistance, a life force, not just anger, negative or destructive. Survivance is a force of nature, a new totem, and it has to be expressed and imagined to create a sense of presence. Survivance stands in contrast to concepts of absence and victimry that are frequently applied to Native communities. (Vizenor, Tuck, & Yang, 2014, p. 113)

Because of the history of troubled and exploitative research conducted in Indigenous communities (L. T. Smith, 1999/2012), concepts of researching back and survivance are bloodlines in Indigenous research methodologies. These resistance-oriented constructs are thus enacted in Indigenous research methods. In each of the exemplars we discuss in this chapter, researching back, survivance, and resistance course through the work.

Dolores Calderon (2014) has described anticolonial methods and methodologies as those that refute the centrality of the experience of colonialism as primary in the configuration of indigeneity. Said another way, anticolonial methods refuse to characterize Indigenous peoples as only peoples contained by their colonial condition. Anticolonial methods call attention to the resistance that Indigenous peoples have always engaged in response to colonization and to the persistence of Indigenous life beyond the colonial reach. We take Calderon's observations to mean that while it is not accurate to describe all Indigenous methods as decolonizing methods (see Chapter 3, this volume), Indigenous methods do work within an anticolonial frame that pushes back against discourses that depict Indigenous peoples as (only) colonial subjects.

INDIGENOUS METHODS OF CRITICAL PLACE INQUIRY

As a result of this importance of Indigenous methods of research, in this chapter we provide in-depth discussions of six Indigenous methods of critical place inquiry. Some of the work discussed here might be more aptly described as approaches or practices rather than methods, yet we attend to them as methods that might provide guidance for other inquiry projects. The methods discussed in the following sections include Indigenous storywork, mapping place-worlds and place-making, (re)mapping, eating the landscape, urban Indigenous land-based pedagogies and community-based design research, and shellmound work. We follow with a discussion about the theoretical commitments we observe across the methods.

Indigenous Storywork

Although it does not provide an extended discussion related to place or land in research, Jo-ann Archibald's (2008) description of Indigenous storywork has major implications for Indigenous methods of critical place research. Several of the methods discussed below use elements of storytelling as core components of Indigenous inquiry, so it makes sense to us to attend to Archibald's generous depictions of what research through storytelling and storylistening, storywork, entails.

At the outset of her discussion, Archibald (2008) recalls Kirkness and Barnhardt's (1991) articulation of the four R's of Indigenous postsecondary education: respect, relevance, reciprocity, and responsibility. These are foundational aspects of Indigenous storywork (Archibald, 2008, p. 1). Archibald writes that in order to find a culturally appropriate research method, she needed to "learn about Stó:lō story principles in order to find Stó:lō story theory" (p. 36). She had a sense that telling stories might be a way to think about interviewing Indigenous research participants. She began with one conversation with an elder, Simon Baker, who allowed her to tape-record their conversation. Before transcription, before working with the storytelling as data, she listened to the tape recording twice. She wanted be sure to attend to what Baker had wanted her to learn about going to elders, listening to them, and showing them respect (p. 43). From this first storywork encounter, Archibald began to see the complexity of responsible story use.

Archibald developed a storywork research protocol that began with meeting with elders to seek permission and guidance. She sought the guidance of elders on whom to ask to participate, which stories she might ask them to tell, how to document the stories, and what might come out of the work (in terms of publication and recognition).

Archibald followed this first permission-seeking meeting with numerous additional meetings with the elders group. In the first meeting, the elders discussed what made a good storyteller, a good story, and good practices of storytelling. In the second, they discussed storytelling for children—this prompted a series of events that led to the third meeting, which focused on dilemmas regarding sacred stories. At the end of this meeting, the elders told Archibald that they "did not have any more to say about storytelling" (2008, p. 64). Two years later, Archibald returned with a draft of a chapter that detailed what she had heard in her meetings with elders. The verification process of this draft took more than one year, with lots of meetings and approval of quotations by all involved individuals.

This painstaking process reflected what was needed in order to conduct ethical and responsible research in this particular community and place. It was what was required for Archibald to learn "to make meaning from stories" (2008, p. 85). Archibald closes her book with discussions for applying and modifying her storywork method in other settings. She also shows how she and other teachers have used storywork as the basis for classroom teaching and learning with young children.

This approach to storywork connects to discussion in Chapter 5 on the role of story in relationship to place. Knowledge of place is held in stories, for example, in name-place stories. In their endurance, stories reinforce connections with people and places and suggest appropriate actions and relationships, including with land (Goeman, 2013). Discussing story as an Indigenous methodology, Kovach (2009) suggests that to privilege story in knowledge-seeking systems means honoring talk through a range of possible methods. Indigenous researchers are using storywork, conversations, interviews, research/sharing circles, and other methods of narration to enable the relation of stories in and of place.

Mapping Place-Worlds and Place-Making

In *The Common Pot: The Recovery of Native Space in the Northeast* (2008), Abenaki author Lisa Brooks provides an etymology of the Abenaki word *awikhigawôgan*, which has roots in words meaning to draw, write, and map (p. xxi). Another root of the word means instrument or tool for image making (p. xxiii). Infusing the word with Craig Womack's reminder that Indigenous uses of language are to invoke as much as evoke, with the potential to "actually cause a change in the physical universe" (Womack, 1999, p. 17), Brooks conveys *awikhigawôgan* as the activity of writing, one that is ongoing and collective.

> Even when it is complete, that instrument can cause a whole new wave of activity to occur. I am absorbed in this process, now, perhaps you are too, as you write notes to me, or to yourself, in the margins of this book or in your own awikhigan, a spiral notebook or a laptop computer. *Awikhigawôgan* is an activity in which we are all engaged. (Brooks, 2008, p. xvii)

Awikhigawôgan is at the center of the method that Brooks creates and enacts in *The Common Pot*. This is a method that maps "how Native people in the northeast used writing as an instrument to reclaim lands and reconstruct communities, but also a mapping of the *instrumental* activity of writing, its role in the rememberment of a fragmented world" (Brooks, 2008, p. xxii, emphasis original). Brooks's method is organized around the introduction of an *awikhigan*,[1] which is then expanded into the "place-world" (Basso, 1996) from which it emerged (Brooks, 2008, p. xxiii). Before we say more about what that means and looks like, we pause to attend to notions of place-worlds and place-making.

Keith Basso (1996) surmises that place-making—the (retrospective) building of place-worlds—is a profoundly human activity (p. 5). It does not require any training or specific skills, just a sense of curiosity about which most other humans are also curious: What happened here? Who was involved? What was it like (p. 5)? These are the questions at the base of place-making. Although it is prevalent and practically ubiquitous, Basso insists that the building of place-words, place-making, is not simple. Rather, the construction of place-worlds is complex, multidimensional, and "highly inventive" (p. 7).

> (R)emembering [what happened here] often provides a basis for imagining. What is remembered about a particular place—including, prominently, verbal and visual accounts of what has transpired there—guides and constrains how it will be imagined by delimiting a field of workable possibilities. These possibilities are then exploited by acts of conjecture and speculation which build upon them and go beyond them to create possibilities of a new and original sort, thus producing a fresh and expanded picture of how things might have been. (Basso, 1996, p. 5)

The building of place-worlds is collective, creative, and generative.

Brooks's employment of Basso's "place-worlds" and "place-making" echoes Basso's emphasis that within Indigenous worldviews, the *where* of events matters as much as the *what* and the consequences of the events themselves (Brooks, 2008, p. xxiii; see also Waziyatawin, 2005). Brooks's *Awikhigawôgan* method also takes guidance from Vine Deloria, Jr.'s argument in *God Is Red*, that

> (C)reation stories are actually much more concerned with geography and spatiality, "what happened here," than with chronological origins and temporality, "what happened then." The stories, he maintains, function practically and artistically as narrative maps of "an exosystem present in a definable place." (Deloria, Jr., 2003, p. 121 in Brooks, 2008, p. xxiii)

Thus, for Basso and for Brooks, building place-worlds, place-making, is also a revisionary act, a re-memory act, in which multiple pasts co-mingle and compete for resonance toward multiple futures. Building and sharing place-worlds, according to Basso (1996),

> is not only a means of reviving former times, but also of revising them, a means of exploring not merely how things have been but also, just possibly, they might have been different than what others have supposed. Augmenting and enhancing conceptions of the past, innovative place-worlds change these conceptions as well. (p. 6)

As with other Indigenous methods discussed in this chapter, place and land are not abstractions. Brooks spent much time walking the land and paddling the waterways that are featured in her book, sometimes alone, other times with friends with whom she would share and swap place-making stories. "To be clear," Brooks writes, "what I am talking about here is not an abstraction, a theorizing about a conceptual category called 'land,' or 'nature,' but a physical, actual, material relationship to an 'ecosystem present in a definable place' (2008, p. xxiv).

The chapters in *The Common Pot* are an elaboration of Brooks's *Awikhigawôgan* method. Each chapter begins with an *awikhigan*, a communicative device of some sort—a map, a photograph (of a shell, a wampum belt, or string), a birch bark scroll, a portrait, a letter—which then spills, floods, into the place-world from which it came forth and has most meaning. The chapters in the book do not have a chronological progression, but instead progress with regard to what the *awikhigan* seeks to accomplish or communicate and how this relates to the one before and after it. Brooks calls this a stylistic progression, but what it serves to do is provide a narrative that works much more like space than time. It begins somewhere, not because it happened first, but because it helps to make sense of what takes place beside it. It is its own orientation. Brooks even says, "I admit that I mean to plunk readers right in the middle of the territory and provide a map to enable navigation. (If you feel a bit disoriented, that's okay. You'll find your way. Use the maps.)" (2008, p. xi, parentheses original).

One of Brooks's most significant points is that the reader should take a participatory role in the *awikhigawôgan* process. She writes,

> Rather than tracing a single argument and forming agreement or argument, I hope you will feel free to interact, deliberate, and grapple with the images and ideas raised herein, stopping at the ends of quotations, sections, and chapters to contemplate the connections between them. My greatest aspiration is that readers will feel themselves entering a place-world and will be compelled to use their minds interactively to try to comprehend it. (2008, p. xxv)

Brooks's hope is that the *awikhigawôgan* method (using Peter Kalifornsky's words) crafts invitations to "'move into a cavity' of your mind" and "complete your complex thought" (1991, pp. 454–55, quoted in Brooks, 2008, p. xxv).

(Re)mapping

(Re)mapping (Goeman, 2013) is a Native feminist discursive method that cannot be detached from material land. Its goal is to unsettle imperial and colonial geographies by refuting how those geographies organize land, bodies, and social and political landscapes (p. 3). Recognizing that colonial geographies "enframe" state borders, assert control over state populations, and overdetermine action and contestation, (re)mapping is a refusal of the

order by disorder (L.T. Smith, 1999/2012) exerted on Indigenous life and land. (Re)mapping is

> the labor Native authors and the communities they write within and about undertake in the simultaneously metaphoric and material capacities of map making, to generate new possibilities. The framing of "re" within parenthesis connotes the fact that in (re)mapping, Native women employ traditional and new tribal stores as a means of continuation or what Gerald Vizenor aptly calls stories of survivance. (Goeman, 2013, p. 3)

Goeman's scribing of (re)mapping, with its use of parenthesis, is deliberate, a pointed way to sidestep the assumption that the past is pure, or can be brought forth into the present.

Goeman's project is to gather together exemplars of how Indigenous women have defined Indigeneity, their communities, and themselves through challenges to colonial spatial order, especially through literary mappings. Goeman does this not to embark upon a (problematic) utopian project of land recovery via "pure ideas of indigeneity" layered atop of colonial mappings. Even if Indigenous boundaries were materially and legally recognized, Goeman does not believe that this alone would sufficiently unsettle colonialism. Goeman recognizes that some element of a recovery project may be expected of a (re)mapping method:

> Recovery has a certain saliency in Native American studies; it is appealing to people who have been dispossessed materially and culturally. I contend, however, that it is also our responsibility to interrogate our ever-changing Native epistemologies that frame our understanding of land and our relationships to it and to other peoples. In this vein, (re) mapping is not just about regaining that which was lost and returning to an original and pure point in history, but instead understanding the processes that have defined our current spatialities in order to sustain vibrant Native futures. (2013, p. 3)

The task is not to recover a static past, but to "acknowledge the power of Native epistemologies in defining our moves toward spatial decolonization" (p. 4).

Goeman engages Massey's (2005) writings as providing conceptual companionship to the notions of space alive in (re)mapping. For Goeman, Massey's call to consider space as a "meeting of histories" rather than a surface upon which human activity occurs, is a useful reframing. Goeman points to Massey's articulations of three functions of space, all of which, according to Goeman, are crucial to decolonization: space as the product of interrelations, space as spheres of possibility, and space as always under construction or a simultaneity of stories so far (Massey, 2005, in Goeman, 2013, p. 6). Together these three functions of space move the discussion away from essentialism, "a common accusation made of Native scholars as we labor to maintain tribal traditions, political grounds, and our lands, in that alternative spatialities are not mired in individual liberalism, but maintain their political viability" (Goeman, 2013, p. 6). Indigenous space within a (re)mapping method always was and is in process—it has and has always had a future in which what happens now matters.

In describing a (re)mapping method, Goeman (2013) also engages McKittrick's (2006) discussion of multiscalar discourses of ownership. Multiscalar discourses of ownership include discourses of "having 'things,' owning lands, invading territories, possessing someone," all "narratives of displacement that reward and value particular forms of conquest" (McKittrick, 2006, p. 3; see also Chapter 2, this volume). Goeman's definition of (re)mapping is particular in its refusal of space as limited to constructions of property: "it is a move toward geographies that do not limit, contain, or fix the various scales of space from the body to the nation in ways that limit definitions of self and community staked out as property" (p. 11). Further,

> My intervention into the various colonial scales and my interrogation of Native women's geographies should not be read as a longing to further construct or revamp that elusive "Indian" that is propped up through racial and gender codes, nor is it a putting of Indians in place or taking them out of it temporally and geographically. Instead, I am concerned with producing decolonized spatial knowledges and attendant geographies that acknowledge colonial spatial process as ongoing but imbued with power struggles. I ask a similar question to that of aboriginal scholar Irene Watson: "Are we free to roam?" and if so, "do I remain the unsettled native, left to unsettle the settled spaces of empire?" (Watson, 2007, p. 15, in Goeman, 2013, pp. 11–12)

Using the descriptors we have used elsewhere in this book (i.e., conceptual, empirical), (re)mapping is a conceptual method, yet Goeman emphasizes the implications of (re)mapping for material *lived* space. Indeed its goal is to enact material change in Indigenous space and the space claimed by the settler colonial nation-state. In part, the method is poised to affect material land because the works engaged by Goeman (all works by Indigenous women) "assert a spatial sovereignty literally grounded in [the women authors'] relationships among land, community, and writing" (2013, p. 13).

> Unlike Western maps whose intent is often to represent the "real," Native maps often conflict, perhaps add to the story, or only tell certain parts. Stories and knowledge of certain places can belong to particular families, clans, or individuals. These maps are not absolute but instead present multiple perspectives—*as do all maps*. While narratives and

maps help construct and define worldviews, they are not determined and always open for negotiation. (Goeman, 2013, p. 25)

Eating the Landscape

Enrique Salmón (2012) discusses eating the landscape as a practice, not exactly as a method. We discuss it here alongside other Indigenous methods of critical place inquiry because although Salmón does not define it in these terms, it could be an approach taken up by other scholars and community researchers as a research method. Salmón locates the practice of eating the landscape in knowledge he learned from his Rarámuri grandmother. He describes the knowledge he learned from his grandmother and other members of his family as a "trove of culturally accumulated ecological knowledge" (p. 2). They painstakingly taught him about plants, focusing on their uses, but also on his kinship to them as individual plants. This kinship extended to the land from which the plants emerged so that when his elders taught him about the plants, "they were introducing me to my relatives" (p. 2). This provided Salmón a reverberating sense of comfort and well-being, a "sense of security that I was bound to everything around me in a reciprocal relationship" (p. 2).

Salmón, an ethnobotanist, endorses the use of stories in the practice of eating the landscape. Stories, he states,

> serve as conduits through which I can express my culture's perceptions of how the natural world developed and why it acts the way it does. The stories also provide metaphors and cultural models from which I can interpret actions and interactions between the people and the plants. (p. 13)

Salmón's practice, like the other Indigenous methods discussed in this chapter, prioritize the significance of place over time.[2] Time tangles on itself in this practice; "Food landscapes remain intact when old recipes are regenerated" (p. 9), Salmón insists. "The food itself, and the landscapes from which it emerges, remembers how it should be cooked" (p. 9). Salmón means this quite literally, referring to how food activates an "encoded memory" of how it should be grown, collected, and prepared (p. 9).

Salmón's practice begins with food; recall Brooks's (2008) method, which begins with an *awikhigan* and then extends into the place-world from which it emerged. Food in Salmón's practice plays a similar role, especially food that comes directly from land. Food is the entré to land, land that is brought into fullness through a combination of stories—some recent, others passed across generations. The stories are often stories of surprising connections between (human) individuals, histories that make themselves known in contemporary time, mistakes made by outsiders just learning to tend to the landscape, and stories that affirm the roles of planting and picking in the cosmos.

Salmón enlists Vandana Shiva's assertion that eating is a political act in order to explain the ways in which eating a landscape is more than eating. Salmón observes that a choice to eat (local, organic, processed) is a choice to support a process. More, eating the landscape is an act of social reaffirmation, enervating kinship and social relationships shared across the (dinner) table. Finally, Salmón asserts that Native agriculture serves an ontological function in Pueblo societies:

> The act of Native agriculture involves much more than knowing when to plow, how to irrigate, and at what depth to sow seed. The responsibility of growing food for one's community is connected to one's identity as a member of the community . . . Raising an ear of corn in this context is a metaphor for helping the children of community grow and survive. Farming is a performance art that reflects one's relationship to place, the cosmos, and the community. (Salmón, 2012, p. 32)

Urban Indigenous Land-Based Pedagogies and Community-Based Design Research

In 2003, two Anishinaabe grandmothers, along with a group of Anishinaabe men and women and allies, walked around Lake Superior in order to bring attention to water pollution of lakes and waterways shared by Anishinaabe, the United States, and Canada; the Great Lakes are the largest freshwater ecosystem in the world. Waters that have long been sources of life are contaminated with chemicals, emissions, and sewage disposal; water quality has been impacted by agricultural runoff and leaking landfills, and made vulnerable by increased residential development. The grandmothers and supporters walked around Lake Michigan in 2004, Lake Huron in 2005, Lake Ontario in 2006, Lake Erie in 2007, Lake Michigan in 2008, and the St. Lawrence River in 2009 (see the Mother Earth Walk Website for more information on the walks). Their walks were inspired, in part, by a prophesy offered by an Anishinaabe, that "In about 30 years, if we humans continue with our negligence, an ounce of drinking water will cost the same as an ounce of gold" (http://www.motherearthwaterwalk.com/, n.d.).

Members of the Chicago inter-tribal American Indian community participated in one of the walks more than ten years ago. Chicago was one of the original "relocation cities," a city where tribes that had been removed from their homelands, often by force, were relocated in the 1940s–1960s. Thus, Chicago's inter-tribal American Indian community includes more than 150 tribes from across North America (Bang et al., 2014). Participation in the water walks and the messages of the water walks inspired a community research project that would bring together more than one hundred Indigenous community members to design and implement innovative science learning environments for Indigenous youth and community in Chicago (Bang et al., 2014).

The project intentionally put Indigenous epistemologies and ontologies at the center; at its heart was a (re)storying of Indigenous relationships to Chicago as always was and will be Indigenous Land. To do this, it was necessary to make evident the settler colonial (il)logic of Chicago as urban and thus ceded land. Part of the work was to refuse the assumption that urban land is inherently no longer Indigenous land.

> Learning about the natural is a critical necessity given the socio-scientific realities (e.g., climate change) that are currently, and will continue to, shape the lands and life that land supports, more specifically for present purposes the lives of both Indigenous and non-Indigenous peoples. For us science education, place-based education, and environmental education are critical sites of struggle because they typically reify the epistemic, ontological, and axiological issues that have shaped Indigenous histories (Castagno & Brayboy 2008). More hopefully, we also see them as sites of potential transformings—forming a nexus between epistemologies and ontologies of land and indigenous futurity. In our view, realizing this transformative potential will require engaging with land-based perspectives and desettling (Bang et al. 2012) dynamics of settler colonialism that remain quietly buried in educational environments that engage learning about, with and in the Land and all of its dwellers. (Bang et al., 2014, p. 39)

The study was organized as a community design based research (CDBR) project and took place over six years. Co-principal investigators modified DBR, a methodological tool used to create learning environments (Brown, 1992), in order to include a broad range of community members "as the decisions makers in the design and enactment of a place-based science-learning environment" (p. 45; see also Bang et al., 2010). Facilitators created an iterative process for community members to participate in a design process that would result in the creation of out-of-school place-based science learning environments for Chicago's Indigenous youth and families. These environments, often shaped as summer programs or Saturday programs, were crafted around three enduring themes: (1) knowing Chicago as the lands of our ancestors and specifically visiting old village sites, (2) knowing Chicago as *wetlands* where many medicinal and edible plants grew and continue to grow, and (3) understanding the impacts of invasive species on these lands (Bang et al., 2014).

The method of CDBR involved "relentless efforts to story land from long views of time and experience" (Bang et al., 2014, p. 49). Project facilitators "worked to make always visible the history and change of the lands we live in, in short, land became our first teacher and our learning environments emerge from there" (p. 49). As Bang et al. explain, the choice of particular words and terms became increasingly important in that storying. The gathered consult from elders about how to explain concepts in ways that were consistent with the Indigenous epistemologies that guided the learning environments. When certain words were consistent with settler epistemologies but not with Indigenous epistemologies, they were discarded; for example, "invasive" species was not compatible with other notions of plants as relatives that were so important to discussions with children and families.

> (T)he term invasive species placed buckthorn, and other plants that were forcibly migrated to Chicago, outside our design principle around naming our plant relatives because while they may not have been *our* relatives, the term disposed them as relatives to any humans. Further, the term failed to make visible the motivation of settlers that brought flora and fauna from their homelands to make these new lands like home—or what has been termed ecological imperialism (McKinley 2007; Crosby 2004). While supporting 'border crossing' (Aikenhead 2001), meaning helping students to learn in western scientific paradigms in addition to Indigenous, did become an important focus for us, it was not where we were yet in the process, thus this insight became another specific example of the ways in which Indigenous erasure can happen in a learning environment—even when we are working hard to be mindful of settler colonialism.

Following [elder] Sarah's advice to find words to express Indian thought, "we fished around" to find a name centered in our own epistemic and ontological centers. In what we view as a form of critical border thinking, we began referring to these plants formerly named "invasive species" as "plants that people lost their relationships with" (Bang et al., 2014, p. 47).

The method of CDBR allowed project facilitators to work with community members as co-theorists in the research. Although the emphasis was always on storying in the long view, the efforts of the co-theorizing work could be observed the very next Saturday or in the shape of the summer programs. Elders, teachers, parents, and other community stakeholders worked together to create and theorize a learning space for their children and families that would allow them to always see Chicago as Native land, something that could not be un-seen later.

Shellmound Work

Chochenyo Ohlone community organizer and educator Corrina Gould says in a 2011 presentation that she began doing "shellmound work" about twelve years prior. Shellmounds have been mischaracterized by geographic historians as middens—large pre-colonial piles of discarded sea shells that have been located throughout the North American continent (Gould 2011a). The shellmounds found throughout the traditional homeland of

Ohlone peoples (the San Francisco Bay Area) are more than heaps of discarded shells; they are in fact the burial grounds of their ancestors. The dead were buried, then covered with soil, shells, and more soil, becoming larger and larger with each generation. The shellmounds ringed the Bay Area. In 1909, an archeologist at UC Berkley found more than 425 shellmounds, each of which was a burial ground that served as monument to the dead for Ohlone and Miwok peoples (Gould, 2011a).

In 1999, Gould co-founded a community organization in Oakland called Indian People Organizing for Change (IPOC) to see if there might be a community use for a recently decommissioned army base. As they began to speak with Native people in the community, they learned that what was really needed was an opportunity to speak to city council and other government leaders about projects, particularly development projects, and how they impacted Native peoples in the Bay Area. In doing this community organizing work, Gould and others were contacted by a person at the housing authority in Alameda, alerting her that in doing maintenance work beneath a home, they unearthed an Ohlone ancestor. A real-estate and development boom was underway, and Gould and other members of IPOC began to be contacted more frequently, often by contractors and developers, as development projects unearthed the remains of other Ohlone ancestors all over the region. Three hundred and sixty-six bodies were recovered in Brentwood; 13 bodies were recovered in San Jose (Gould, 2012).

One of the largest shellmounds was at the site of the proposed Emeryville Mall. It was more than 60 feet high and 350 feet in diameter—so large that it was marked on an 1852 Coast Survey Map. It was used as a navigational point of reference and took on this aspect of significance in addition to it being a sacred burial ground and memorial. The Emeryville mound held/holds the remains of thousands of Ohlone ancestors, but had been desecrated over the years by toxic dumping containing arsenic and other carcinogens. During the dotcom influx of money and development period, Emeryville was identified as a brownfield that could be cleaned up—but to clean it meant the removal of the remains of those thousands of Ohlone ancestors. Upon learning about the plans to place a shopping mall on the site, Gould and IPOC petitioned developers to halt their plans and instead create a suitable memorial to Ohlone peoples at the shellmound. The developers refused and went ahead with their plans, digging up hundreds of remains in the process. Many remains were simply hauled off to waste dumps, with no notification to Ohlone peoples (Gould, 2011a). In particular, they excavated a site where infants and children were buried in order to install the movie theaters and parking garage (Gould, 2012). Every year, IPOC organizes a protest on black Friday (the day after Thanksgiving in the United States, a big day for shopping) to educate shoppers on their participation in the continued mistreatment of sacred grounds.

Soon after, Gould and IPOC also began organizing shellmound walks to educate themselves; other Ohlone, Bay Miwok, and Indigenous peoples; and allies about the shellmounds, their locations, and the continued presence even beneath the asphalt, shopping centers, and condominiums. The first time they did a shellmound walk they used Nelson's 1909 map of the 425 shellmounds and did a three-week route of 280 miles, from Sogorea Te to San Jose, praying and learning all the way. They were joined by people from all over the world who were moved to learn and commemorate the land and the ancestors. They have completed this walk numerous times, often making different tracings across the land to visit and acknowledge each site. They also now organize shorter walks—perhaps visiting several sites in just one city—to pray and visit the shellmounds now covered by buildings, streets, and parking lots.

At the same time, IPOC has been responding to a growing issue at Sogorea Te, also known as Glen Cove, California. Sogorea Te has been known by Ohlone people and several other groups of Indigenous peoples as sacred ground since time immemorial. It was used at least in part as burial ground, but also has always been a site to gather, pray, and reflect (Gould, 2011a). In 1984, developers moved earth dug up from another site (where condominiums were being built) to Segorea Te; that earth included remains and funerary objects from more than 3,500 years ago.

In 2011, the city of Vallejo, California, waived the permits for developers to grade the land and place a parking lot and public bathroom atop of the open ground of Segorea Te. Developers refuse to admit that human remains are at Segorea Te, and before they could break ground, Gould, Wounded Knee DeOcampo, other members of IPOC, and members of the Ohlone and Miwok peoples took occupation of the sacred land. The land they are wanting to preserve includes about 15 acres along important waterways used by various tribes for trade and ceremony.

The people took occupation of Segorea Te on April 14, 2011, and stayed there through the month of July. In a press release from the occupation participants on July 20, 2011, a cultural easement and settlement agreement was announced. It said, in part,

> Yesterday, the Yocha Dehe and Cortina tribes established a cultural easement and settlement agreement with the City of Vallejo and the Greater Vallejo Recreation District (GVRD). The agreement sets a legal precedent for granting Native peoples jurisdiction over their sacred sites and ancestral lands. The cultural easement forever guarantees that the Yocha Dehe and Cortina tribes will have legal oversight in all activities taking place on the sacred burial grounds of Sogorea Te/Glen Cove. It also represents a significant step forward in enacting tribal sovereignty, as the first such easement under CA Senate Bill 18 to be negotiated at the city and recreational district levels.
>
> The agreement's terms include elimination of the formerly planned restroom facility and relocation of a downsized 2-space parking lot to an area thoroughly tested to confirm that it contains no human remains or cultural remnants.

While the specifics of the deal leave some ambiguity about how GVRD's park development project can and cannot proceed, the Committee is hopeful that Yocha Dehe and Cortina will use their newfound influence to make sure that the resting place of the ancestors is not further disturbed or desecrated.

"The cultural easement is an important victory, however we are concerned about the lack of specific language that would prevent grading on the western portion of the site," states Corrina Gould. "We will be communicating this to the tribes and we have faith that they will take all necessary measures to ensure that ancestral remains and cremations are left undisturbed."

Gould continued, "We appreciate and are humbled by the vast support that we have received in protecting our ancestors. It is our responsibility to continue to do the work to make certain that all of our sacred places are protected." (Gould, 2011b)

A closing ceremony was held on July 30, 2011, and participants and organizers were recognized and honored. In January, 2012, Corrina Gould sent this message to participants and other readers concerned with what would happen next:

Each time someone walked onto that land and paid respects to the fire, it strengthened the community as a whole. The miracle was not in just protecting the site, but in protecting each other and allowing the space to include almost anyone who came with a good heart and good intentions. Over the months that we lived together, we endured weather hardships, boredom, laughter, tears, celebrations, and disappointments. We created bonds that will stay with us forever; sometimes with people we would have never imagined being in our lives before Sogorea Te.

We were truly blessed by the ancestors, because we took a stand and because we opened our hearts and allowed a healing to happen. No one and nothing can take away these gifts. Our lives have been transformed and we can never be the same, nor should we want to be. We were all a part of something more than history; we were a part of a miracle, a complete transformation. When that sacred fire that burned for 109 days finally went out in the physical sense, it continued to burn in each of us individually. When we come together, our shared experience rekindles those flames and reminds us that we are human beings with a purpose.

Over the last few months, people have posted alarming pictures on Facebook and have written things about the desecration of Sogorea Te, stirring up great concern amongst those who hold this sacred land close to our hearts. We, the Committee to Protect Sogorea Te, have tried to look into each issue as it has arisen and want to be transparent with all of the people who involved their time and lives in protecting the land.

Some of the Committee kept watch over Sogorea Te during the early stages of GVRD's park development project, while others, including myself, didn't see what had happened to the land until October, when we were able to end the 2011 Peacewalk there.

Let us not mince words. The sight of what had been done to our beloved land was devastating. We knew when we parted ways and crossed that gate on July 31st that Sogorea Te would never look the same again. But what we saw upon returning was nothing short of getting kicked in the gut. It literally took my breath away.

We mourn what once was. We celebrated a victory in July, and yet, looking at the land now makes this victory taste bitter in my mouth. Out of all that GVRD wanted to do with the land, we only asked for three things: that they not build bathrooms, not include a 15-car parking lot, and not grade a hill that contains] burials/cremations. These are for the most part what we won.

They are not going to build a bathroom, the parking lot is only two handicap parking places and will be located adjacent to the sidewalk. We were aware that GVRD planned to take out the invasive species of plants and tear down the mansion and, yes, even put in trails. However, when I went there several weeks ago, what I saw was that the entire site had been molested. The creek is virtually exposed, all of the trees have been cut down, and, to our dismay, the grading has occurred. (Gould, 2012)

When the park opened on June 16, 2012, participants in the occupation attended the opening ceremony. They wore black t-shirts and held signs that read "No celebration for desecration." Much was accomplished, but the victories were tempered by the overdevelopment of the site.

Gould's letter from January, 2012, closes in a way that makes clear what she has taken away from the occupation of Segorea Te:

A tribal sovereign government is still a government. It is also a fact that this same tribal government allowed for the desecration of Sogorea Te in decades past and continues to make concessions to other developers, allowing desecration of other burial and sacred sites. Together we must decide what needs to be done to stop the on-going desecration of all of our sacred places.

The story of Sogorea Te is ours collectively. We each make up a part of the history that was a miracle. It is our voices that need to reach out to everyone. We stood up and led a good fight. We protected a sacred site, and, at the same time, we protected ourselves and each other. We each brought to Sogorea Te our best and became better human beings because of this experience.

We all continue to mourn not just the loss of parts of the sacred site, but also the community we created and left behind. Human beings need to be needed, and for some, this sacred place gave us a place to belong, a place that we each had worth, and a place where prayers are answered. Our ancestors continue to bless us in so many ways. (Gould, 2012)

Although it is clearly relevant to discussions of Indigenous methods of critical place research, readers may not immediately see how Corinna Gould's shellmound work can be characterized as a research method. Even though the shellmound work was not conducted by people with elite academic credentials and findings were not shared in peer-reviewed publications, the shellmound work would meet most standards in definitions of research: it generated original and useful knowledge, it was conducted systematically, and it was dispersed among a community that found it meaningful.

We included a lengthy description of this work to show that the shellmound work can and should be understood as research method, within the tradition of what Eve Tuck and Monique Guishard (2013) have called Decolonial Participatory Action Research (DPAR). DPAR "is useful in contesting the assumed legitimacy of scientifically based research, but also in generating research that is concerned with the redistribution of power, knowledge, and place, and the dismantling of settler colonialism" (Tuck & Guishard, 2013, p. 5). DPAR is conducted in and with (not on) communities, using an explicit anticolonial approach.

> Decolonial PAR is a public science, meaning it seeks to be accountable to real people, to tangible relationships, and it disbelieves the permanence of the settler-colonial nation state. In part, the project of decolonial PAR is to expose the matrices of settler colonialism, and the ways in which neoliberal logic—the most recent iteration of settler colonialism—works to undermine and dispossess the public sphere. It is to make that which is concealed apparent, and to attend to the lines of power that course through settler colonial nation-states. Decolonial PAR projects are crafted to provide participants and community members with multiple points of entry, and multiple opportunities to draw meaning, value, and action from the work. They are designed to have continuity between the research and community life, and for collaboration to move in recursive ways. Decolonial PAR is anticipatory and proactive (not reactive) with respect to ethical quandaries, and comprises an ethical framework including components of reflexivity, expertise, humility, dignity, action, and relationality. (Tuck & Guishard, 2013, pp. 16–17)

DPAR is reflexive with regard to purposes, stance, theories of change, and potential risks of action and research. It seeks to interrupt existing knowledge hierarchies, taking seriously the expertise that is derived of lived experience. It requires humility and vulnerability, contestation and creative production (see Torre & Ayala, 2009). DPAR makes space for collective work that is defined by self-determination, "in which members speak what is otherwise silenced, make transparent that which is otherwise concealed, and make meaningful that which is otherwise forgotten or devalued. There is dignity in the work of creating a space for ourselves, the kind of space that has been systematically denied to us" (Tuck & Guishard, 2013, p. 20).

DPAR is rooted in action, which takes place early and often over the course of a project. The shellmound work is an example of work that blurs the lines between method and action so that actions are pedagogical or provocative and serve as dynamic interventions to unfair practices for all contributors (Tuck, 2009a; Tuck & Guishard, 2013). Perhaps most importantly, the shellmound work was organized in a way that sidestepped making people/participants into objects by making them the subjects of research (Tuck & Guishard, 2013).

DESCRIBING INDIGENOUS METHODS OF CRITICAL PLACE INQUIRY

Coming to the end of this engagement with Indigenous methods of critical place inquiry, some questions may linger. Clearly, especially when read alongside the methods discussed in Chapter 5, the Indigenous methods that appear in these chapters resonate and reverberate with methods arising from other non-Indigenous traditions. What exactly makes these methods Indigenous methods? Are they Indigenous methods only because they have been made by Indigenous peoples for Indigenous communities? "Yes" is a first but partial answer.

These methods are distinct from other non-Indigenous methods of critical place inquiry because of the theoretical work beneath them. That is, as we get beneath the activities of research, the theories that shape them are what makes them Indigenous. As we read across these exemplars, we observe three theoretical commitments that set Indigenous methods of critical place inquiry apart from non-Indigenous methods: the role of refusals, the non-abstraction of land, and service to Indigenous sovereignty. We discuss each of these theoretical commitments in turn.

Refusal

Audra Simpson (2007) asks the following questions of her own ethnographic work with members of her Nation: "Can I do this and still come home; what am I revealing here and why? Where will this get us? Who benefits from this and why?" (p. 78). These questions force researchers to contend with the strategies of producing legitimated knowledge based on the colonization of knowledge (Tuck & Yang, 2014). Simpson's (2007) article is in many ways the backstory on her ethnography on Mohawk nationhood and citizenship and is a layered example of refusal centered in Kahnawake

Nation, within which she herself is a member. Simpson opens her article with a critique of the need to know as deeply connected to a need to conquer, a need to govern. There are three concurrent dimensions of refusal in Simpson's analysis—in Simpson's words, her ethnography "pivoted upon refusal(s)" (p. 73). The first dimension is engaged by the interviewee, who refuses to disclose further details: "I don't know what you know, or what others know . . . no-one seems to know." The second dimension is enacted by Simpson herself, who refuses to write on the personal pain and internal politics of citizenship.

> It very interesting to me that he would tell me that "he did not know" and "no one seems to know"—to me these utterances meant, "I know you know, and you know that I know I know . . . so let's just not get into this." Or, "let's just not say." So I did not say, and so I did not "get into it" with him, and I won't get into it with my readers. What I am quiet about is his predicament and my predicament and the actual stuff (the math, the clans, the mess, the misrecognitions, the confusion and the clarity)—the calculus of our predicaments. (2007, p. 77)

The interviewee performs refusal by speaking in pointedly chosen phrases to indicate a shared/common knowledge, but also an unwillingness to say more, to demarcate the limits of what might be made public, or explicit. The second dimension of refusal is in Simpson's accounting of the exchange, in which she installs limits on the intelligibility of what was at work, what was said and not said, for her readers. Simpson tells us, "in listening and shutting off the tape recorder, in situating each subject within their own shifting historical context of the present, these refusals speak volumes, because they tell us when to stop" (2007, p. 78). In short, researcher and researched refuse to fulfill the ethnographic want for a speaking subaltern. Both of these refusals reflect and constitute a third dimension—a more general anti-coloniality and insistence of sovereignty by Kahnawake Nation—and for many, a refusal to engage the logic of settler colonialism at all (see also Tuck & Yang, 2014).

As Eve Tuck has written about with K. Wayne Yang (2014), Simpson's articulations of refusal show how refusals are theoretically generative (Simpson, 2007, p. 78), are expansive. Refusal is not just a "no," but a redirection to ideas otherwise unacknowledged or unquestioned (Tuck & Yang, 2014, p. 239).

In her (re)mapping method, Goeman (2012) refuses the recovery narratives that dot the landscape of Indigenous research. She does this relentlessly, insisting that the point is not to return to some pure point of historical past (an impossible task), but instead to understand the "processes that have defined our current spatialities in order to sustain vibrant Native futures" (p. 3). (Re)mapping is an Indigenous futurity project, concerned with how what we do now makes possible evermore futures, not with recollecting a static and one dimensional past.

Bang et al.'s (2014) discussion of their CDBR project also performed a key refusal of one of the assumed goals of place-based education, to learn to live properly on (a piece of) land; they write,

> As Indigenous people, we do not need to re-inhabit or learn to dwell in the places in which we have always dwelt (see Bowers 2009). For the teachers involved in this project, the process was not about re-inhabitation—it was learning from land to restore(y) it and ourselves as original inhabitants—that is living our stories in contested lands (Somerville 2007) and restoring land as the first teacher even in 'urban' lands. Narratives in which Indigenous people are absent, or relegated to a liberal multiculturalism that subsumes Indigenous dominion to occupancy, and narratives and positionings of land as backdrop for anthropocentric life, will only help to produce new narratives of territorial acquisition and fail to bring about needed social change. (Bang et al., 2014, p. 49)

Refusal is a powerful characteristic of Indigenous methods of inquiry, pushing back against the presumed goals of knowledge production, the reach of academe, and the ethical practices that protect institutions instead of individuals and communities. Again, refusal is more than just a no; it is a generative stance situated in a critical understanding of settler colonialism and its regimes of representation (Tuck & Yang, 2014).

Non-Abstractions of Land

Another theoretical commitment that girds Indigenous methods of critical place inquiry is the non-abstraction of land, as has been discussed. Goeman (2012), Brooks (2008), Bang et al. (2014), Salmón (2012), and Gould (2011a) all emphasize that their work is concerned with generating real and lived impacts for specific groups of Indigenous peoples on specific expanses of land. Land is not a conceptual floatation device—although it could be because it figures so prominently in Indigenous literatures. Instead, each of the methods sets purposes about repatriation, rearticulation, and reclamation of Indigenous land. This land is locatable, walkable, material.

Indigenous Sovereignty

Finally (and this point is certainly related to the prior point on non-abstractions of land), Indigenous methods of critical place inquiry seek to recognize, maintain, and expand Indigenous sovereignty. This may be through practices of self-determination and decision making, establishing bases for land claims, reorganizing prior chronological tellings of land into more useful organizations that show deep and sustaining connections, or through the reimagining of land through the foods it provides. Indigenous methods of critical place inquiry take seriously the sovereignty of Indigenous tribes and communities and seek to be useful in word and action.

AMENDING THE DEFINITION OF CRITICAL PLACE INQUIRY

Taken together, the three theoretical commitments of Indigenous methods of critical place inquiry help to explain how and why incommensurabilities between Indigenous and non-Indigenous approaches may persist. Elsewhere, Eve Tuck has argued that academic disciplines that do not acknowledge and actively resist settler colonialism are bound to be invested in settler futurities, which by design cannot make space for Indigenous futurities or Black futurities (Tuck & Gaztambide-Fernández, 2013). This is not true for Indigenous futurities, which do not require the erasure of those who now participate in settler-colonial societal structures as settlers (see Chapter 3, this volume, for more on settler-colonial societal structures).

The critical intellectual tradition has not always been accountable to Indigenous peoples (Grande, 2004). The assumed social justice projects of the critical intellectual tradition compete with Indigenous justice projects related to sovereignty and decolonization (Grande, 2004; Tuck & Yang, 2012). The task of critical place inquiry is to organize itself around commitments to Indigenous sovereignty, refusal, and the non-abstraction of land—not as peripheral points or extra considerations, but as foundational to its praxis. We consider some of the shapes this might take at length in our final chapter.

NOTES

1. "*Awikhigan* is a tool for image making, for writing, for transmitting an image or idea from one mind to another, over waterways, over time" (Brooks, 2008, p. xxii).
2. To explain this, Salmón later writes that rather than a focus on heroes as in Western cultural history, Rarámuri cultural history emphasizes the landscape. "The heroes [in Rarámuri history] are the trees, plants, animals, and children. The land, plants, and people share the landscape rather than dominate it" (2012, p. 14).

7 Ethical Imperatives of Critical Place Inquiry

The foundational axiom of this book is that place is significant in social science research but is rarely treated as such. As we note in the introduction, other scholars have made this observation and argument before us[1] (Harvey, 1996; N. Smith, 1984/2008; Soja, 2010). For example, Soja's *Seeking Spatial Justice* (2010) works to show how "an assertive and explanatory spatial perspective helps us make better theoretical and practical sense of how social justice is created, maintained, and brought into questions for democratic social action" (p. 2). Soja's project is concerned with describing the "consequential spatiality" of social justice (p. 5). His approach goes further than to just

> claim that "space matters," as geographers like me have been arguing for decades. It arises more ambitiously from a deeply held belief that *whatever your interests may be, they can be significantly advanced by adopting a critical spatial perspective*. Spatial thinking in this sense cannot only enrich our understanding of almost any subject but has the added potential to extend our practical knowledge into more effective actions aimed at changing the world for the better. (Soja, 2010, p. 2, italics original)

Soja's cry to the world resonates with us—he is urging social scientists to recognize and attend to the significance of space, and to find ways to more meaningfully engage space in theory, methodology, and method. This book has traced the ways in which some, but no where near the majority of, social scientists have (knowingly or unknowingly) responded to Soja's call.

In Chapter 1, we present a discussion of some of the treatments of place that stand in the way of more earnest attendings. These include approaches that relegate place to the role of backdrop in social science research—while usually mentioning the place names of research sites (or pseudonyms for them), the ways in which places permeate identities, social contexts, or research practices, and vice versa, are left unconsidered in many studies across a range of social science fields. We discuss the ways in which the "spatial turn" has meant many more researchers are now considering how space and place influence the sites and methods of inquiry. However, there has been a dichotomizing of space and place through centering on the global mobility of the spatial realm, with some researchers suggesting that place is a static and bounded concept that is antiquated in contemporary globality. The more recent "new materialist" or "ontological turn" is also promising in its focus on materiality, and in Chapter 1, we suggest the need to develop approaches that focus on land and other species, as well as to not lose sight of political and macro considerations in analyses of materiality. We argued that scholarship across these and related trajectories of social science research needs to take place and land more seriously to do better research—because better research matters for places and for lives lived in places.

To respond to and help deepen existing treatments of place, we have used the pages of this book to articulate critical place inquiry. We forward this as an approach to place in research that is explicitly political in its intentions and ethical obligations to land, people, and other species. We theorize such an orientation to place in Chapter 2, where we suggest how places themselves can be understood as mobile, as both shaping and shaped by social practice, as interactive and dynamic, and as embedded with power relations, including those of (settler) colonialism. We also discussed how consideration of place needs to extend beyond the social to consider the land itself and its nonhuman inhabitants as they determine and manifest place. Finally, we discussed the potential politics of places enabled through such conceptualizations, including place-based politics and associated social movement building across places.

As we discussed conceptualizations of place and implications for methodologies and methods of research, we extended our definition of critical place inquiry so that it is more accountable to issues of land, sovereignty, and resistance as understood within Indigenous frameworks. We attended to this throughout the chapters of the book in discussion with non-Indigenous trajectories and approaches to critical place research, and also deepened the discussion of decolonizing considerations and conceptualizations of place in Chapter 3 and of Indigenous methods of critical place inquiry in Chapter 6.

Through these various discussions we have endeavored to outline theories, methodologies, and methods of research in relationship to one another and as forms of critical place inquiry. We hope the mapping, combining, and juxtaposing of concepts and approaches within these pages is productive for other researchers wanting to make their research more attentive and responsive to place. Yet, questions still linger about why the call for more attention to place and space has, for the most part, gone unheeded in social science? Or, put another way, why is it so easy for most social scientists to ignore place in their inquiries? This is a question that haunts as we conclude this volume.

One partial answer to the question can be traced to the roots of the Western intellectual tradition, in Descartes's (1637) cleaving of the mind from the body, and of the individual from society and nature, with the declaration "Cogito ergo sum."[2] The implications of this cleaving are countless: it separated human consciousness from the material world; it initiated a preponderance of binaries; it amplified man's dominion over the earth and its animals; it made the Western tradition simultaneously anthropocentric and removed humans from their own understandings of ecosystems. Much of the work in areas of environmental scholarship in the late twentieth century and early twenty-first century has set out to undo the epistemological consequences of Descartes's cleaving, yet, as Marcia McKenzie has observed with her colleagues, too many areas of environmental and critical research continue to maintain and perpetuate these divisions (McKenzie, Hart, Bai, & Jickling, 2009). Indigenous studies has always existed outside, perhaps in spite of, the fallout of these separations of mind from body, individual from community and place.

As discussed in the introduction, Neil Smith (1984/2008) argues that capitalism expanded an ideology of nature as separate from humanity. He writes that the "positing of nature as an external object is neither arbitrary nor accidental" (p. 15). Building on roots in the philosophies of Bacon and Newton (contemporaries of Descartes), capitalism rests on an assumption of an external, objectified nature:

> In the labor process, human beings treat natural materials as external objects of labor to be worked up as commodities. Producers put the "mechanical arts" between themselves and the objects of labor in order to increase the productiveness of the labor process, and so if science is to function as the means for developing these "mechanical arts," then it too must treat nature as an external object. (N. Smith, 1984/2008, p. 1)

Smith concludes that it is the coproduction of capitalism and science that have ideologically located humans as separate from nature, or better said to reflect the anthropocentricity of this ideology, nature as outside of humans. Continued Western embeddedness in the logics of Enlightenment rationalities of prioritizing mind over body, individual over community, humans over nature, is thus a partial answer to why place has not been more significantly taken up in social science research to date.

Another partial and related answer may be connected to the proliferation of postmodern and post-positivist theories of the late twentieth century. In focusing on the role of language in mediating social life, postmodernism and associated social theories struggled with the attendant loss of knowledge of the real and implications for understanding human identity or subjectivity, culture, and the role of research in contributing to such understandings. This enabled the interruption of linearities of modernism and positivism, as well as the dismantling of hegemonies based on essentialist understandings of identity or culture. However, with an emphasis on the discursive, or the mediated aspects of social life such as language and institutional practices, many postmodern social theories focused on epistemology at the expense of the ontological or material, emphasizing the social construction and effects of places, if considering place and land at all.

A final partial answer comes from settler colonial studies, a field that has emerged in the two decades. In posing the question, "why is it so easy for most social scientists to ignore place in their inquiries?" we are also posing the question more broadly: "why do some societies ignore place?" There is no reason to expect that Western social scientists would operate from worldviews not their own, and as outlined in the previous partial answers, the land has not been prioritized in Western thinking and practice. This is not to say that all social scientists operate within a Western intellectual tradition, but to note its influence in academe as well as in Western culture writ large. Western societies exhibit deep behaviors of ignorance toward land, water, environment, and sustainability, as evidenced in fuel extractions, agricultural practices, pollution and toxic dumping, hyperdevelopment, and water use. Of course, it is not only Western societies that exhibit these behaviors of ignorance, which are enacted in large-scale all over the globe.

Indeed, what first drew Eve Tuck to settler colonial studies was that it provided an explanation for the inability of settler societies to recognize land and water in any way that was significant enough to lead to a change in course of direction. Settler colonial studies seeks to understand the particular features of settler colonialism and how its shapes and contours of domination (such as those in the United States, Canada, Australia, Brazil, New Zealand, Israel, and Chinese Tibet) differ from other forms of coloniality. As we discuss in Chapter 3, settler colonialism is a form of colonialism in which outsiders come to make a new home on land that is already inhabited by other humans. In this form of colonialism, it is land, place, that is the ultimate pursuit, rather than extractions (spices, gold, or labor) as in other forms of colonialism.

It is interesting to note that the proliferation of settler colonial nation-states coincides with the emergence of a global North/South dynamic. Jodi Byrd (2011) argues that it was the "breakaway" speed formation of settler colonies that produced the global North. Part of the North/South dynamic is that the global North heaves the brunt of its militaristic, economic, and environmental needs on the global South. Thus, another one of the general characteristics of settler colonialism is the maintenance of "internally contradictory quagmires where human rights, equal rights, and recognitions are predicated on the very systems that propagate and maintain the dispossession of indigenous peoples for the common good of the world" (Byrd, 2011, p. xix). This is a way that settler colonialism has replicated itself as a global phenomenon.

An additional general feature of settler colonialism is that in many contexts it has simultaneously taken form as "Slave estates" (Spillers, 2003; Wilderson, 2010) requiring the forced labor of stolen peoples on stolen land. In many cases, settlement required/s the labor of chattel slaves and guest workers, who must be kept landless and estranged from their homelands (see McKittrick, 2006). Indeed, settler colonialism "works" by making Indigenous land into property, and making the bodies of slaves property, or chattel (Tuck & Yang, 2012).

Thus, settler colonialism involves a daedal arrangement of justifications and unhistories in order to deny genocide and brutality. This is what Veracini (2011) means when he writes that settler colonialism must cover its tracks, and does so by making its structuring natural, inevitable, invisible, and immutable (see also Tuck & Yang, 2012). Veracini's notion that settler colonialism must cover its tracks has major implications for how settler societies narrate themselves and their relationships to the stolen lands they occupy. Most people living in settler societies have never learned how settler colonialism differs from other forms of colonialism. In the United States, for example, school children are more likely to learn about colonialism in India (what many would characterize as a form extraction colonialism) than they are to learn about settler colonialism. People living in settler-colonial societies are unlikely to ever hear their societies described in those terms. They are even less likely to think of their societies as continuing to be organized around settler colonialism in contemporary time, not just as part of the founding story of their nation.

In Chapter 3, we discussed the ways in which settler colonialism reduces human relationships to land to relationships of an owner to property, as a crucial part of the logic of settler colonialism. Together, these two characteristics of settler colonialism—that it covers its tracks and remakes land into property—help to answer our question "why do some societies ignore place?" Settler societies are designed to not consider place—to do so would require consideration of genocide (Grande, 2004), but also ongoing displacement and dispossession. "Culture, underpinned as usual by faith, law, and revisionary history, has proven only too capable of doing what main force could not, which is to make the colonizer capable of sleeping at night or reaching across the dinner or communion table without recoiling from the sense of the blood of the 'Other' on his hands" (Findlay, 2000, p. x).

Turning towards place necessitates acknowledgement and reparations based on these histories: of (settler) colonialism, capitalism, and of Cartesian and (post)modern separations of mind from body, body from land. As humans make our planet increasingly toxic, unlivable, and at the same time increasingly inequitable, at what point might this cleavage be sewn back together, might we account for our pasts and to future generations? Are we capable of "post carbon social theories" of place (Elliot & Urry, 2010) that address ongoing obsessions with expansion and capitalism; never mind are we capable of living post carbon social lives? We believe that theorizing and practicing place more deeply is at least a step in the direction of such a path.

In the remainder of this closing chapter we discuss how the "legitimacy" or validity of social science research can be approached through critical place inquiry.

RECONFIGURING LEGITIMACY IN CRITICAL PLACE INQUIRY

Legitimacy is an integral concept/worry in all research, whether acknowledged or not. The words more often used to convey legitimacy in social science research—reliability, validity, consistency, test-retest, inter-method—have to do with inquiry being considered trustworthy. Although it refers to a distinct characteristic, the culture of social science also prefers research to be generalizable; that is, for a finding to be trustworthy and useful, what is true in one place must be true in another place. For these reasons, the notion of generalizability may work against meaningful engagement in place in social science inquiry.

One now-classic critical conception of legitimacy that is helpful in considering critical place inquiry is catalytic validity (Reason & Rowan, 1981; Lather, 1984, 1991a). Lather writes,

> Catalytic validity represents the degree to which the research process re-orients, focuses, and energizes participants toward knowing reality in order to transform it . . . The argument for catalytic validity lies not only within recognition of the reality-altering impact of the research process, but also in the desire to consciously channel this impact so that the respondents gain self-understanding and, ultimately, self-determination through research participation. (Lather, 1991a, p. 68)

Catalytic validity plays out as *meaningfulness* to communities involved in the research, and in addition, in participatory research, meaningfulness to a collective of co-researchers. Catalytic validity is an approach that attempts to invert the landscapes of meaning-making so that the foci of meaning are located in the experiences and knowledges of the community.

Catalytic validity can be intersected by Michelle Fine's concepts of *theoretical generalizability* and *provocative generalizability* (Fine, 2008, pp. 227–230). Fine's contributions confront the prevalence of large, randomized, "blind" trials in knowledge production and assert a series of turns toward thinking about what can be lifted up and listened across in deeply place-based, locally meaningful inquiries that, when mapped as counter-topographies (Katz, 2001), reveal structural, systematic dispossession, exploitation, and domination (Fine, 2008). Theoretical generalizability contends with the ways in which theory meaningfully travels from rich context to rich context, even against all odds of easy transfer. It requires what Eve Tuck, Fine, and Sarah Zeller-Berkman have identified as obligations and opportunities of jumping scale: integrity with home spaces, active respect for sovereignty, relationship, understanding competing responsibilities, and resisting homogenization (Fine, Tuck, & Zeller-Berkman, 2007).

Fine's (2008) provocative generalizability, drawing on Maxine Greene's calls to "fight the numbness of oppression,"

> refers to researchers' attempts to move their findings toward that which is not yet imagined, not yet in practice, not yet in sight. This form of generalizability offers readers an invitation to launch from our findings to what might be, rather than only understanding (or naturalizing) what is. Greene's desire for social and ethical imagination rises as a standard for social research: does the work move readers to act? (p. 229)

The intersection of catalytic validity and theoretical and provocative generalizabilities marks the potential for critical place inquiry that is both generative and iterative, expansive and seeking, but with an ethic of meaningfulness for home.

Connecting to these aims, Bronwyn Davies (2014) identifies two common yet contrasting definitions of legitimacy in social science research. The first, the one employed most often in social science research discourse, is concerned with conforming to established standards. It is conferred via design and findings that can be replicated. The second definition, which Davies says is employed in post-critical and post-realist research, is concerned with filial relationship. That is, "legitimacy comes not from obedience to prescribed rules, but from a relationship of respect and love, in which those who go before provide a horizon of possibilities that do not foreclose thought, but open it up" (Davies, 2014).[3] Taking up the idea of legitimacy as resting on a validity conferred through relationship, Davies suggests how filial relationships (of parents to children, and we would add other relationships as well) encompass elements of growth and surprise. She writes,

> Children are not necessarily obedient to their parents' rules, but can nonetheless be recognized by them and encouraged to flourish in diverse, surprising and unexpected ways, taking up what they've learned from their parents and using it elsewhere—in a move that exceeds what the parents could imagine. In such a model, "agency exceeds the power by which it is enabled" (Butler 1997: 15). Engaging in post-critical, post-realist research requires a capacity to engage creatively with the possibilities opened up by others. (p. 444)

Thus in this connotation, Davies suggests that legitimacy is conferred through the embracing of trajectories of knowing, of multiplicity, of specificity, of the intersectional, of movement. What is made possible in critical place inquiry when it is this second definition of legitimacy that provides guidance?

SO WHAT AND SO WHERE? RELATIONAL VALIDITY

Drawing from this concept of research legitimacy understood as sharing characteristics with filial relationships, as well as from understandings of the legitimacy of research based on its catalytic or provocative ability to impel action and be of use, we propose relational validity for consideration in forms of critical place inquiry. This does not entail a hierarchy of roles as might be assumed with some connotations of filial; we also expand beyond the filial to consider relational ethics more broadly. In what follows we suggest several precepts and implications of a relational approach to validity.

1) *Relational validity is based on paradigmatic understandings of the relationality of life.* Discussing the words of his father Stan Wilson (2001), Opaskwayak Cree scholar Shawn Wilson (2008) discusses the concept of self as relationship in Indigenous research. He writes,

> Identity for Indigenous peoples is grounded in their relationships with the land, with their ancestors who have returned to the land and with future generations who will come into being on the land. Rather than viewing ourselves as being *in* relationship with other people or things, we *are* the relationships that we hold and are part of. (p. 80)

Similar orientations can be found echoed in Indigenous epistemologies around the globe. Dominant Western trajectories of the past centuries have actively undermined the recognition and valuing of forms of relational knowledge and accountabilities, as has been well documented by Indigenous and feminist scholars, ethicists, and increasingly, by other domains of science, social science, and the humanities (e.g., Kawagley, 2006; L. T. Smith, 1999/2012; Barad, 2007; Ingold, 2011; Plumwood, 1993; Rowe, 1990; Cahill, 2004). Ironically, the human induced collapse of ecosystems that has been enabled through non-relational understandings of validity is functioning as a form of the earth "talking back" in ways that may compel the greater uptake of relational understandings and approaches to legitimacy in research and social life (L. T. Smith, 1999/2012). This is not at all to advocate for the collapse or assimilation of Indigenous and non-Indigenous epistemologies. Rather, it is to prioritize the reality that human life is connected to and dependent on other species and the land, and to suggest the necessity of working across differences in solidarities that share this prioritization (Grande, 2004; Gruenewald, 2003; see also Tuck & Yang, 2012, on contingent collaborations).

2) *Relational validity is based on an understanding that the prioritization of "economic validity" is harmful for people and places.* The Intergovernmental Panel on Climate Change (IPCC; 2013) indicates global temperatures have risen by 0.78 degrees Celsius since the pre-industrial period with an additional 0.7 degrees Celsius of warming already in the atmosphere even if we stopped emitting greenhouse gasses tomorrow. At our current rates of fossil fuel consumption, a 4 percent temperature increase is expected by 2100, causing circumstances such as the extinction of a third of all species and a nearly ice-free Arctic Ocean (summer minimum) by 2050, reductions in September Arctic sea ice extent between 43% and 94% (IPCC, 2013), and worldwide extreme drought conditions by 2100 (Dai, 2011), causing famine, reduced access to water, increases in climate refugees, and increased global conflict (Lynas, 2007). While only a few years ago a discourse of climate change denial was prevalent and growing (Leiserowitz, Maibach, Roser-Renouf, & Hmielowski, 2012), we have entered a new stage where it has become possible to discuss the realities of human extinction from the planet. (Sarmiento, Sean, Tola, & Hantel, 2014)

The economic, individualist, and anthropocentric paradigm of Western (post)modernism continues to expand in its current globalizing and neoliberal forms (Peck, 2013). In its global reach it binds increasing numbers of governance practices to the support of fossil fuel and other extractive industries, resulting in the neglect of a fiduciary responsibility to ensure the fulfillment of the right to clean water, air, and land. Legislation that ignores those rights and prioritizes economic growth over environmental protection and human rights is a condition of neoliberalization that increasingly operates through territory and science and technology. A clear example of this are the recent omnibus budget bills in Canada that have struck down the ability to protect these rights through environmental legislation (Land, 2013), solidifying Canada's ranking near the bottom of OECD countries in environmental protection (Waldie, 2013). Pierce (2012) discusses the mergings of government to territory and science as "biocapitalism" and suggests that what makes the union between science and neoliberal forms of governmentality constituting biocapitalism particularly dangerous are the ways in which biological life has becomes integral to economic growth in ways never before imagined. As a result, "the tensions of capitalism are being played out on a global, biospheric scale and thus implicate the future of life on earth" (Cooper, 2008, p. 49 in Pierce, 2012, p. 24). This is an economic paradigm that banks its future on scientific and technological advances designed to capitalize on forms of life (Pierce, 2012).

Biocapitalism thus functions as neocolonialism in much of the world, for example, in exploitive and damaging Canadian mining operations in countries around the world, as well as in maintaining settler colonialism in nations such as Canada and the United States, as territory continues to be the site of exploitation, assimilation, and abuse. The conditions of exploitative relations to land already most influence Indigenous peoples, people of color, rural communities, the poor, people in the Global South, and other populations who are on the receiving end of a disproportionate amount of the social and environmental harms perpetuated through extractive and other polluting industries, and things are only going to get worse (Agyeman, Cole, Delay, & O'Riley, 2009; Walker, 2012). Climate change induced extreme weather events such as flooding and hurricanes, health impacts through disease and climate-related illness, the location of nuclear and other waste, and a range of other circumstances are already perpetuating massive climate and environmental injustices, including loss of life, that most affect already marginalized populations and regions (Klein & Simpson, 2013; Walker, 2012).

There are also interspecies implications of the abuses of fracking, oil spills, chemical pollutants, climate change, nuclear reactor fallout, nuclear waste storage, plastic ingestion, industrial agriculture practices, genetic modification of foods, animal testing, and other associated issues. These impacts have increasingly been documented by science; research is conclusive in indicating unprecedented human impact on not only other animals and plants, but also on the geological characteristics of the planet itself (Palsson et al., 2013). Some areas of social science, such as critical animal studies or education (e.g., Best, 2009; Kahn, 2010), have prioritized these discussions, but in many areas of social science anthropocentrist underpinnings result in continued assumptions that a focus in social science research on other species is "flaky" and/or limited to the purview of white environmentalists (Gosline & Teelucksingh, 2008).

3) *Relational validity implies that research is not only about understanding or chronicling the relationality of life and the inadequacy of economic validity, but also that research necessarily influences these conditions in small or significant ways; it thus impels action and increased accountability to people and place.* Because no action *is* an action, and because not acting has implications, a more adequate response is required to current and future injustices. An important aspect of critical place inquiry is accountability to community, as discussed in Chapter 5 on research methods. This entails research that is conducted in and with community, not on communities (Tuck & Guishard, 2013). This includes following ethical protocols of engaging with Indigenous communities in research on Indigenous land (L. T. Smith, 1999/2012). As Barad writes,

> Responsibility, then, is a matter of the ability to respond. Listening for the response of the other and an obligation to the other,

who is not entirely separate from what we call the self. This way of thinking ontology, epistemology, and ethics together makes for a world that is always already an ethical matter. (Barad in Dolphijn & van der Tuin, 2012, p. 69)

We close the book by turning to look at points of inspiration and consideration for relational ethics on the ground.

CONCLUSION: RELATIONAL VALIDITY IN ETHICAL PRACTICE

Research ethics that promote and safeguard relational validity shift focus away from the linear procedural considerations of risk, benefit, and signatures of informed consent that now characterize the discourse on ethics of social science toward ecological considerations of mutual benefit, honoring, recognition, and the long view. Much of what is now included in discussions of research ethics and in graduate courses on ethical conduct is concerned with protecting the institution from accusations of mistreatment. Many of the institutional provisions for protecting human subjects arose from egregious abuses of trust, authority, and humanity; existing ethical considerations are reactive rather than proactive with regard to envisioning what might comprise respectful and meaningful research conduct (see also Tuck & Guishard, 2013, on decentering the Institutional Review Board (IRB) as the arbiter of research conducted with humans).

Centering relational validity in ethical practice is not an easy thing to do. The culture of academe is not ideal for the cultivation of an ethical practice based on relational validity; existing research protocol review processes, professional benchmarks like tenure and promotion, and funding timelines may indeed work against the cultivation of relational ethics. Inquiry based on relational validity must take inspiration from different sources than the application forms required by IRBs or Human Research Ethics Boards (HREBs). It is important that institutional approval is obtained, but it cannot comprise the entirety of one's consideration of ethical practice. Instead, in this section we offer some emerging (and sometimes challenging) points of inspiration.

At the Saskatchewan Citizens' Hearings on Climate Change in November 2013, Marcia McKenzie listened to 34 speakers over two days speak to the existing and expected impacts of climate change on the lives and ecosystems of local communities. Included were presentations on the impacts of climate change on agriculture and water security, and possible approaches to adaptation, on engineering and policy solutions to reduce greenhouse gas (GHG) emissions, and on the impacts of climate change and tar sands extraction on First Nations and Métis communities. Speakers from across sectors and perspectives powerfully brought home the human, interspecies, and land-based impacts of climate change, and the alliances between oil and state that are working against transitions to feasible alternative energy systems (e.g., see Höhne, van Breevoort, Deng, Larkin, & Hänsel, 2013, on how we could phase out GHG emissions by mid-century). A closing talk by Christian Holz of Climate Action Network Canada (2014) emphasized that reducing GHG emissions requires the separation of oil and state and that effort needs to focus on exposing the current links between the two: "We need to build an alliance which can say, 'we need system change, not climate change.' " As Holz indicated, and as described in earlier sections of the book, this is not a technical problem; it is a problem of capitalism.

Holz (2013) highlighted three dimensions of injustice wrought by climate change: the inequities associated with global environmental change (e.g., disproportionate impacts on Global South and on Indigenous communities), interspecies injustice (i.e., the effects on other species and the land), and intergenerational injustice (i.e., the effects on future generations). We have used these categories to organize the following discussion of emerging and challenging points of inspiration as ethical obligations of research to people across places, to land, and to future generations. In summary, as Holz (2013) said, "we need to put human life before economic growth; mother earth before corporate success; people before profit, because that is what is necessary for people's survival in our children and grandchildren's generations."

To People across Places

Tatek Abebe (2009) observes that research ethics/ethical protocols emerging from the global North involve standard practices that are difficult or even perhaps absurd to apply elsewhere. "Different geographies demand different and reflexive ways of negotiating roles and ethical spaces" (p. 462). From Abebe, we learn that ethical practices must be place-specific, place-responsive, place-resonant. This is true not only because of the fluidity of inquiry and its likelihood to flow in unanticipated directions (part of what makes inquiry worth doing), but also because universalized ethical guidelines (read: those developed in the global North) can never do enough to both protect safety and dignity, and to promote meaningful interactions, in all places.

In Chapter 2 we discussed conceptualizations of power and place (pp. 35–40), attending to ways in which spatial organizations give coherence and rationality to maldistributions of power and resources (McKittrick, 2006; see also Fortmann, 1995), geographic processes that result in what David Harvey (2003) has called accumulation by dispossession. The mistake made by many sociologists and other social scientists, according to Connell (2007), is twofold: they neglect to see the configuration of the metropole in the coproduction of globalization, and they see globalization as both economic strategy and ontology (pp. 51–52). These slippages—thinking that the metropole is the whole, thinking that globalization is complete—obscure the vantage point of social scientists from seeing the disproportionate burdens of globalization on the global South and on the Indigenous world;

indeed, they prevent social science from being able to observe the global politics of accumulation by dispossession. Thus, a relational obligation to place would include a robust analysis of the metropole; at the same time it remembers that globalization—like neoliberalism, like settler colonialism—is always an already incomplete process because of the ongoing, even banal, resistance of everyday people and because of the vitality of other ways of being that persist.

Beyond this point, recently, there has been a cluster of scholarship and public critique about the notion of solidarity, which might otherwise seem like an appealing vernacular for researchers wishing to engage relational validity. The twitter hashtag #solidarityisforwhitewomen, coined in 2013 by feminist of color blogger Mikki Kendall to critique actions by white feminists (and the rantings of one self-labeled "male feminist" in particular[4]) quickly prompted thousands of tweets from all over the ethernet, featuring apt, often funny, often cutting hypocrisies amid white feminism and cisgender roles, but also the project of solidarity itself. As the hashtag trended globally in August 2013, tweets sliced open the ways in which solidarity offers a false promise across unevenly powered locations. Rubén Gaztambide-Fernández (2012) offered a critique of solidarity for its tendency to reinscribe settler colonial logics and absolve those who benefit from settler structures of their complicity in ongoing settlement (see also Mohanty, 2003).

Writing with K. Wayne Yang about decolonization, Eve Tuck has advocated for the notion of contingent collaborations over the false promises of solidarity (2012). Contingent collaborations are those temporary partnerships that are organized not by sameness, but an

> ethic of incommensurability, which recognizes what is distinct, what is sovereign for project(s) of decolonization in relation to human and civil rights based social justice projects. There are portions of these projects that simply cannot speak to one another, cannot be aligned or allied. [In some cases there are only] opportunities for what can only ever be strategic and contingent collaborations, [because forming] lasting solidarities may be elusive, even undesirable. (Tuck & Yang, 2012, pp. 28–29)

A relational ethics that is accountable to place sees what can be problematic about promises of solidarity, and instead seeks to establish contingent collaborations based on shared aims and visions.

A third useful idea when considering a relational ethics to place is the notion of mutual implication. Mutual implication, or *nos-otras*, is a way of describing how the colonized and the colonizer, the oppressor and the oppressed "'leak' into each other's lives" (Torre & Ayala, 2009, p. 390, citing Anzaldúa, 1987) after centuries of contact. Fine (1994) writes that much of qualitative research has reproduced a colonizing discourse of the Other. The hyphen, she says, is where self-Other join, that which both separates and merges personal identities with our inventions of Others. Working the hyphen, then, for Fine, means that researchers probe how we are in relation to the contexts we study and with our informants, understanding that we are all multiple in those relations (p. 72). Working the hyphen means to unravel, critically, the blurred boundaries in our relation, and in our texts; to understand the political work of our narratives; to decipher how the traditions of social science serve to inscribe; and to imagine how our practice can be transformed to resist acts of othering (p. 75).

Alison Jones and Kuni Jenkins (2008), theorizing the hyphen in the context of settler colonialism in New Zealand, observe that "the hyphen between coloniser-indigene always and necessarily reaches back into our shared past" (p. 473). "Research in any colonized setting," they continue, is a

> struggle between interests, and between ways of knowing and ways of resisting, and we attempt to create a research and writing relationship based on that tension, not on its erasure. Indeed, we seek to extend the tension, and examine its possibilities. In doing this, we cautiously reject the usual suggestion that indigene-coloniser/settler research relationships should be based in 'mutual sharing', or 'understanding', or even collaboration when understood in such terms. These injunctions can be understood as calling on certain postures of empathetic relating which aim at *dissolving, softening* or *erasing* the hyphen, seen as a barrier to cross-cultural engagement and collaboration. (p. 475)

Thus, when Maria Torre and Jennifer Ayala (2009) theorize the hyphenated relationship of *nos-otras*, Anzaldúa's term, they theorize nos-otras not as mutual sharing, but as mutual implication. Torre and Ayala engage Anzaldúa's hyphen, nos-otras, as a marker of the ways in which the colonized and colonizers have leaked into each others' lives, creating a "geography of hybrid selves" (2009, p. 390, building from Anzaldúa's language). Torre and Ayala observe that mutual implication requires social science research design that seeks "knowledge *entremundos,* between the cracks of multiple experiences, underscoring relationship and interdependence" (2009, p. 391).

To Land

Included in such a relational, dialogical ethics are broadened understandings of who and what needs protection through ethics protocols. In work with Malia Villegas (forthcoming), Eve Tuck developed a set of recommendations for ethical and responsible research on Indigenous land that disrupt anthropocentric norms of many ethics review boards. They write,

> We have framed these recommendations in terms of research on Indigenous land to include not only research on and with Indigenous communities, but also on Indigenous human remains and human tissue;

our sacred places, flora, and fauna; our stories, histories, literature and art; our knowledge and knowledge systems; and data, including test scores, graduation rates, birth and mortality rates, employment rates, and other life outcomes. The guidelines apply to evaluations of institutions, programs, and curricula.

We appreciate that much of research is currently divided between research involving human subjects, and research that does not involve human subjects. Our guidelines apply to both sides of this divide because we contend that it is a false divide. This divide does not apply to how we understand the relationships between people, flora, fauna, and place. They emerge from a belief in the power of life in all its forms; and a recognition that human concerns and benefits must be balanced with the concerns and benefits of other life. (Tuck & Villegas, forthcoming)

This emergent articulation of a relational orientation to research expands the range of materials requiring approval from tribes and institutions in order to recognize the consequences of research on human tissue, literature, and graduation rates for Indigenous futurities. The statement cites the problematic practices and assumptions of prior generations of researchers in order to call for an elevated set of considerations and ethical obligations. It speaks to concerns for interspecies justice, for land justice, for justice that reflects the cosmological understandings of a particular place and people. It suggests the need for different forms of community-based and institution-based protocols for social science inquiry that better take into consideration accountability to land and interspecies justice (Elliot & Urry, 2010).

To Future Generations

Taking relationality as a premise of life and research, and recognizing the perpetuation of harms in and of place, relational validity requires reparations and repatriations based on these histories and current contexts as well as accountabilities to the future. The notion of futurity is distinct from the notion of future because futurity includes how current practices shape and make possible the future (Tuck & Gaztambide-Fernández, 2013). Thus, a relational ethics to future generations would de-center a settler futurity because settler futurities depend on the remaking of land and life into property and because settler futurities foreclose all others. There are other futurities to consider and enact. There are also very present concerns related to the futurities of (drinkable) water, water salination and temperature, soil contamination and overproduction, shrinking shorelines, and the reduction of important pollinating species (such as honeybees) and species of cultural significance. These imminent concerns require immediate and sustained action.

In Chapter 3, we briefly discuss the late 2013 events at Elsipogtog, part of Mi'gmaw land. At Elsipogtog, Mi'kmaq resistors to fracking have been attacked with dogs and tear gas by Royal Canadian Mounted Police, shot with rubber bullets, and arrested for defending their land and expressing their outrage over fracking, but also the overall dispossession of Indigenous peoples from their homelands. Most of the Mi'kmaq protesters are grandmothers and mothers carrying drums and feathers.

The protests at Elsipogtog are taking place within the broader political and environmental movement Idle No More, and during a wider conversation about reconciliation between the Canada nation-state and First Nations peoples. Yellowknives Dene scholar Glen Coulthard has been a vocal critic of the project of reconciliation, and observes,

> What the recent actions of the Mi'kmaq land and water defenders at Elsipogtog demonstrate is that direct actions in the form of Indigenous blockades are both a negation and an affirmation. They are a crucial act of negation insofar as they seek to impede or block the flow of resources currently being transported from oil and gas fields, refineries, lumber mills, mining operations, and hydro-electric facilities located on the dispossessed lands of Indigenous nations to international markets. These forms of direct action, in other words, seek to negatively impact the economic infrastructure that is core to the colonial accumulation of capital in settler political economies like Canada's. Blocking access to this critical infrastructure has historically been quite effective in forging short-term gains for Indigenous communities. Over the last couple of decades, however, state and corporate powers have also become quite skilled at recuperating the losses incurred as a result of Indigenous peoples' resistance by drawing our leaders off the land and into negotiations where the terms are always set by and in the interests of settler capital. (Coulthard, 2013, n.p.)

The very terms of change, the most effective paths, the opportunities to secure not just a future but a futurity that makes possible the well-being of the next generations, are dramatically shifting. We are indeed at a threshold, one that separates the current unsustainable time-space practices of uneven development, settler colonialism, late capitalism, and environmental degradations from a still yet-to-be defined set of time-space practices. Will they be practices of desperation? More scarcity? More fear? Will they be practices of recovery? Of resuscitation? These are questions that the next generation will answer if we don't. Doreen Massey (2005) expresses the urgency of place this way:

> What is special about place is not some romance of a pre-given collective identity or of the eternity of the hills. Rather, what is special about place is precisely that throwntogetherness, the unavoidable challenge of negotiating a here-and-now (itself drawing on a history and a geography of thens and theres); and a negotiation which must take place

within and between both human and nonhuman. This in no way denies a sense of wonder: what could be more stirring than walking the high fells in the knowledge of the history and the geography that has made them here today. This is the event of place. (Massey, 2005, p. 140)

This prompts us to consider as researchers, how we are contributing to place as event through our research. Leanne Simpson writes of the mothers and grandmothers protesting at Elsipogtog: "Our bodies should be on the land so that our grandchildren have something left to stand upon" (Klein & Simpson, 2013, n.p.).[5] To make our bodies, to make our work, to make our questions be on the land so that our grandchildren have something left to stand upon is our call. If we don't answer it, the next generation will.

NOTES

1. Massey acknowledges that less attention has been paid attention to space than time in social sciences, but her response is not to advocate for the prioritization of space over time. Instead, her project is concerned with the ways in which space is imagined (2005, p. 18).
2. Benedict Spinoza as early as 1677 refused this cleaving, insisting repeatedly that the mind and the body are the same thing (Dolphijn & van der Tuin, 2012, p. 94).
3. Davies (2014) sidesteps the problematics of an understanding of filial legitimacy as resting on whether a child is born in or out of "wedlock."
4. See http://www.huffingtonpost.com/2013/08/13/solidarityisforwhitewomen-creator-mikki-kendal-women-of-color-feminism-_n_3749589.html
5. See also Chapter 3.

Author Biographies

Eve Tuck is an Associate Professor of Educational Foundations and Coordinator of Native American Studies at State University of New York at New Paltz. Her publications are concerned with the ethics of social science research and educational research, Indigenous social and political thought, decolonizing research methodologies and theories of change, and the lived and placed consequences of settler colonialism and neoliberalism. She is the author of *Urban Youth and School Pushout: Gateways, Getaways, and the GED* (Routledge, 2012), co-editor with K. Wayne Yang of *Youth Resistance Research and Theories of Change* (Routledge, 2014), and co-author of *Theory and Educational Research: Toward Critical Social Explanation* (Routledge, 2009) with Jean Anyon, Michael Dumas, Darla Linville, Kathleen Nolan, Madeline Perez, and Jen Weiss. With Kate McCoy and Marcia McKenzie, she is co-editor of a special issue of *Environmental Education Research* (2014) titled "Land education: Indigenous, postcolonial, and decolonizing perspectives on place and environmental education research."

Marcia McKenzie is an Associate Professor in the Department of Educational Foundations and Director of the Sustainability Education Research Institute at the University of Saskatchewan (www.seri.usask.ca). She is principal investigator on two SSHRC-funded projects: the Sustainability and Education Policy Network (www.sepn.ca) and the Digital Media Project: Youth Making Place. Her interdisciplinary research focuses on the intersections of environment and critical education, educational policy and practice, youth identity and place, and the politics of social science research. She is co-editor of *Fields of Green: Restorying Culture, Environment, and Education* (2009).

References

Abebe, T. (2009). Begging as a livelihood pathway of street children in Addis Ababa. *Forum for Development Studies, 36*(2), 275–300.

Aberley, D. (Ed.). (1993). *Boundaries of home: Mapping for local empowerment.* Gabriola Island, BC: New Society Publishers.

Abrams, L. (2010). *Oral history theory.* London: Routledge.

Alfred, T. (2013, November 19). What does the land mean to us? [Weblog article]. Indigenous Nationhood Movement Weblog. Retrieved from http://nationsrising.org/what-does-the-land-mean-to-us/

Agnew, J. (2005). Sovereignty regimes: territoriality and state authority in contemporary world politics. *Annals of the Association of American Geographers, 95*(2), 437–461.

Agnew, J. (2011). Space and place. In J.A. Agnew & D. Livingstone (Eds.), *Sage handbook of geographical knowledge.* London: SAGE.

Agnew, J.A. (Ed.). (2003). *Geopolitics: Re-visioning world politics.* London: SAGE.

Agrawal, A. (2002). *Indigenous knowledge and the politics of classification.* Oxford: Blackwell.

Agyeman, J., Cole, P., Delay, R.H., & O'Riley, P. (Eds.). (2009). *Speaking for ourselves: Environmental justice in Canada.* Toronto: UBC Press.

Aikenhead, G. (2001). Integrating western and Aboriginal sciences: Cross-cultural science teaching. *Research in Science Teaching, 31*(3), 337–355.

Alexander, C., Beale, N., Kesby, M., Kindon, S., McMillan, J., Pain, R., & Ziegler, F. (2007). Participatory diagramming: A critical view from North East England. In S. Kingdon, R. Pain, & M. Kesby (Eds.), *Participatory action research approaches and methods: Connecting people, participation and place* (pp. 112–121). London: Routledge.

Amsden, J., & VanWynsberghe, R. (2005). Community mapping as a research tool with youth. *Action Research, 3*(4), 357–381.

Anderson, B., & Harrison, P. (Eds.). (2010). *Taking-place: Non-representational theories and geography.* Farnham, UK: Ashgate.

Anderson, J. (Ed.). (2010). *Understanding cultural geography: Places and traces.* London: Routledge.

Anderson, J., & Jones, K. (2009). The difference that place makes to methodology: uncovering the 'lived space' of young people's spatial practices. *Children's geographies, 7*(3), 291–303.

Anzaldúa, G. (1987). *Borderlands/La Frontera: The new Mestiza.* San Francisco, CA: Aunt Lute Books.

Appadurai, A. (Ed.). (1986). *The social life of things: Commodities in cultural perspective.* Cambridge, UK: Cambridge University Press.

Appadurai, A. (1996). *Modernity at large: Cultural dimensions of globalization.* Minneapolis: University of Minnesota Press.

Archibald, J. (2008). *Indigenous storywork: Educating the heart, mind, body, and spirit.* Vancouver, BC: UBC Press.

Arvin, M., Tuck, E., & Morrill, A. (2013). Decolonizing feminism: Challenging connections between settler colonialism and heteropatriarchy. *Feminist Formations, 25*(1), 8–34.

Augé, M. (1995). *Non-places: Introduction to an anthropology of supermodernity.* London: Verso.

Bakhtin, M. (1981). *The dialogic imagination: Four essays.* Austin: University of Texas Press.

Baldwin, A. (2012).Whiteness and futurity: Towards a research agenda. *Progress in Human Geography, 36*(2), 172–187.

Ball, S. (2012). *Networks, new governance and education.* Bristol, UK: Policy Press.

Bang, M., Curley, L., Kessel, A., Marin, A., Suzukovich, E., & Strack, G. (2014). Muskrat theories, tobacco in the streets, and living Chicago as Indigenous land. In K. McCoy, E. Tuck, & M. McKenzie (Eds.), Special issue on land education: Indigenous, postcolonial, and decolonizing perspectives on place and environmental education research, *Environmental Education Research,* 37–55.

Bang, M., Medin, D., Washinawatok, K., & Chapman, S. 2010. Innovations in Culturally- based Science Education through Partnerships and Community. In *New science of learning: Cognition, computers and collaboration in education,* 569–592. New York: Springer.

Barad, K. (2007). *Meeting the universe halfway: Quantum physics and the entanglement of matter and meaning.* Durham, NC: Duke University Press.

Barker, J. (Ed.). (2005). *Sovereignty matters: Locations of contestation and possibility in Indigenous struggles for self-determination.* Lincoln: University of Nebraska Press.

Barrera, J. (2013, March 26). Journey of Nishiyuu walker's names now "etched" into "history of this country." Aboriginal Peoples Television Network National News. Last accessed December 9, 2013, at http://aptn.ca/pages/news/2013/03/26/journey-of-nishiyuu-walkers-names-now-etched-into-history-of-this-country.

Basso, K.H. (1996). *Wisdom sits in places: Landscape and language among the western Apache.* Albuquerque: University of New Mexico Press.

Belmessous, S. (Eds.). (2012). *Native claims: Indigenous law against empire, 1500–1920.* New York: Oxford University Press.

Béneker, T., Sanders, R., Tani, S., & Taylor, L. (2010). Picturing the city: Young people's representations of urban environments. *Children's Geographies, 8*(2), 123–140.

Bennett, J. (2001). *The enchantment of modern life: Attachments, crossings, and ethics.* Princeton, NJ: Princeton University Press.

Bennett, J. (2010a). A vital stopover on the way to a new materialism. In D. Coole & S. Frost (Eds.), *New materialisms: Ontology, agency and politics* (pp. 47–69). Durham, NC: Duke University Press.

Bennett, J. (2010b). *Vibrant matter: A political ecology of things.* Durham, NC: Duke University Press.

Best, S. (2009). The rise of critical animal studies: Putting theory into action and animal liberation into higher education. *Journal for Critical Animal Studies, VII*(1), 9–52.

Billick, I., & Price, M.V. (2010). *The ecology of place: Contributions of place-based research to ecological understanding.* Chicago, IL: University of Chicago Press.

Bird, S. E. (1996). Introduction: Constructing the Indian, 1830s–1990s. In S.E. Bird (Ed.), *Dressing in feathers: The construction of the Indian in American popular culture* (pp. 1–12). Boulder, CO: Westview Press.

Bird, S.E. (2002). It makes sense to us : Cultural identity in local legends of place. *Journal of Contemporary Ethnography, 31,* 519–547.

Black, D.J. (2012). Native authenticity, rhetorical circulation, and neocolonial decay: The case of Chief Seattle's controversial speech. *Rhetoric & Public Affairs, 15*(4), 635–645.

Borgatti, S. P., & Halgin, D. S. (2011). On network theory. *Organization Science*, 22(5), 1168–1181.

Borgatti, S. P., Mehra, A., Brass, D. J., & Labianca, G. (2009). Network analysis in the social sciences. *Science*, 323, 892–895.

Bourdieu, P. (1990). *The logic of practice*. Redwood City, CA: Stanford University Press.

Bowers, C. A. (2009). *Educating for an ecologically sustainable future: The conceptual basis for reforming teacher education and curriculum Studies*. CA Bowers.

Boym, S. (2001). *The future of nostalgia*. New York: Basic Books.

Braun, B., & Whatmore, S. (Eds.). (2010). *Political matter: Technoscience, democracy, and public life*. Minneapolis: University of Minnesota Press.

Brennan-Horley, C., Luckman, S., Gibson, C., & Willoughby-Smith, J. (2010). GIS, ethnography, and cultural research: Putting maps back into ethnographic mapping. *The Information Society*, 26(2), 92–103.

Brooks, L. (2008). *The common pot: The recovery of native space in the northeast*. Minneapolis: University of Minnesota Press.

Brown, A. L. 1992. Design experiments: Theoretical and methodological challenges in creating complex interventions in classroom settings. *The Journal of the Learning Sciences*, 2(2), 141–178.

Bruyneel, K. (2007). *The third space of sovereignty: The postcolonial politics of U.S.-indigenous relations*. Minneapolis: University of Minnesota Press.

Bryant, L. R., Srnicek, N., & Harman, G. (2011). *The speculative turn: Continental materialism and realism*. Melbourne, Australia: Re.Press.

Burkhart, B. Y. 2004. What Coyote and Thales can teach us: An outline of American Indian epistemology. In A. Waters (Ed.), *American Indian thought: Philosophical essays* (pp. 15–26). Malden, MA: Blackwell Publishing.

Burns, O. M., & Smith, A. B. (2011). Editors' introduction. Cosmos and History. *The Journal of National and Social Philosophy*, 7(1), 1–6.

Butler, J. (1997). *The psychic life of power*. Stanford: Stanford University Press.

Byrd, J. (2011). *The transit of empire: Indigenous critiques of colonialism*. Minneapolis: University of Minnesota Press.

Cahill, C. (2004). Defying gravity? Raising consciousness through collective research. *Children's Geographies*, 2(2), 273–286.

Cahill, C. (2007). Doing research with young people: Participatory research and the rituals of collective work. *Children's Geographies*, 5(3), 297–312.

Cajete, G. (Ed.). (1994). *Look to the mountain: An ecology of indigenous education*. Durango, CO: Kivaki Press.

Cajete, G. (1999). *Native science: Natural laws of interdependence*. Santa Fe, NM: Clear Light Books.

Cajete, G. (2000). Indigenous knowledge: The pueblo metaphor of Indigenous education. In M. Battiste (Ed.), *Reclaiming indigenous voice and vision*. Vancouver, BC: UBS Press.

Calderon, D. (2014). Speaking back to manifest destinies: A land education-based approach to critical curriculum inquiry. In K. McCoy, E. Tuck, & M. McKenzie (Eds.), Special issue on land education: Indigenous, postcolonial, and decolonizing perspectives on place and environmental education research, *Environmental Education Research*, 20(1), 24–36.

Carr, W., & Kemmis, S. (1986). *Becoming critical: Education, knowledge, and action research*. London: Falmer.

Carspecken, P. F. (1995). *Critical ethnography in educational research: A theoretical and practical guide*. London: Routledge.

Casey, E. S. (Ed.). (2009). *Getting back into place: Toward a renewed understanding of the place-world*. Bloomington: Indiana University Press.

Castagno, A., & Brayboy, B. M. J. (2008). Culturally responsive schooling for indigenous youth: A review of the literature. *Review of Educational Research*, 78(4), 941–993.

Castree, N. (2007). *Neoliberal environments: A framework for analysis*. Manchester: Centre for the Study of Political Economy, Manchester University. [Online]. Retrieved From: http://www.socialsciences.manchester.ac.uk/PEI/publications/wp/documents/Castree.pdf

Cele, S. (2006). *Communicating place: Methods for understanding children's experiences of place*. Stockholm, Sweden: Acta Universitatis Stockholmiensis.

Chamberlin, J. E. (2004). *If this is your land, where are your stories? Reimagining home and sacred space*. Cleveland, OH: Pilgrim Press.

Chamberlin, J. E. (2001). From hand to mouth: The postcolonial politics or oral and written traditions. In M. Battiste (Ed.), *Reclaiming Indigenous Voice and Vision* (pp. 124–141). Vancouver: UBC Press.

Chawla, L. (2007). Childhood experiences associated with care for the natural world: A theoretical framework for empirical results. *Children, Youth and Environments, 17*(4), 144–170.

Chilisa, B. (2011). *Indigenous research methodologies*. London: SAGE.

Cieri, M., & McCauley, R. (2007). Participatory theatre: 'Creating a source for staging an example' in the USA. In S. Kindon, R. Pain, & M. Kesby (Eds.), *Participatory action research approaches and methods: Connecting people, participation and place* (pp. 141–149). London: Routledge.

Clandinin, D. J., & Rosiek, J. (2007). Mapping a landscape of narrative inquiry: Borderland spaces and tensions. *Handbook of narrative inquiry: Mapping a methodology, 35–75.*

Clifford, J., & Marcus, G. E. (Eds.). (1986). *Writing culture: The poetics and politics of ethnography*. Berkeley: University of California Press.

Coleman, S., & Collins, P. J. (Eds.). (2006). *Locating the field: Space, place and context in anthropology*. ASA Monographs Series. Oxford: Berg.

Collin, M. (2007). *The time of the rebels: Youth resistance movements and 21st century revolutions*. London: Serpent's Tail.

Connell, R. (2007). *Southern theory: The global dynamics of knowledge in social science*. Sydney: Allen & Unwin Australia; Cambridge: Polity Press.

Cooke, B., & Kothari, U. (2001). *Participation: The new tyranny?* London: Zed Books.

Coole, D., & Frost, S. (Eds.). (2010). *New materialisms: Ontology, agency and politics*. Durham, NC: Duke University Press.

Cooper, M. (2008). *Life as surplus: Biotechnology and capitalism in the neoliberal era*. Seattle: University of Washington Press.

Coulthard, G. (2013, November 5). For our nations to live, capitalism must die. *Voices Rising*. Retrieved November 25, 2013, from http://nationsrising.org/for-our-nations-to-live-capitalism-must-die/

Coulthard, G. S. (2007). Subjects of empire: Indigenous peoples and the 'politics of recognition' in Canada. *Contemporary Political Theory, 6*(4), 437–460.

Creswell, J. W. (1994). *Research design*. Thousand Oaks, CA: SAGE.

Cresswell, T. (2003). Landscape and the obliteration of practice. In K. Anderson, M. Domosh, S. Pile, & N. Thrift (Eds.), *Handbook of cultural geography* (pp. 269–280). London: SAGE.

Cresswell, T. (2004). *Place: A short introduction*. Malden, MA: Blackwell.

Cresswell, T., & Merriman, P. (2013). *Geographies of mobilities: Practices, spaces, subjects*. Farnham, England: Ashgate.

Cronon, W. (1992). Kennecott journey: The paths out of town. In W. Cronon, G. Miles, & J. Gitlin (Eds.), *Under an open sky* (pp. 28–51). New York: Norton.

Crosby, A. W. (Eds.). (2004). *Ecological imperialism: The biological expansion of Europe, 900–1900*. Cambridge, UK: Cambridge University Press.

Curry, M. R. (1998). *Digital places: Living with geographic information technologies*. London: Routledge.

Dai, A. (2011). Drought under global warming: A review. *Wiley Interdisciplinary Reviews: Climate Change*, 2(1), 45–65.

Dando, C. E. (2010). The map proves it: Map use by the American women suffrage movement. *Cartographica: The International Journal for Geographic Information and Geovisualization*, 45(4), 221–240.

Davies, B. (2014). Legitimation in post-critical, post-realist times, or whether legitimation? In A. D. Reid, E. P Hart & M. A. Peters (Eds.) *A companion to research in education* (pp. 443–450). Dordrecht: Springer.

Débord, G. (1958). *Theory of the derive*. Retrieved from http://www.bopsecrets.org/SI/2.derive.htm

De Certeau, M. (1984). *The practice of everyday life*. Berkeley: University of California Press.

Dé Ishtar, Z. (2005). *Holding yawulyu: White culture and black women's law*. North Melbourne, Australia: Spinifex Press.

Deleuze, G., & Guattari, F. (1987). *A Thousand Plateaus: Capitalism and Schizophrenia*. Minneapolis: University of Minnesota.

Deloria, V. (1991). Perceptions and maturity: Reflections on Feyerabend's point of view. In *Beyond Reason* (pp. 389–401). Netherlands: Springer.

Deloria, Jr., V. (Ed.). (1973/2003). *God is red: A native view of religion* . New York: The Putnam Publishing Group.

Deloria, Jr., V., & Wildcat, D. R. (2001). *Power and Place: Indian Education in America*. Goldon, CO: Fulcrum Publishing.

Denzin, N., Lincoln, Y., & Smith, L. T. (2008). *Handbook of critical Indigenous methodology*. Thousand Oaks, CA: SAGE.

Denzin, N. K., & Lincoln, Y. S. (Eds.). (2000). *Handbook of qualitative research*. Thousand Oaks, CA: SAGE.

Denzin, N. K., & Lincoln, Y. S. (Eds.). (2005). *The Sage handbook of qualitative research* (3rd ed.). Thousand Oaks, CA: SAGE.

Denzin, N. K., & Lincoln, Y. S. (Eds.). (2011). *The Sage handbook of qualitative research*. Thousand Oaks, CA: SAGE.

Derrida, J. (1976). *Of grammatology* (G. C. Spivak Trans.). Baltimore, MD: Johns Hopkins University Press.

Descartes, R. (1637). *Discours de la méthode*. Retrieved from DissertationsGratuites.com.

Deyhle, D. (2009). *Reflections in place: Connected lives of Navajo women*. Tucson: University of Arizona Press.

Dillabough, J., & Kennelly, J. (2010). *Lost youth in the global city. Class, culture on the urban imaginary*. New York: Routledge.

Dillard, C. B. (2000). The substance of things hoped for, the evidence of things not seen: Examining an endarkened feminist epistemology in educational research and leadership. *International Journal of Qualitative Studies in Education*, 13(6), 661–681.

Dolphijn, R., & van der Tuin, I. (2012). *New materialism: Interviews and cartographies*. Ann Arbor, MI: Open Humanities Press.

Donald, D. (2012). Forts, colonial frontier logics, and Aboriginal-Canadian relations: Imagining decolonizing educational philosophies in Canadian Contexts. In A. Abdi (Eds.), *Decolonizing philosophies of education* (pp. 91–111). Amsterdam: Sense Publishers.

Elliot, A., & Urry, J. (2010). *Mobile lives*. London: Routledge.

Ellis, C. (2004). *The ethnographic I: A methodological novel about autoethnography*. Walnut Creek, AB: Mira Press.

Ellsworth, E. (1989). Why doesn't this feel empowering? Working through the repressive myths of critical pedagogy. *Harvard Educational Review*, 59(3), 297–325.

Elwood, S., & Martin, D. (2000). 'Placing' interviews: Location and scales of power in qualitative research. *Professional Geographer, 52*(4), 649–657.

Elwood, S., Feliciano, R., Gems, K., Gulasingam, N., Howard, W., Mackin, R., . . . & Sierra, S. (2007). Participatory GIS: The Humboldt/West Humboldt Park Community GIS Project, Chicago, USA. In S. Kingdon, R. Pain, & M. Kesby (Eds.), *Participatory action research approaches and methods: Connecting people, participation and place* (pp. 170–178). London: Routledge.

Engel, S., Mauro, D., & Carroll, K.K. (2014). An African-centered approach to land education. In K. McCoy, E. Tuck, & M. McKenzie (Eds.), Special issue on land education: Indigenous, postcolonial, and decolonizing perspectives on place and environmental education research, *Environmental Education Research*, 70–81.

Erdrich, L. (Eds.). (2003). Books and islands in Ojibwe country: Traveling through the land of my ancestors. New York: National Geographic.

Evans, M. M. (2002). "Nature" and environmental justice. In J. Adamson, M.M. Evans, & R. Stein (Eds.), The environmental justice reader: Politics, poetics, and pedagogy (pp. 181–193). Tucson: University of Arizona Press.

Evans, J., & Jones, P. (2011). The walking interview: Methodology, mobility and place. *Applied geography, 31*, 849–858.

Fals-Borda, O. (2006). The North-South convergence: A 30-year first-person assessment of PAR. *Action research, 4*(3), 351–358.

Fanon, F. (1961). *The wretched of the earth.* New York: Grove Press.

Fanon, F. (1967). *Black skins, white masks.* New York: Grove Press.

Farinelli, F. (2000). Friedrich Ratzel and the nature of (political) geography. *Political Geography, 19*(8).

Fenwick, T., Edwards, R., & Sawchuck, P. (2011). *Emerging approaches to educational research: Tracing the sociomaterial.* Abingdon, UK: Routledge.

Fincham, B., McGuinness, M., & Murray, L. (Eds.). (2010). *Mobile methodologies.* London: Palgrave Macmillan.

Findlay, L.M. (2000). Forward. In M. Battiste (Ed.), *Reclaiming Indigenous voice and vision* (pp. ix–xiii).Vancouver, BC: University of British Columbia Press.

Fine, M. (1994). Working the hyphens: Reinventing self and other in qualitative research. In N.K. Denzin & Y.S. Lincoln (Eds.), *Handbook of qualitative research* (pp. 70–82). Thousand Oaks, CA: SAGE.

Fine, M. (2008). An Epilogue, of Sorts. In J. Cammarota, & M. Fine (Eds.), *Revolutionizing education: Youth participatory action research in motion* (pp. 213–234). New York: Routledge.

Fine, M., & Barreras, R. (2001). To be of use. *Analyses of Social Issues and Public Policy, 1*(1), 175–182.

Fine, M., Tuck, E. & Zeller-Berkman, S. (2007). Do You Believe in Geneva? Methods and ethics at the global local nexus. In C. McCarthy, A. Durham, L. Engel, A. Filmer, M. Giardina, & M. Malagreca (Eds.), *Globalizing cultural studies: Ethnographic interventions in theory, method, and policy* (pp. 493–525). New York: Peter Lang Publications.

Fine, M., Weis, L., Weseen, S., & Wong, L. (2000). For whom? Qualitative research, representations, and social responsibilities. In N.K. Denzin & Y.S. Lincoln (Eds.), *Handbook of qualitative research* (2nd ed.) (pp. 107–132). Thousand Oaks, CA: SAGE.

Fortmann, L. (1995). Talking claims: discursive strategies in contesting property. *World Development, 23*(6), 1053–1063.

Friedel, T.L. (2008). (Not so) crude text and images: Staging *Native* in 'big oil' advertising. *Visual Studies, 23*(3), 238–254.

Friedel, T.L. (2011). Looking for learning in all the wrong places: Urban Native youths' cultured response to Western-oriented place-based learning. *International*

Journal of Qualitative Studies in Education, Special Issue – Youth Resistance Revisited, 24(5), 531–546.

Friedman, T. L. (2005). *The world is flat: A brief history of the Twenty-First Century.* New York: Farrar, Straus and Giroux.

Friedman, T. L. (2007). *The world is flat: A brief history of the twenty-first century.* London: Macmillan.

Fuhse, J., & Mützel, S. (2011). Tackling connections, structure, and meaning in networks: quantitative and qualitative methods in sociological network research. *Qualitative and Quantitative, 45*, 1067–89.

Futch, V. A., & Fine, M. (2014). Mapping as a method: History and theoretical commitments. *Qualitative Research in Psychology, 11*(1), 42–59.

Gaztambide-Fernández, R. A. (2012). Decolonization and the pedagogy of solidarity. *Decolonization: Indigeneity, Education & Society, 1*(1).

Gieseking, J. J. (2008). Mental mapping as a methodology: Its evolution, its usefulness, and the ways in which they may be analyzed them. *Royal Geographical Society with the Institute of British Geographers.* Paper presentation.

Gieseking, J. J. (2013a). Where we go from here: The spatial mental mapping method and its analytic components for social science data gathering. *Qualitative Inquiry, 19*(9), 712–724.

Gieseking, J. J. (2013b). *Living in an (in)visible world: Lesbians' and queer women's spaces and experiences of justice and oppression in New York City, 1983–2008* (Doctoral dissertation). Graduate Centre, City University of New York, New York.

Gilmore, R. W. (1999). You have dislodged a boulder: Mothers and prisoners in the post Keynesian California landscape. *Transforming Anthropology, 8*(1–2), 12–38.

Gilmore, R. W. (2002). Fatal couplings of power and difference: Notes on racism and geography. *The Professional Geographer, 54*(1), 15–24.

Gilmore, R. W. (2006). *Golden gulag: Prisons, surplus, crisis, and opposition in globalizing California* (Vol. 21). Berkeley: University of California Press.

Glyn, A. (2006). *Capitalism unleashed: Finance, globalization, and welfare.* New York: Oxford.

Goeman, M. (2008). From place to territories and back again: Centering storied land in the discussion of indigenous nation-building. *International Journal of Critical Indigenous Studies, 1*(1), 23–34.

Goeman, M. (2012). The tools of a cartographic poet: Unmapping settler colonialism in Joy Harjo's poetry. *Settler Colonial Studies, 2*(2), 89–112.

Goeman, M. (2013). *Mark my words: Native women mapping our nations.* Minneapolis: University of Minnesota Press.

Gosline, A., & Teelucksingh, C. (2008). Representing nature and environmentalism. In A. Gosline & C. Teelucksingh (Eds.), *Environmental justice and racism in Canada: An introduction* (pp. 89–116). Toronto, ON: Emond Montgomery Publications.

Gould, C. (2011a, June 22). *Glen cove struggle.* Public lecture. Vallejo Naval & Maritime Museum. Retrieved from http://www.indybay.org/newsitems/2011/07/06/18683990.php

Gould, C. (2011b, July 20). *Press release: A victory for protection of Sogorea Te.* Retrieved from http://protectglencove.org/2011/easement-press-release/#more-3732

Gould, C. (2012, January 7). *An update for supporters and friends of Sogorea Te.* Retrieved from http://protectglencove.org/2012/update-letter/#more-4057

Grande, S. (2004). *Red pedagogy: Native American social and political thought.* Oxford, UK: Rowman & Littlefield Publishers.

Greene, J. C. (2013). On rhizomes, lines of flight, mangles, and other assemblages. *International Journal of Qualitative Studies in Education, 26*(6), 749–758.

Grosz, E. A. (1994). *Volatile bodies: Toward a corporeal feminism.* Crows Nest, NSW: Allen & Unwin.

Gruenewald, D. A. (2003). The best of both worlds: A critical pedagogy of place. *Educational Researcher, 32*(4), 3–12.

Gulson, K., & Symes, C. (2007). Knowing one's place: space, theory and education. *Critical Studies in Education, 48*(1), 97–110.

Gulson, K. N., & Parkes, R. J. (2009). In the shadows of the mission: Education policy, urban space, and the 'colonial present' in Sydney. *Race Ethnicity and Education, 12*(3), 267–280.

Haluza-Delay, R., O'Riley, P., Cole, P., & Agyeman, J. (2009). Speaking for ourselves, speaking together: Environmental justice in Canada. In J. Agyeman, P. Cole, R. Haluza-Delay and P. O'Riley (Eds.), *Speaking for ourselves: Environmental justice in Canada* (pp. 1–26). Vancouver: UBC Press.

Haraway, D. (1985). Manifesto for cyborgs: Science, technology, and socialist feminism in the 1980s, *Socialist Review 80,* 65–108.

Haraway, D. (1988). Situated knowledges: The science question in feminism and the privilege of partial perspective. *Feminist Studies, 14*(3), 575–599.

Haraway, D. (1997). *Modest_Witness@Second_Millennium: FemaleMan©_Meets_OncoMouseTM.* New York: Routledge.

Harvey, D. (1989). *The condition of postmodernity.* Oxford: Blackwell.

Harvey, D. (1996). *Justice, nature and the geography of difference.* Oxford: Blackwell.

Harvey, D. (2000). *Spaces of hope.* Oakland: University of California Press.

Harvey, D. (2001). *Spaces of capital: Towards a critical geography.* New York: Routledge.

Harvey, D. (2003). *The new imperialism.* Oxford: Oxford.

Harvey, D. (2005). *A brief history of neoliberalism.* New York: Oxford University Press.

Hawkins, G. (2010). Plastic materialities. In B. Braun, & S. Whatmore (Eds.), *Political matter: Technoscience, democracy, and public life* (pp. 119–138). Minneapolis: University of Minnesota Press.

Heidegger, M. (1971). *Poetry, language, thought.* New York: Harper & Row.

Henry George Institute. (n.d.). We May Be Brothers After All: Speech of Chief Seattle, January 9, 1855. Retrieved from http://www.landreform.org/seattle0.htm

Hergenrather, K. C., Rhodes, S. D., Cowan, C. A., Bardhoshi, G., & Pula, S. (2009). Photovoice as community-based participatory research: A qualitative review. *American Journal of Health Behaviour, 33*(6), 686–698.

Hinkinson, J. (2012). Why settler colonialism? *Arena Journal, 37/38*(1).

Höhne, N., van Breevoort, P., Deng, Y., Larkin, J., & Hänsel, G. (2013). *Feasibility of GHG emissions phase-out by mid-century.* Ecofys. Retrieved December 8, 2013: http://www.ecofys.com/files/files/ecofys-2013-feasibility-ghg-phase-out-2050.pdf

Holz, C. (2014). Oil and education. Keynote presentation, Annual Meeting of the Sustainability and Education Policy Network, January, 29, 2014, Montréal, Québec.

Howes, D. (Ed.). (2005). *Empire of the senses: The sensual culture reader.* London: Bloomsbury Academic.

Howes, D., & Classen, C. (1991). Conclusion: Sounding sensory profiles. In D. Howes (Ed.), *The varieties of sensory experience: A sourcebook in the anthropology of the senses* (pp. 257–288). Toronto, ON: University of Toronto Press.

Hume-Cook, G., Curtis, T., Potaka, J., Tangaroa Wagner, A., Woods, K., & Kindon, S. (2007). Uniting people with place through participatory video: A Ngaati Hauiti journey. In S. Kindon, R. Pain, & M. Kesby (Eds.), *Participatory Action*

Research: Connecting People, Participation and Place (pp. 160–169). London: Routledge.

Huss, E. (2008). Shifting spaces and lack of spaces: Impoverished Bedouin women's experience of cultural transition through arts-based research. *Visual Anthropology, 21,* 58–71.

Husserl, E. (1913/1982). *Ideas pertaining to a pure phenomenology and to a phenomenological philosophy* (F. Kersten, Trans.). Dordrecht, Netherlands: Kluwer Academic Publishers.

Ingold, T. (2000). *The perception of the environment: Essays in livelihood, dwelling and skill.* London: Psychology Press.

Ingold, T. (2008). Bindings against boundaries: Entanglements of life in an open world. *Environment and Planning, 40,* 1796–1810.

Ingold, T. (2011). *Being alive: Essays on movement, knowledge and description.* London: Routledge.

Ingold, T., & Vergunst, J. L. (Eds.). (2008). *Ways of walking.* Farnham, UK: Ashgate.

Intergovernmental Panel on Climate Change (IPCC). (2013). *Climate Change: The physical science basis.* http://www.ipcc.ch/report/ar5/wg1/#.UqKpvfRDuuI

Irwin, R. L., Bickel, B., Triggs, V., Springgay, S., Beer, R., Grauer, K., & Sameshima, P. (2009). The city of Richgate: A/r/tographic cartography as public pedagogy. *Jade, 28*(1), 61–70.

Jackson, A. Y., & Mazzei, L. A. (2012). *Thinking with theory in qualitative research: Viewing data across multiple perspectives.* London: Routledge.

Jensen, C. B. (2010). *Ontologies for developing things: Making health care futures through technology.* Rotterdam: Sense.

Jessop, B., Brenner, N., & Jones, M. (2008). Theorizing sociospatial relations. *Society and Space, 26,* 389–401.

Jones, A., & Jenkins, K. (2008). Rethinking collaboration: Working the indigene-colonizer hyphen. In K. Denzin, Y. S. Lincoln, & L. T. Smith (Eds.), *Handbook of critical and indigenous methodologies* (pp. 471–486). Thousand Oaks, CA: SAGE.

Jones, K. (2008). "It's well good sitting in the storecupboard just talking about what we do": Considering the spaces/places of research within children's geographies. *Children's Geographies, 6*(3), 327–332.

Jones, P., Bunce, G., Evans, J., Gibbs, H., & Hein, J. R. (2008). Exploring space and place with walking interviews. *Journal of Research Practice, 4*(2), 1–9.

Jones, Q., & Grandhi, S. A. (2005). P3 systems: Putting the place back into social networks. *IEEE Internet Computing* (Sept–Oct), 38–46.

Jordon, J. (1989). Poem about my rights. In *Naming our destiny: New and selected poems.* New York: Thunder's Mouth Press.

Kahn, R. (2010). Critical pedagogy, ecoliteracy, and the planetary crisis: The ecopedagogy movement. New York: Peter Lang.

Katz, C. (2004). *Growing up global: Economic restructuring and children's everyday lives.* Minneapolis: University of Minnesota Press.

Katz, C. (2001). On the grounds of globalization: A Topography for feminist political engagement. *Sign, 26*(4), 1213–1234. Kaufmann, V. (2006). *Guy Debord: Revolution in the service of poetry.* Minneapolis: University of Minnesota Press.

Kaufman, J. S., Ewing, M. S, Hyle, A. E., Montgomery, D., & Self, P. A. (2006). Women and nature: Using memory-work to rethink our relationship to the natural world. *Environmental Education Research, 12*(3), 309–326.

Kawagley. A. O. (2006). *A Yupiaq worldview: A pathway to ecology and spirit* (2nd ed.). Long Grove, IL: Waveland Press.

Kawagley, A. O. (2010). Foreword. In R. Barnhardt & A. O. Kawagley (Eds.), *Alaska Native education: Views from within* (pp. 1–5). Fairbanks: Alaska Native Knowledge Network, Center for Cross-cultural Studies, University of Alaska.

Kawagley, A. O. (2006). *A Yupiaq worldview: A pathway to ecology and spirit.* Prospect Heights, IL: Waveland Press.

Kayira, J. (2013). *Re-learning our roots: Youth participatory research, indigenous knowledge, and sustainability through agriculture* (Doctoral dissertation). School of Environment and Sustainability, University of Saskatchewan, Saskatoon, SK.

Kindon, S., Pain, R., & Kesby, M. (2007). *Participatory action research approaches and methods: Connecting people, participation and place.* Oxon, UK: Routledge.

Kirkness, V., & Barnhardt, R. (1991). First Nations and higher education: The four R's—respect, relevance, reciprocity, responsibility. *Journal of American Indian Education, 30*(3), 1–15.

Klein, N., & Simpson, L. (Mar 05, 2013). Dancing the world into being: A conversation with Idle No More's Leanne Simpson. *YES! Magazine.* Last accessed December 9, 2013 at http://www.yesmagazine.org/peace-justice/dancing-the-world-into-being-a-conversation-with-idle-no-more-leanne-simpson

Korteweg, L., & Oakley, J. (2014). Eco-heroes out of place and relations: Decolonizing the narratives of *Into the Wild* and *Grizzly Man* through Land education. In K. McCoy, E. Tuck, & M. McKenzie (Eds.), Special issue on land education: Indigenous, postcolonial, and decolonizing perspectives on place and environmental education research, *Environmental Education Research*, 131–143.

Kovach, M. E. (2009). *Indigenous methodologies: Characteristics, conversations, and contexts.* Toronto, ON: University of Toronto Press.

Kretzmann, J. P., & McKnight, J. L. (1993). *Building communities from the inside out: A path toward finding and mobilizing a community's assets.* Chicago, IL: Acta Publications.

Krieg, B., & Roberts, L. (2007). Photovoice: Insights into marginalisation through a 'community lens' in Saskatchewan, Canada. In S. Kingdon, R. Pain, & M. Kesby (Eds.), *Participatory action research approaches and methods: Connecting people, participation and place* (pp. 150–159). London: Routledge.

Krueger, P. (2011). *Navigating the gaze: Young people's intimate knowledge with surveilled spaces at school* (Doctoral dissertation). The Graduate Center, City University of New York.

Krueger-Henney, P. (forthcoming). Co-researching school spaces of dispossession: A story of survival. *Association of Mexican American Educators Journal.*

Kuhn, T. S. (1970). *The structure of scientific revolutions.* Chicago, IL: University of Chicago Press.

Kullman, K. (2012). Experiments with moving children and digital cameras. *Children's Geographies, 10*(1), 1–16.

Kwok, J. Y. C., & Ku, H. B. (2008). Making habitable space together with female Chinese immigrants to Hong Kong: An interdisciplinary participatory action research project. *Action Research, 6*(3), 261–283.

LaDuke, W. (1999). *All our relations: Native struggles for land and life.* Cambridge: South End Press.

Land, L. (2013). A summary of current federal legislative amendments affecting First Nations. Retrieved March 23, 2013, from http://www.oktlaw.com/wp-content/uploads/2013/01/summaryconcerns.pdf

Larsen, S. C., Sorenson, C., McDermott, D., Long, J., & Post, C. (2007). Place perception and social interaction on an exurban landscape in central Colorado. *The Professional Geographer, 59*(4), 421–422.

Lashua, B. D., & Fox, K. (2007). Defining the groove: From remix to research in "The Beat of Boyle Street." *Leisure Sciences, 29,* 143–158.

Lather, P. (1984). Critical theory, curricular transformation and feminist mainstreaming. *Journal of Education, 66*(1), 49–62.

Lather, P. (1991a). Deconstructing/deconstructive inquiry: The politics of knowing and being known. *Educational Theory, 41*(2), 153–173.

Lather, P. (1991b). *Getting smart: Feminist research and pedagogy with/in the post-modern*. New York: Routledge.

Lather, P. (2006). Paradigm proliferation as a good thing to think with: Teaching research in education as a wild profusion. *International journal of qualitative studies in education, 19*(1), 35–57.

Lather, P. (2013). Methodology 2.1: What do we do in the afterward? *International Journal of Qualitative Studies in Education, 26*(6), 634–645.

Lather, P., & Smithies, C.S. (1997). *Troubling the angels: Women living with HIV/AIDS*. Boulder, CO: Westview Press.

Latour, B. (2005). *Reassembling the social: An introduction to actor-network theory*. Oxford: Oxford University Press.

Lavery, C. (2005). The pepys of London E 11: Graeme Miller and the politics of linked. *New Theatre Quarterly, 21*(2), 148–160.

Lavoie, J. (2013, May 22). It's Pkols, not Mount Douglas, marchers proclaim. *Times Colonist*. Retrieved May 27, 2013, from http://www.timescolonist.com/news/local/it-s-pkols-not-mount-douglas-marchers-proclaim-1.228920

Law, J. (2004). *After method: Mess in social science research*. Oxon, UK: Routledge.

Lee, S. (2009). *Narrated landscape as counterweight to perception of placelessness in contemporary urban landscape: Re-visioning place in Gwangbok-dong and Nampo-dong, Busan, South Korea*. Unpublished Doctoral Dissertation. University of Illinois, Urbana-Champaign.

Leiserowitz, A., Maibach, E., Roser-Renouf, C., & Hmielowski, J. (2012). *Global warming's Six Americas, March 2012 & Nov. 2011*. Yale University and George Mason University. New Haven, CT: Yale Project on Climate Change Communication.

L'Eplattenier, B.A. (2009). An argument for archival research methods: Thinking beyond Methodology. *College English, 72*(1), 67–79.

Letiecq, B., & Schmalzbauer, L. (2012). Community-based participatory research with Mexican migrants in a new rural destination: A good fit?. *Action Research, 10*(3), 244–259.

Lipman, P. (2011). *The new political economy of urban education: Neoliberalism, race, and the right to the city*. New York: Routledge.

Lipsitz, G. (1998). *The possessive investment in whiteness*. Philadelphia, PA: Temple University Press.

Lipsitz, G. (2011). *How racism takes place*. Philadelphia, PA: Temple University Press.

Lorde, A. (1984). *Sister outsider: Essays and speeches*. Trumansburg, NY: Crossing Press.

Lowan, G. (2009). Exploring place from an Aboriginal perspective: Considerations for outdoor and environmental education. *Canadian Journal of Environmental Education, 14*, 42–58.

Lynas, M. (2007). *Six degrees: Our future on a hotter planet*. Hammersmith, UK: Fourth Estate.

MacLure, M. (2013). Researching without representation?: Language and materiality in post-qualitative methodology. *International Journal of Qualitative Studies in Education, 26*(6), 658–667.

Malpas, J.E. (1999). *Place and experience: A philosophical topography*. Cambridge, UK: Cambridge University Press.

Maneja Zaragoza, R., Boada, M., Barrera-Bassols, N., & McCall, M. (2009). Children and teenagers' sociological perceptions: Environmental education proposals. *Utopia y Praxis Latinoamerica 14*(44), 39–51.

Marcus, A.P. (2009). (Re)creating places and spaces in two countries: Brazilian transnational migration processes. *Journal of Cultural Geography, 26*(2), 173–198.

Marcus, G. (2009). Notes towards an ethnographic memoir of supervising graduate research through Anthropology's decades of transformation. In J. Faubion & G. Marcus (Eds.), *Fieldwork is not what it used to be: Learning anthropology's method in a time of transition* (pp. 1–32). Ithaca, NY: Cornell University Press.

Marcus, G. E. (1995). Ethnography in/of the world system: The emergence of multi-sited ethnography. *Annual Review of Anthropology, 24*, 95–117.

Marres, N. (2010). Front-staging nonhumans: Publicity as a constraint on the political activity of things. In B. Braun & S. Whatmore (Eds.), *Political matter: Technoscience, democracy, and public life* (pp. 178–210). Minneapolis: University of Minnesota Press.

Marx, K. (1969). *Theses on Feuerbach*. In K. Marx & F. Engels (Eds.), *Selected works* (W. Lough, Trans.; Vol. 1, pp. 13–15). Moscow: Progress. (Original work published 1888).

Massey, D. (1984). *Spatial divisions of labour*. Basingstoke: Macmillan.

Massey, D. (1991). A global sense of place. *Marxism Today* (38), 24–29.

Massey, D. (1994). *Space, place, and gender*. Minneapolis: University of Minnesota.

Massey, D. (2005). *For space*. London: SAGE.

Massey, D. (2008). When theory meets politics. *Antipode, 40*(3), 492–497.

Massey, D. (2009). The possibilities of a politics of place beyond place? A conversation with Doreen Massey. *Scottish Geographical Journal, 125*(3–4), 401–420.

McCann, E., & Ward, K. (2012). Assembling urbanism: following policies and 'studying through' the sites and situations of policy making. *Environment and Planning, 44*(1) 42–51.

McCann, E. J. (2011). Urban policy mobilities and global circuits of knowledge: Toward a research agenda. *Annals of Association of American Geographers, 101*(1), 107–130.

McCoy, K. (2014). Manifesting Destiny: a land education analysis of settler colonialism in Jamestown, Virginia, USA. *Environmental Education Research, 20*(1), 82–97.

McCoy, K., Tuck, E., & McKenzie, M. (Eds.). (2014). Special issue on land education: Indigenous, postcolonial, and decolonizing perspectives on place and environmental education research. *Land education: Indigenous, postcolonial, and Environmental Education Research, 20*(1).

McIntyre, A. (2003). Through the eyes of women: Photovoice and participatory research as tools for reimagining place. *Gender, Place and Culture, 10*(1), 47–66.

McKay, D. (2005). Migration and the sensuous geographies of re-emplacement in the Philippines. *Journal of Intercultural Studies, 26*(1–2), 75–91.

McKenzie, M. (2009). Scholarship as intervention: Critique, collaboration and the research imagination. *Environmental Education Research, 15*(2), 217—226.

McKenzie, M., Butcher, K., Fruson, D., Knorr, M., Stone, J., Allan, S., & Kayira, J. (2013). Suited: Participatory research and relational learning. In M. Brody, J. Dillon, R.B. Stevenson, & A.E. J. Wals (Eds.), *International handbook for research on environmental education* (pp. 487–497). New York: American Educational Research Association.

McKenzie, M., Hart, P., Bai, H., & Jickling, B. (Eds.). (2009). *Fields of green: Restorying culture, environment, and education*. Cresskill, NJ: Hampton Press.

McKinley, E. (2007). Indigenous Students. *Handbook of research on science education, 199*.

McKittrick, K. (2006). *Demonic grounds: Black women and the cartographies of struggle*. Minneapolis: University of Minnesota Press.

McKnight, J., & Kretzmann, J. (1993). *Building communities from the inside out: A path toward finding and mobilizing a community's assets*. Chicago, IL: ACTA Publications.

McLeod, J. (2003). Why we interview now—reflexivity and perspective in a longitudinal study. *International Journal of Social Research Methodology*, 6(3), 201–211.

McLeod, J., & Thomson, R. (2009). *Researching social change: Qualitative approaches*. London: SAGE.

McLeod, J., & Yates, L. (2006). *Making modern lives: Subjectivity, schooling, and social change*. Albany, NY: SUNY Press.

McRuer, J. (forthcoming). Topical review: Approaches to research organizational networks to advance collaboration for sustainability and social change. *Environmental Education Research*.

Merleau-Ponty, M. (1945/2002). *The phenomenology of perception*. London: Routledge.

Merriman, P. (2013). Rethinking mobile methods. *Mobilities*, 1–20.

Meyer, M. A. (2003). *Ho'oulu: Our time of becoming: Collected early writings of Manulani Meyer*. Honolulu, Hawai'i: Ai Pohaku Press.

Meyer, M. A. (2008). Hawaiian epistemology and the triangulation of meaning. In K. Denzin, Y. S. Lincoln, & L. T. Smith (Eds.), *Handbook of critical and indigenous methodologies* (pp. 217–232). Thousand Oaks, CA: SAGE.

Middleton, J. (2010). Sense and the city: Exploring the embodied geographies of urban walking. *Social & Cultural Geography*, 11(6), 575–596.

Miller, D. (2008). *The comfort of things*. Cambridge. UK: Polity.

Miller, G. (2003). Linked (audio walk). London: Museum of London.

Mitchell, C. (2008). Getting the picture and changing the picture: Visual methodologies and educational research in South Africa. *South African Journal of Education*, 28(3), 365–383.

Mohanty, C. T. (2003). *Feminism without borders: Decolonizing theory, practicing solidarity*. New Delhi, India: Zubaan.

Moores, S., & Metykova, M. (2009). Knowing how to get around: Place, migration, and communication. *The Communication Review*, 12(4), 313–326.

Moores, S., & Metykova, M. (2010). "I didn't realize how attached I am": On the environmental experiences of trans-European migrants. *European Journal of Cultural Studies*, 13, 171–189.

Moreton-Robinson, A. (2009). Introduction: Critical Indigenous theory special issue. *Cultural Studies Review*, 15(2), 11.

Morgensen, S. L. (2012). Destabilizing the settler academy: The decolonial effects of Indigenous methodologies. *American Quarterly*, 64(4), 805–808.

Morgensen, S. L. (2011). The Biopolitics of settler colonialism: Right here, right now. *Settler Colonial Studies*, 1(1), 52–76.

Morgensen, S. L. (2009). Un-Settling Settler Desires. In Unsettling Minnesota Collective (Eds.) Unsettling ourselves: Reflections and resources for deconstructing colonial mentality. [Online sourcebook]. Retrieved July 15, 2014, from http://unsettling minnesota.files.wordpress.com/2009/11/um_sourcebook_jan10_revision.pdf

Murthy, D. (2008). Digital ethnography: An examination of the use of new technologies for social research. *Sociology*, 42(5), 837–855.

Myers, M. (2010). "Walk with me, talk with me": The art of conversive wayfinding. *Visual Studies*, 25(1), 59–68.

Nayak, A. (2003). *Race, place and globalization: Youth cultures in a changing world*. Oxford, UK: Berg.

Nayak, A., & Jeffrey, A. S. (2011). *Geographical thought: An introduction to ideas in human geography*. Upper Saddle River, NJ: Pearson Prentice Hall.

Neeganagwedgin, E. (2012). Chattling the Indigenous other: A historical examination of the enslavement of Aboriginal Peoples in Canada. *AlterNative*, 8(1), 15–26.

O'Donoghue, D. (2010). Classrooms as installations: A conceptual framework for analyzing classroom photographs from the past. *History of Education*, 39(3), 401–415.

Opondo, M., Dolan, C., Wendoh, S., & Kathuri, J. N. (2007). Gender and employment: Participatory social auditing in Kenya. In S. Kindon, R. Pain, & M. Kesby (Eds.), *Participatory action research approaches and methods: Connecting people, participation and place* (pp. 80–87). Oxon, UK: Routledge.

Otero, R. L., & Cammarota, J. (2011). Notes from the ethnic studies home front: Student protests, texting, and subtexts of oppression. *International Journal of Qualitative Studies in Education, 24*(5), 639–648.

Pain, R. (2009). Globalized fear? Towards an emotional geopolitics. *Progress in Human Geography, 33,* 466–486.

Palsson G, Szerszynski B, Sörlin S, Marks J, Avril B, Crumley C, Hackmann H, Holm P, Ingram J, Kirman A, et al. (2013). Reconceptualizing the 'anthropos' in the anthropocene: Integrating the social sciences and humanities in global environmental change research. *Enviro Sci Policy, 28,* 3–13

Paperson, L. (2014). A ghetto land pedagogy is an antidote for settler environmentalism. In K. McCoy, E. Tuck, & M. McKenzie (Eds.), Special issue on land education: Indigenous, postcolonial, and decolonizing perspectives on place and environmental education research, *Environmental Education Research,* 115–130.

Parrish, S. S. (2010). Rummaging/In and out of holds. *American Literary History, 22*(2), 289–301.

Patel, L. (2012). *Youth held at the border: Immigration, education and the politics of inclusion.* New York: Teachers College Press.

Patterson, O. (1982). *Slavery and social death: Comparative study.* Cambridge: Harvard University Press.

Peck, J. (2013). Explaining (with) neoliberalism. *Territory, Politics, Governance, 1*(2), 132–157.

Peck, J., & Theodore, N. (2010). Mobilizing policy: Models, methods, and mutations. *Geoforum, 41,* 169–174.

Perry, T. (1972). Chief Seattle Speech, film script for *Home* [prod. by the Southern Baptist Radio and Television Commission, 1972]. Last accessed December 8, 2013, at http:// www.washington.edu/uwired/outreach/cspn/Website/Classroom%20Materials/ Reading%20the%20Region/Texts%20by%20and%20about%20Natives/ Texts/8.html

Pierce, C. (2012). The promissory future(s) of education: Rethinking scientific literacy in the era of biocapitalism. *Educational Philosophy and Theory, 44*(7). doi: 10.1111/j.1469–5812.2010.00736.x

Pihama, L. (2005). Kaupapa Māori theory: Asserting indigenous theories of change. In J. Barker (Ed.), *Sovereignty matters: Locations of contestation and possibility in indigenous struggles for self-determination.* Lincoln: University of Nebraska Press.

Pink, S. (2007). *Doing visual ethnography* (2nd ed.). London: SAGE.

Pink, S. (2009). *Doing sensory ethnography.* London: SAGE.

Plumwood, V. (1993). *Feminism and the mastery of nature.* New York: Routledge.

Posner, R. A. (2001). *Public intellectuals: A study of decline.* Cambridge, MA: Harvard University Press.

Povinelli, E. A. (2011). *Economies of abandonment: Social belonging and endurance in late liberalism.* Durham, NC: Duke University Press.

Pratt, L. M. (1992). *Imperial eyes: Travel writing and transculturation.* New York: Routledge.

Pulido, L. (2000). Rethinking Environmental Racism: White privilege and urban development in Southern California. *Annals of the Association of American Geographers, 90*(1), 12–40.

Radstone, S. (Ed.). (2000). *Memory and methodology.* Oxford, UK: Berg.

Ramos, F. S. (2007). Imaginary pictures, real life stories: The FotoDialogo method. *International Journal of Qualitative Studies in Education, 20*(2), 191–224.

Ramsay, N. (2009). Taking-place: Refracted enchantment and the habitual spaces of the tourist souvenir. *Social & Cultural Geography, 10*(2), 197–217.

Rapport, N., & Overing, J. (2000). *Social and cultural anthropology: The key concepts.* London: Routledge.

Reason, P., & Rowan, J. (1981). Issues of validity in new paradigm research. In P. Reason & J. Rowan (Eds.), *Human inquiry: A sourcebook of new paradigm research* (pp. 23–262). New York: John Wiley.

Reed, T. V. (2002). Towards an environmental justice ecocriticism. In J. Adamson, M. M. Evans, & R. Stein (Eds.), *The environmental justice reader: Politics, poetics & pedagogy* (pp. 146–162). Tucson: University of Arizona Press.

Relph, E. (1976). *Place and placelessness.* London: Pion.

Richardson, L. (2000). New writing practices in qualitative research. *Sociology of Sport Journal, 17,* 5–20.

Rishbeth, C., & Finney, N. (2006). Novelty and nostalgia in urban greenspace: Refugee perspectives. *Tijdschrift voor Economische en Sociale Geografie, 97*(3), 281–295.

Rosaldo, R. (1993). *Culture & truth: The remaking of social analysis.* Boston, MA: Beacon Press.

Rose, G. (1993). *Feminism and geography: The limits of geographical knowledge.* Cambridge: Polity.

Rose, N. (1999). *Powers of freedom: Reframing political thought.* Cambridge, UK: Cambridge University Press.

Rowe, J. S. (1990). *Home place.* Edmonton, Alberta: NeWest.

Salmón, E. (2012). *Eating the landscape: American Indian stories of food, identity, and resilience.* Tucson: University of Arizona Press.

Sandercock, L., & Attili, G. (2010). Digital ethnography as planning praxis: An experiment with film as social research, community engagement and policy dialogue. *Planning Theory & Practice, 11*(1), 23–45.

Sanderson, E., with Holy Family Settlement Research Team, Newport, R., & Umaki Research Participants. (2007). Participatory cartographies: Reflections from research performances in Fiji and Tanzania. In S. Kingdon, R. Pain, & M. Kesby (Eds.), *Participatory action research approaches and methods: Connecting people, participation and place* (pp. 122–131). London: Routledge.

Sarmento, J. (2009). A sweet and amnesic present: The postcolonial landscape and memory makings in Cape Verde. *Social & Cultural Geography, 10*(5), 523–544.

Sarmento, J. (2011). *Fortifications, Post-colonialism and Power: Ruins and Imperial Legacies.* Burlington, VT: Ashgate Publishing.

Sarmiento, E., Sean, T., Tola, M., & Hantel, M. (2014). *Science, politics, and social natures in the Anthropocene.* New Brunswick, NJ: Rutgers University.

Sassen, S. (1991). *The global city: New York, London, Tokyo.* Princeton, NJ: Princeton University Press.

Sassen, S. (2006). *Territory, authority, rights: From medieval to global assemblages.* Princeton, NJ: Princeton University Press.

Sassen, S. (2007). *A sociology of globalization.* New York: W.W. Norton.

Sassen, S. (2012). Analytic Tactics: Geography as Obstacle Keynote presentation at American Association of Geographers Annual Meeting. Annual Meeting in New York. Retrieved from http://www.aag.org/cs/annualmeeting/videos/2012_new_york/honorary_geographer_saskia_sassen

Scheurich, J. J. (1997). *Research method in the postmodern.* London: UK: Falmer Press.

Scott, S. L. (2009). Discovering what the people knew: The 1979 Appalachian Land Ownership Study. *Action Research, 7*(2), 185–205.

Seamon, D. (1979). *A geography of the lifeworld: Movement, rest, and encounter.* London: Croom Helm.

Seamon, D. (1980). Body-subject, time-space routines, and place-ballets. In A. Buttimer and D. Seamon (Eds.), *The human experience of space and place* (pp. 148–165). London: Croom Helm.

Seidman, I. (1998). *Interviewing as Qualitative Research* (2nd. ed.). New York: Teachers.

Simonsen, K. (2004). Networks, flows, and fluids—reimagining spatial analysis? *Environment and Planning A, 36*(8), 1333–1337.

Simpson, A. (2007). On ethnographic refusal: Indigeneity, 'voice' and colonial citizenship. *Junctures, 9*, 67–80.

Sin, C. H. (2003). Interviewing in 'place': The socio-spatial construction of interview data. *Area, 35*(3), 305–312.

Smith, D. W. (2007). *Husserl*. London: Routledge.

Smith, J. (2011). Postcolonial Māori television? The dirty politics of indigenous cultural production. *Continuum: Journal of Media & Cultural Studies, 25*(5), 719–729.

Smith, J. M. (2008). Identities and urban social spaces in Little Tokyo, Los Angeles: Japanese Americans in two ethno-spiritual communities. *Geografiska Annaler: Series B, Human Geography, 90*(4), 389–408.

Smith, L. T. (1999/2012). *Decolonizing methodologies: Research and indigenous peoples*. London: Zed Books.

Smith, N. (1984/2008). *Uneven development: Nature, capital, and the production of space*. Athens: University of Georgia Press.

Smith, N., & Katz, C. (1993). Grounding metaphor: Towards a spatialized politics. In M. Keith, & S. Pile (Eds.), *Place and the Politics of Identity*, (pp. 67–83). London: Routledge.

Soja, E. (2001). *Postmodern geographies. The reassertion of space in critical social theory*. London: Verso.

Soja, E. W. (1999). Thirdspace: Expanding the scope of the geographical imagination. In D. Massey, J. Allen, & P. Sarre (Eds.), *Human geography today* (pp. 260–278). Cambridge: Policy.

Soja, E. W. (2010). *Seeking spatial justice*. Minneapolis: University of Minnesota.

Somerville, M. (2007). Place literacies. *Australian Journal of Language and Literacy, 30*(2), 149–164.

Somerville, M. (2013). *Water in a dry land: Place-learning through art and story*. London: Routledge.

Spillers, H. (2003). *Black and white in color: Essays on American literature and culture*. Chicago: University of Chicago Press.

Stewart, A. (2008). Whose place, whose history? Outdoor environmental education pedagogy as 'reading' the landscape. *Journal of Adventure Education & Outdoor Learning, 8*(2), 79–98.

Stewart, K. (2007). *Ordinary effects*. Durham, NC: Duke University Press.

Stoller, P. (1986). The reconstruction of ethnography. In P. P. Chock & J. R. Wyman (Eds.), *Discourse and the social life of meaning* (pp. 51–74). Washington, D.C.: Smithsonian Institution Press.

Stoller, P. (1989). *The taste of ethnographic things: The senses in anthropology*. Philadelphia: University of Pennsylvania Press.

St. Pierre, E. A. (2011). Post qualitative research: The critique and the coming after. *Handbook of qualitative research, 4*, 611-626.

St. Pierre, E. A. S., & Pillow, W. S. (Eds.). (2000). *Working the ruins: Feminist poststructural theory and methods in education*. New York: Routledge.

Striffler, S. (2007). Neither here nor there: Mexican immigrant workers and the search for home. *American Ethnologist, 34*(4), 674–688.

Styres, S., Haig-Brown, C., & Blimkie, M. (2013). Toward a pedagogy of Land: The urban context. *Canadian Journal of Education/Revue Canadienne de l'Education, 36*(2), 188–221.

Styres, S., & Zinga, D. (2013). The community-first land-centered theoretical framework: Bringing a good mind to Indigenous education research. *Canadian Journal of Education/Revue Canadienne de L'éducation, 36*(2), 284–313.

TallBear, K. (2013). *Native American DNA*. Minneapolis: University of Minnesota Press.

Tamboukou, M. (2008). Re-imagining the narratable subject. *Qualitative Research, 8*(3), 283–292.

Tedlock, D. (1983). *The spoken word and the work of interpretation*. Philadelphia: University of Pennsylvania Press.

Temenos, C., & McCann, E. (2013). Geographies of policy mobilities. *Geography Compass, 7*(5), 344–357.

Terrance, L. L. (2011). Resisting colonial education: Zitkala-Sa and Native Feminist archival refusal. *International Journal of Qualitative Studies in Education, 24*(5), 621–626.

The Henry George Institute (n.d.). We May Be Brothers After All: Speech of Chief Seattle, January 9, 1855. Retrieved from Liberation Theology and Land Reform website last accessed July 15, 2014 at http://www.landreform.org/reading0.htm

Thomas, J. A. (2009). The evidence of sight. *History and Theory, 48*(4), 151–168.

Threadgold, T. (2000). Poststructuralism and discourse analysis. In C. Poynton & A. Lee (Eds.), *Culture & text: Discourse and methodology in social research and cultural studies* (pp. 40–58). Plymouth, UK: Rowman & Littlefield.

Thrift, N. (2008). *Non-representational theory: Space, politics, affect*. London: Routledge.

Tolia-Kelly, D. P. (2007). Fear in paradise: The affective registers of the English Lake District landscape re-visited. *The Senses and Society, 2*(3), 329–351.

Torre, M. E., & Ayala, J. (2009). Envisioning participatory action entremundos. *Feminism & Psychology, 19*(3), 387–393.

Trell, E. M., & van Hoven, B. (2010). Making sense of place: Exploring creative and (inter) active research methods with young people. *Fennia-International Journal of Geography, 188*(1), 91–104.

Tuan, Y. (1974). *Topophilia: A study of environmental perceptions, attitudes, and values*. Englewood Cliffs, NJ: Prentice-Hall.

Tuan, Y. F. (1974). *Topophilia: A study of environmental perception, attitudes, and values*. Englewood Cliffs, NJ: Prentice-Hall.

Tuan, Y. F. (1977). *Space and place: The perspective of experience*. Minneapolis: University of Minnesota Press.

Tuck, E. (2009a). Re-visioning action: Participatory action research and Indigenous theories of change. *Urban Review, 41*(1),47–65.

Tuck, E. (2009b). Suspending damage: A letter to communities. *Harvard Educational Review, 75*(3), 409–427.

Tuck, E. (2009c). Theorizing back: An approach to participatory policy analysis. In J. Anyon, M. J. Dumas, D. Linville, K. Nolan, M. Perez, E. Tuck, & J. Weiss, *Theories and educational research: Toward critical social explanation* (pp. 111–130). New York: Routledge.

Tuck, E., & Fine, M. (2007). Inner angles: A range of ethical responses to/with Indigenous and decolonizing theories. In N. K. Denzin & M. D. Giardina (Eds.), *Ethical futures in qualitative research: Decolonizing the politics of knowledge* (pp. 45–168). Walnut Creek, CA: Left Coast Press.

Tuck, E., & Gaztambide-Fernández, R. (2013). Curriculum, replacement, and settler futurity. *Journal of Curriculum Theorizing, 29*(1), 72–89.

Tuck, E., & Guishard, M. (2013). Uncollapsing ethics: Racialized sciencism, settler coloniality, and an ethical framework of decolonial participatory action research. In T. M. Kress, C. S. Malott, & B. J. Portfilio (Eds.), *Challenging status quo retrenchment: New directions in critical qualitative research* (pp. 3–27). Charlotte, NC: Information Age Publishing.

Tuck, E., McKenzie, M., & McCoy, K. (2014). Introduction to special issue on Land education: Indigenous, postcolonial, and decolonizing perspectives on place and environmental education research. *Land Education: Indigenous, Postcolonial, and Environmental Education Research, 20* (1), 1–23.

Tuck, E., & Ree, C. (2013). A glossary of haunting. In S. H. Jones, T. E. Adams, & C. Ellis (Eds.), *Handbook of autoethnography* (pp. 639–658). Walnut Creek, CA: Left Coast Press.

Tuck, E., & Villegas, M. (forthcoming). *A statement on research that takes place on Indigenous land.*

Tuck, E., & Yang, K. W. (2012). Decolonization is not a metaphor. *Decolonization: Indigeneity, Education and Society, 1*(1), 1–40.

Tuck, E., & Yang, K. W. (Eds.). (2014). *Youth resistance research and theories of change.* New York: Routledge.

Urry, J. (2007). *Mobilities.* Cambridge: Polity.

Valentine, G. (2000). Exploring children and young people's narratives of identity. *Geoforum, 31,* 257–267.

Van Wyck, P. C. (2008). An Emphatic Geography: Notes on the Ethical Itinerary of Landscape. *Canadian Journal of Communication, 33*(2), 171.

Veracini, L. (2011). Introducing settler colonial studies. *Settler Colonial Studies, 1,* 1–12. Retrieved from http://ojs.lib.swin.edu.au/index.php/settlercolonialstudies/article/view/239.

Vizenor, G. R. (1994). *Manifest manners: Postindian warriors of survivance.* Middletown, CT: Wesleyan University Press.

Vizenor, G. R. (1998). *Trickster discourse.* Norman: University of Oklahoma Press.

Vizenor, G. R. (1999). *Manifest manners: Narratives on postindian survivance.* Winnipeg, MB: Bison Books.

Vizenor, G., Tuck, E., & Yang, K. W. (2014). Resistance in the blood. In E. Tuck & K. W. Yang (Eds.), *Youth resistance research and theories of change.* London: Routledge.

Waldie, P. (18 Nov, 2013). Canada dead last in ranking for environmental protection. London. *The Globe and Mail.* http://www.theglobeandmail.com/news/world/canada-dead-last-in-oecd-ranking-for-environmental-protection/article15484134/?mkt_tok=3RkMMJWWfF9wsRokuazLZKXonjHpfsX56eok Xqe%2FlMI%2F0ER3fOvrPUfGjI4DSMdhI%2BSLDwEYGJlv6SgFS7jNMbZk z7gOXRE%3D

Walker, G. (2012). *Environmental justice: Concepts, evidence and politics.* New York: Routledge.

Wallach, Y. (2011). Trapped in mirror-images: The rhetoric of maps in Israel/Palestine. *Political Geography, 30,* 358–369.

Wang, C. C., Morrel-Samuels, S., Hutchison, P. M., Bell, L., & Pestronk, R. M. (2004). Photovoice: Community building among youths, adults, and policymakers. *American Journal of Public Health, 94*(6), 911–913.

Watson, I. (2007). Settled and unsettled spaces: Are we free to roam? In A. Moreton-Robinson (Ed.), *Sovereign subjects: Indigenous sovereignty matters* (pp. 15–34). Crows Nest, NSW, Australia: Allen & Unwin.

Waziyatawin, A. W. (2005). *Remember this! Dakota decolonization and the Eli Taylor narratives.* Lincoln: University of Nebraska Press.

Weiss, J. (2011). Valuing youth resistance before and after public protest. *International Journal of Qualitative Studies in Education, 24*(5), 595–599.

Whitehouse, H., Watkin, F. L., Sellwood, J., Barrett, J. M., & Chigeza, C. (2014). Sea country: Navigating Indigenous and colonial ontologies in Australian environmental education. In K. McCoy, E. Tuck, & M. McKenzie (Eds.), Special issue on land education: Indigenous, postcolonial, and decolonizing perspectives on place and environmental education research, *Environmental Education Research*, 59–69.

Wilderson, F. (2010). *Red, White, and Black: Cinema and the Structure of US Antagonisms*. Durham, NC: Duke University Press.

Williams, R. (1958). Moving from high culture to ordinary culture. In N. McKenzie (Ed.), *Convictions*. London: MacKibbon & Kee.

Williams, R. (1961). *The long revolution*. Harmondsworth: Penguin.

Willis, P. E. (1977). *Learning to labour: How working class kids get working class jobs*. New York: Columbia University Press.

Wilson, S. (2001). What is Indigenous research methodology? *Canadian Journal of Native Education, 25*(2), 175–180.

Wilson, S. (2008). *Research as ceremony: Indigenous research methods*. Blackpoint, NS: Fernwood Publishing.

Winlow, H. (2009). Mapping the contours of race: Griffith Taylor's zones and strata theory. *Geographical Research, 47*(4), 390–407.

Wolfe, P. (1999). *Settler colonialism and the transformation of anthropology: The politics and poetics of an ethnographic event*. New York: Cassell.

Wolfe, P. (2006). Settler colonialism and the elimination of the native. *Journal of Genocide Research, 8*(4), 387—409.

Wolfe, P. (2011). After the frontier: Separation and absorption in US Indian policy. *Settler Colonial Studies, 1*(1), 13–51.

Womack, C. S. (1999). *Red on red: Native American literary separatism*. Minneapolis: University of Minnesota Press.

Worster, A. M., & Abrams, E. (2005). Sense of place among New England commercial fishermen and organic farmers: Implications for socially constructed environmental education. *Environmental Education Research, 11*(5), 525–535.

Wyck, P. C. (2008). An emphatic geography: Notes on the ethical itinerary of landscape. *Canadian Journal of Communication, 33*(2), 171–191.

Yang, K. W. (2008, March 7). Organizing MySpace: Youth Walkouts, Pleasure, Politics, and New Media. *Educational Foundations, 21*, 9–28.

Žižek, S. (2010). *Living in the end of times*. London: Verso.

Index